THE DOUBLEDAY
DEVOTIONAL CLASSICS

VOLUME III

Other books by E. Glenn Hinson

THE DOUBLEDAY
DEVOTIONAL CLASSICS

VOLUME III

———•———

Edited by E. Glenn Hinson

A DOUBLEDAY-GALILEE ORIGINAL

DOUBLEDAY & COMPANY, INC.
GARDEN CITY, NEW YORK
1978

The editor and publisher express their appreciation for permission to use the material indicated:

> From pp. 27–219 of *Purity of Heart* by Søren Kierkegaard, translated by Douglas V. Steere. Copyright, 1938, 1948 by Harper & Row, Publishers, Inc.
>
> *A Testament of Devotion* by Thomas R. Kelly. Copyright, 1941 by Harper & Row, Publishers, Inc.
>
> *On Listening to Another* by Douglas V. Steere. Copyright, 1955 by Harper & Row, Publishers, Inc.

By permission of Harper & Row, Publishers, Inc.

CONTENTS

CLASSIC I

CLASSIC II

CLASSIC III

PURITY OF HEART
Is to Will One Thing

by Søren Kierkegaard

Translated by Douglas V. Steere

EDITOR'S INTRODUCTION TO *PURITY OF HEART*

Purity of Heart is a disturbing classic, the kind we feel more comfortable not reading but, once read, are thankful we paid the price. With pen and ink Kierkegaard, would-be pastor and priest, puts us in a confessional booth and forces us to scrutinize our commitment. He lays bare our every subterfuge and closes off every escape route which would allow us to remain divided in our allegiance. He takes us out of our hiding places and makes us see how far we fall short of real Christianity. He wants us to have "purity of heart," and we can have it only if we "will one thing," the good, that which God wills. Halfway commitment will not suffice. It is as good as no commitment at all.

Purity of Heart

Purity of Heart is one of Kierkegaard's *Edifying Discourses,* the first translated into English but not the first he wrote. It was composed in 1846, a year in which he was earnestly struggling with a desire to be a pastor. After first throwing off the idea of pastoral ministry which his father wanted him to pursue, he later changed his mind and passed his theological examinations in 1840. But for several years afterwards he continued his vocational search. In 1846 his vocation reached a new stage, beyond the literary one. On February 7 he wrote in his journal, "My idea is now to prepare myself for Holy Orders. I have prayed to God for several months to give me further help, for it has been clear to me for a long time past that I ought not to continue any longer as an author, which I either wish to be entirely and absolutely, or not at all."[1] On November 5 he stated a desire to be "a country parson" as one of two ideals—"to live quietly in the country and devote my life to the little circle of those around me. . . ."[2] But his calling turned out otherwise. A year later he had resigned himself to the fact that he would never be a pastor.

In lieu of sermons Kierkegaard wrote what he later called "Christian Addresses." In his journal he differentiated these in this way: "A Christian Address deals to a certain extent with doubt—A Sermon operates absolutely and entirely through authority, that of Holy Writ and of Christ's apostles. It is therefore neither more nor less than heresy to entertain doubt in a sermon, however well one might be able to handle it."³ As this distinction suggests, Kierkegaard functioned as a Socratic gadfly, dialectically pricking the bubble of complacent Christianity wherever he could. Earlier, he did this as an aesthetic writer; now he did it as a religious one. He addressed himself to "that solitary individual" who might read his discourses aloud, as Kierkegaard read sermons aloud, for purposes of edification.

The *Journals* show that when Kierkegaard composed *Purity of Heart* he was very much preoccupied with the matter of confession and forgiveness. Without naming his father, he related how the latter, as a little boy, had stood on a hill and cursed God and, at age eighty-two, could not forget it even then. To that, as we will see later, were added other sins. Kierkegaard himself wrestled all his life with the melancholia which derived from his father's guilt. Only after his "conversion" experience in 1848 did he learn that God not only forgives but even forgets. At this particular juncture he saw a solution not in concealing guilt or even forgetting it but in remorse, repentance, and confession. These are "Eternity's emissaries, to humanity." It is by these that we overcome double-mindedness and will one thing.

Purity of Heart is a confessional meditation based on James iv. 8—"Draw near to God and he will draw near to you. Cleanse your hands, you sinners, and purify your hearts, you men of double mind." In his relentless way Kierkegaard turns these words around and around and gauges every implication. In section 12, where the reader should perhaps start reading in order to get a clear idea of what is happening, he demands that we picture ourselves as individuals on a stage with God as the audience, asking ourselves, "What kind of life am I living? Do I or do I not truthfully, sincerely, honestly, will one thing?" We must not imagine others present. We stand alone before God. Indeed, the address asks whether we live in such a way as to be conscious of being an individual, that "one solitary individual." The fact that we consider this being done *before God* makes it all the more serious, of *ultimate* seriousness. No other person dares to intrude. There is no hiding

place in the crowd. In eternity each has to answer *as an individual.*
That is the stance of confession, that of eternity. Eternity asks us
only *as individuals* whether we will one thing. It asks us about our
occupations, not whether they are this or that, successful or un-
successful, but whether they are what God wills. It asks us about
the means that we use to carry out our vocations, for in eternity
means and ends are the same. It doesn't matter whether we reach
the goal, it matters only whether we shot straight at the target.
Eternity asks too whether, in pursuing our occupations, we treated
others as we would have had them treat us. It asks only whether, in
suffering, we are faithful or faithless, not how much or whether we
have suffered.

In the preceding comments we can see Kierkegaard himself
wrestling to solve his vocational dilemma. An attack on him in *The
Corsair* in 1845 and 1846 brought the matter to a head. He recognized that he had to stand as a solitary individual. On March 9 he
wrote in his journal, "Two things in particular occupy me: (1)
that, whatever the cost, I should remain intellectually true, in the
Greek sense, to my life's idea; (2) that religiously it should be as
ennobling as possible. For the second I pray to God."[4] The isolation
he experienced caused excruciating pain. Even children poked fun
at him on the street. Thanking God that there is "deep within a
man a place where all this can be completely forgotten in communion with thee,"[5] he analyzed the disposition and experiences which
had equipped him to bear the suffering attendant on his choice.
There was first "a disproportion between soul and body" which
gave his mind "a tensile strength that is rare." There was the melancholia which he had inherited from his father and shared with
him. There was the rift with Regina Olsen, whom he loved but
from whom he separated so as to free himself "to the service of an
idea." His physician had told him he could never resolve the ten-
sion in his life and advised him not to set his whole will power in
motion lest he "should burst everything asunder." But that became
the moment of choice. He would resign himself to the suffering of
that one solitary individual.[6]

In *Purity of Heart,* therefore, Kierkegaard comes to us in his role
as a priestly gadfly. On the Feast of Confession he challenges us to
put aside our double-mindedness and will one thing. He, formerly
an author but momentarily a priest, though never ordained as one,

is preoccupied with helping us discover and face the mixture of our motives, barriers to willing one thing, and thus muster up the courage to pay the price of willing it. He is a clever analyst of motives, for his own brilliant and supple mind furnished him with plenty of them. He doesn't bother with obvious denials and dodges. He peers more deeply into our lives. All qualified and confused motives are symptomatic of double-mindedness—eagerness for variety and great moments, desire for reward, fear of punishment, egocentric service of the good, and halfway commitment. If we will the Good while *also* willing any of these, we do not will *one* thing. Purity of heart requires that we will *only* one thing.

What Kierkegaard does as he forces us to examine our motives, of course, is to confront us with the fact that we are not really Christian. He will not claim that even for himself. To be genuinely Christian would mean to pay a high price for willing one thing. It would mean commitment, loyalty, and readiness to suffer all for the Good. Willingness to suffer, to take up the Cross, is, for Kierkegaard, the key. It confirms whether or not we will really follow. Although this insight was one which Kierkegaard shared with others, it took on special meaning for him, and no other person, unless John of the Cross, gave it more emphasis. He knew both physical and emotional suffering throughout his life, having a psyche deeply scarred by the discovery of his father's sin. He suffered on account of the attacks and ridicule of others, far more than his attackers knew. The perception which grew within him through all of this was that, rather than fleeing suffering, he should embrace it by willing one thing. He would not employ his cleverness to avoid paying this price; rather, he would accept suffering "as the high price at which Almighty God sold me an intellectual power which has found no equal among my contemporaries."[7] Cleverness would help him expose evasions rather than contrive them. It is not disgraceful to be clever. It is only disgraceful to use cleverness to support double-mindedness. The goal is that *"the sufferer who sincerely wills the Good, uses this very cleverness to cut off evasions and hence to launch himself into the commitment* and to escape the disillusionments of choosing the temporal way" (section 11).

Even in the splendid translation of Douglas Steere used in this volume, *Purity of Heart* is not an easy book to read. It requires strict concentration and rereading, even reading aloud as Kierkegaard intended. One difficulty is that Kierkegaard demands a level of Christian commitment which boggles our minds. He puts us before God himself. He strips away those excuses which drop so glibly from our lips, those rationalizations which leap so quickly into our minds. This makes us writhe and squirm. Before dismissing him as a harsh master who reaps where he has not sown, however, let us recognize that he acted, as he thought, out of love and in our best interest. The separation of sin has gotten in the way of our commitment. In a time of confession we have an opportunity to accuse ourselves. We pray, as he instructs us, "Oh, Thou that givest both the beginning and the completion, give Thou victory in the day of need so that what neither a man's burning wish nor his determined resolution may attain to, may be granted unto him in the sorrowing of repentance: to will only one thing."

Søren Aabye Kierkegaard

We will neither understand nor appreciate fully the thoroughly Christian character of Kierkegaard's message and vocation without looking at his experience. As he himself perceived, he was equipped from birth to play the role of an Anti-Climacus, who would "make men aware of Christianity, . . . deceive people, in a true sense, into entering the sphere of religious obligation which they have done away with. . . ."[8]

The greatest single contributor to this vocation was Søren's father, Michael Pedersen Kierkegaard. He doted on his son, born in his fifty-sixth year, on May 5, 1813. From the time of Søren's birth, Michael Pedersen honed his brilliant progeny's powers of observation and critical reason. Because Søren was frail and sickly, unable to go out of doors, the father devoted hours to entertaining and educating him by walking up and down the room hand in hand with him on imaginary journeys. Kierkegaard described the process vividly in a story he composed in 1842 entitled "Johannes Climacus or *De omnibus dubitandum est*," explaining the roots of his prodigious capacity for argument.

So they went out of doors to a nearby castle in Spain, or out to the seashore, or about the streets, wherever Johannes wished to go, for his father was equal to anything. While they went up and down the room his father described all that they saw; they greeted passers by, carriages rattled past them and drowned his father's voice; the cakewoman's cakes were more enticing than ever. He described them so accurately, so vividly, so explicitly even to the least details, everything that was known to Johannes and so fully and perspicuously what was unknown to him, that after half an hour of such a walk with his father he was as much overwhelmed and fatigued as if he had been a whole day out of doors. Johannes soon learned from his father how to exercise his magical power.[9]

At the same time, Kierkegaard goes on to say, Michael Pedersen shaped his son's powers of critical reason by allowing him to witness arguments with others.

His father always allowed his opponent to state his whole case, and then as a precaution asked him if he had nothing more to say before he began his reply. Johannes had followed the opponent's speech with strained attention, and in his way shared an interest in the outcome. A pause intervened. The father's rejoinder followed, and behold! in a trice the tables were turned. How that came about was a riddle to Johannes, but his soul delighted in the show. The opponent spoke again. Johannes could almost hear his heart beat, so impatiently did he await what was to happen.—It happened; in the twinkling of an eye everything was inverted, the explicable became inexplicable, the certain doubtful, the contrary evident.[10]

Michael Pedersen also cultivated his son's self-image, his pride. He taught Søren, both in word and example, that one can do what he or she wills. Søren tells how, as a child, he would lock himself in his room and say in a loud, clear voice, "I will it!"

But these account for only one side of Søren Kierkegaard's complex personality and sense of mission. Michael Pedersen also passed on to his son his deeply rooted melancholy. The young Søren discerned a contradiction here. The same father who took him deep into the fantasy land of imagination, shredded opponents with his critical acumen, and told him he could do what he truly willed often betrayed a profound sense of personal impotence and unworthiness. But the magnitude of this contradiction did not become evident to him until 1830 or '31, the year of "the great earthquake."

There is unanimous agreement that the "earthquake" involved a smashing revelation of a sin which Michael Pedersen had committed and which he was convinced had left him accursed for the rest of his life. The disclosure came unplanned and unexpected. It blew away the nimbus, the near aura of divinity, which the young genius saw over his father's head. It plunged him into a state of depression equivalent to his father's, and eventually caused him to leave home. Indeed, it infected not only Søren but his entire family, creating a sense of foreboding that the father was cursed to outlive every one of them. When, one by one, the children, save Peter and Søren, preceded their father in death, it seemed to confirm the curse. Kierkegaard described this overwhelming sense of despair in graphic terms.

> Then I suspected that my father's great age was not a divine blessing but rather a curse; that the outstanding intellectual gifts of our family were only given to us in order that we should rend each other to pieces: then I felt the stillness of death grow around me when I saw my father, an unhappy man who was to outlive us all, a cross on the tomb of all his hopes. There must be guilt upon the whole family, the punishment of God must be on it; it was to disappear, wiped out by the powerful hand of God, obliterated like an unsuccessful attempt, and only at times did I find a little alleviation in the thought that my father had been allotted the heavy task of calming us with the consolation of religion, of ministering to us so that a better world should be open to us even though we lost everything in this world, even though we were overtaken by the punishment which the Jews always called down up their enemies: that all recollection of us should be utterly wiped out, that we should no longer be found.[11]

What was the shattering revelation of Michael Pedersen Kierkegaard? Many have assumed that it was the incident, often cited by Søren, when, as a youth in the Jutland heath, the elder Kierkegaard stood on a hillside and cursed God. Johannes Hohlenberg, however, has questioned this interpretation and argued instead that the "earthquake" had to do with "further sins," which Søren associated with the figure of Hamlet and which caused him to be preoccupied with confession. The specific cause of Michael Pedersen Kierkegaard's guilt was likely connected with the fact that Søren's mother, his second wife, bore him her first child about five months after they married. Hohlenberg has theorized that the father's relationship to his second wife, at that time a servant in the Kierkegaard household, may have begun with an act of rape. He points especially to a note inserted by S.K. in his journal in February 1837, pondering the statement that indulgences can forgive *all* sins, *"etiam si matrem virginem violasset"* ("even if one has violated the virgin mother"). This might explain why Michael Pedersen always regarded his first wife as his *real* wife, despite the fact that Anne Sørensdatter Lund, who also had a Jutland peasant background, bore all his children. In fact, his violation of Anne Lund may have been an act of angry defiance of God in reaction to his first wife's death. Thus, a chain of events produced the profound sense of guilt which, when disclosed by accident to S.K., overwhelmed him as well.[12]

Kierkegaard's violent separation from his father shoved him out into the world on his own. He had intellectual moorings, but he did not know what his vocation was. He was searching for the "great idea" to which he could attach himself. The confusion and uncertainty, compounded with his melancholy, plunged him into near despair. For several years, 1830–36, he lived the life of a prodigal. He studied at the University of Copenhagen, but there is scant evidence of diligence. His interest focused on three ideas—Don Juan, Faust, and the wandering Jew—all of which were more or less symbolic of his state of mind at the time, "life outside religion in its three-fold direction. . . ."[13] Although he moved out of his father's house, he continued to maintain an extravagant standard of living by running up debts and charges, which his father, after their reconciliation, paid off for him. He drank heavily, and, in one of his drunken spells, friends took him to a brothel. About 1836 he evidently "bottomed out," seriously contemplating suicide. "I have just returned from a party of which I was the life and soul," he noted in his journal for March 1836; "wit poured from my lips, everyone laughed and admired me—but I went away—and the dash should be as long as the earth's orbit————————————————————and wanted to shoot myself."[14]

Sometime after this, Kierkegaard began to go uphill again by way of a moral reformation. The antipathy and hostility he had manifested toward Christianity as well as toward his father diminished. On May 19, 1838, he recorded what is probably to be interpreted as a mystical experience of conversion, reminiscent of Pascal's, although S.K. was reluctant to admit direct experience of God could occur.

May 19. *Half-past ten in the morning.* There is an indescribable joy which enkindles us as inexplicably as the apostle's outburst comes gratuitously: "Rejoice I say unto you, and again I say unto you rejoice."— Not a joy over this or that but the soul's mighty song "with tongue and mouth, from the bottom of the heart:" "I rejoice through my joy, in, at, with, over, by, and with my joy"—a heavenly refrain, as it were, suddenly breaks off our other song; a joy which cools and refreshes us like a breath of wind, a wave of air, from the trade wind which blows from the plains of Mamre to the everlasting habitations.[15]

On July 7 he entered another exultant notation about his transformation. "God creates out of *nothing*, wonderful, you say: yes, to be sure, but he does what is still more wonderful: he makes saints out of sinners."[16]

Behind this experience lay some kind of intervention by S.K.'s father, which possibly cost the latter his life. Three days after his father died, on August 8, at the age of eighty-two, Kierkegaard wrote, "I had so very much wished that he might live a few years longer, and I look upon his death as the last sacrifice which he made to his love for me; for he did not die from me but *died for me* in order that if possible I might still turn into something." Walter Lowrie has theorized that Michael Pedersen may have intervened decisively on Søren's twenty-fifth birthday, May 5, 1838, when, by Danish law, the latter would have come of age. No one knows what transpired, but, Lowrie adds, "the greatest and most costly sacrifice this close-mouthed old man could have made to save his son was to open his heart to him completely." This alone could have saved him.[17]

Whatever happened here, from this point on, S.K.'s vocation began little by little to emerge with clarity. He would be "that solitary individual," intent on bringing Christianity into Christendom, however much sacrifice that required. This mission resulted, by his choice, in increasing isolation.

The first painful phase of his mission was connected with his winning and then rejecting of Regina Olsen. Though ten years older than she, he fell in love with Regina and she, awed by his intellect, with him at first sight in May 1837. After he had passed his theological examination in the summer of 1840, ignoring the fact that she was engaged already to Fritz Schlegel, S.K. proceeded to visit her and try to win her with his charm and wit. Even during a brief absence from Copenhagen during a visit to Jutland, August 9–September 8, 1840, he loaned the family books and suggested that they read certain passages, evidently to keep them mindful of him. Upon his return he declared his love in a private meeting and on September 10, asked for her hand. Both she and her father gave consent. Immediately, the very next day, however, S.K. realized he had made a dreadful error. "A penitent such as I was, my *vita ante acta,* my melancholy, that was enough. I suffered unspeakably at that time."

Regina did not suspect S.K.'s dilemma for a while. His vexation with her only caused her to worship him all the more. This put the entire burden of a break solely on S.K.'s shoulders, "God's punishment upon [him]." He truly loved her, contrary to what some have judged. Only his perception of himself and his calling compelled him to take the drastic step he did. "If I had not been a penitent, had not had my *vita ante acta,* had not been melancholy, my union with her would have made me happier than I had ever dreamed of being. But in so far as I was what, alas, I was, I had to say that I could be happier in my unhappiness without her than with her; she had moved me and I would have liked, more than liked, to have done everything for her."[18] A "divine protest" stood in the way. Or a powerful fear. In a journal entry in 1843 Kierkegaard explained that, had he gone on with the engagement, he

> would have had to initiate her into terrible things: my relation to my father, his melancholy, the eternal darkness that broods deep within, my going astray, pleasures and excesses which in the eyes of God are not perhaps so terrible, for it was dread that drove me to excess, and where was I to look for something to hold on to when I knew, or suspected that the one man I revered for his power and strength had wavered.[19]

Assailed by such thoughts, he wrote her and sent her back the ring. He had to summon up his last ounce of will power to repel her efforts to sustain the engagement. "If I had not believed that God had lodged a veto," Kierkegaard admitted, "she would have been victorious."[20] Two months later, she conceded the inevitable. Even her father's warnings that she might take her life failed to shake S.K.'s decision. He did go to see her and leave one last word of consolation. Though he parted nonchalantly for appearance's sake, he cried the whole night and, for a time, he went to Berlin, intending to stay a year and a half but actually staying six months. His early return roused her hopes that he had come to himself, but he repulsed her advances. Eventually, in 1843, she became engaged again to Schlegel, but right up to that time she held out hopes of a reconciliation. Always concerned to show the finality of the decision, S.K. attended the wedding in 1847.

The break with Regina set Søren Kierkegaard free to pursue his vocation. For several years he tried to fulfill his father's wish that he become a pastor. Before he began to woo Regina he had passed the theological examination *cum laude*. Until 1847 he entertained a strong desire to become a country parson. His real vocation, however, was that of scholar and writer. As a student he had dabbled in aesthetic pursuits. In September 1841 he obtained the M.A., equivalent to the modern Ph.D., with a thesis entitled "The Concept of Irony." Following his breach with Regina, he inaugurated his tireless efforts as an author, one work after another pouring from his pen until his momentous experience of 1848 in which he committed himself still more expressly to a Christian vocation. From this experience on, he set himself the task of "introducing Christianity to Christendom," a task which culminated in his virulent attack upon established Christianity, "especially in Protestantism, and more especially in Denmark." True to his own perception during a second trip to Berlin in May of 1843, he turned out to be a stormy petrel—a bird which appears when storm clouds gather.[21]

Kierkegaard himself understood his entire literary effort as a Christian endeavor. It is evident, however, that his perspective and approach evolved as he pursued his mission and answered the fire of his attackers. Drawing upon Kierkegaard's own statements, Walter Lowrie posited first a withdrawal from the aesthetical and from speculation (1841–46), then a turning to Christianity with increasing fervor (1846–49), and finally an onslaught against Christendom (1849–55). In *The Point of View of My Life as an Author*, composed in 1848 in response to increasingly hostile attacks, Kierkegaard himself argued that what had changed was not his basic sense of purpose but both his writing style and his style of life. At the same time that he had published *Either/Or*, he also published *Two Edifying Discourses* (1843). In the former he had used an aesthetic style to win a hearing, he said, for his audience consisted of aesthetes. His deception, which he carried over into his personal life—for example, in making fleeting appearances at the theater—was an *indirect* method of reaching people. If he had addressed them *directly* on behalf of Christianity, when they knew so little about it, they would have tuned him out. Even his pseudonyms assisted in this indirection.

The year 1848, however, brought a transformation in the life and writing of Søren Kierkegaard, which had been impending for some time. A factor in it was doubtless a foreboding about death, in the face of which he wanted to come to grips with himself and his melancholy. On August 16, 1847, he wrote, "I now feel the need of approaching nearer to myself in a deeper sense, by approaching nearer to God in the understanding of myself. . . . I must come to closer grips with my melancholy." He proceeded to observe that his writing, valuable as it was and approved by God, had kept him from facing himself.

> But now God wishes things otherwise. Something is stirring within me which points to a metamorphosis. For that very reason I dare not go to Berlin, for that would be to procure an abortion. I shall therefore remain quiet, in no way working too strenuously, hardly even strenuously, not begin on a new book, but try to understand myself, and really think out the idea of my melancholy together with God here and now. That is how I must get rid of my melancholy and bring Christianity closer to me.[22]

The "metamorphosis" occurred in April 1848, following a stock market crash which virtually depleted Kierkegaard's fortune in royal bonds left him by his father. Many have been destroyed emotionally by such an event; Kierkegaard was liberated by it. He discerned that a God of love not only can forgive but also forget our sins! On Ash Wednesday, April 18, 1848, he exulted in his journal:

> My whole being is changed. My reserve and self-isolation is broken —I must speak.
>
>   Lord give thy grace.
> It is indeed true, what my father said of me: "you will never be anything so long as you have money." He spoke prophetically, he thought that I would lead a riotous and debauched life. But that is just where he was wrong. But with an acuteness of mind and a melancholy such as mine, and then to have had money: what an opportunity for developing all the agonies of self-torture in my heart.[23]

In May he reflected back over his experience. Faith, he discerned, meant to "believe by virtue of the absurd that God will help [one] temporally." That is what forgiveness of sins means, a help in present human experience. "But belief in the forgiveness of sins means to believe that here in time the sin is forgotten by God, that it is really true that God forgets."[24] Musing over his unhappy years, he added, "It is wonderful how God's love overwhelms me. . . ."[25] He now saw clearly that God had arranged his whole life—melancholy and all. Since Easter, he went on to confide, "a hope has awakened in my soul that God may desire to resolve the fundamental misery of my being." To him the experience signified that he was "in faith in the profoundest sense."[26]

S.K.'s change of fortune forced him to sell the family house, where he had lived from 1844 through 1847, and move into a small apartment. This move coalesced with a radical shift in his approach to his vocation. Henceforth, to the end of his life, he spoke directly. If previously his critics could complain that they did not understand him, they would no longer have cause to do so.

In his self-imposed isolation Kierkegaard directed his attention fully to the task of introducing Christianity to Christendom. What especially offended was the fact that he aimed his salvos not merely at the lethargic but at a group of reformers, among whom his brother Peter was a leader. He criticized Luther. As an advocate of genuine reform, Kierkegaard wrote in 1849 that "the closer I examine Luther the more convinced do I become that he was muddleheaded." Luther introduced "a comfortable kind of reforming which consists in throwing off burdens and making life easier," while true reform "always means to make life more difficult, to lay on burdens" and the true reformer is always put to death as an enemy of mankind. Worse still, "in Lutheranism faith has simply become a fig-leaf behind which people skulk in the most unchristian way."[27] Luther "overthrew the Pope and set the public on the throne."[28]

Kierkegaard also offended by his life-style. Having been liberated by his financial misfortune, he did nothing to meet the usual standards of success. Indeed, he slapped polite sensibilities smack in the face by conversing publicly with common folk—gardeners, coachmen, and others. He was playing to the hilt the role of a solitary individual.

All of this was excruciatingly painful to Kierkegaard, but he persisted in his calling anyway, convinced by his experience in 1848 that "the highest of all is not to understand the highest but to act upon it."[29] The problem was the absence of Christianity from Christendom, especially Danish Christendom. In Denmark, he observed in 1854, Christianity "can only be compared to the lowest forms of paganism." People have even forgotten the point of Christianity—viz., self-denial—"while worldly well-being and soft-hearted mediocrity are idolised."[30]

Little by little, Kierkegaard began to see in Bishop Jacob Peter Mynster, his father's old friend and counselor, a symbol of the depravity of Danish Christianity. So long as Mynster lived, however, S.K. had to treat him gently. Mynster's death on January 30, 1854, freed him. The extravagant funeral eulogy of Mynster by his successor Hans Larsen Martensen, long an object of Kierkegaard's attacks, gave him an occasion to speak. Painfully, but with a profound sense of obligation, he spent the final year of his life attacking Martensen in an effort to reintroduce discipleship, costly discipleship, into Christendom.

To the very end Kierkegaard remained true to his painful protest. On his death bed he refused to receive communion from the hands of an ordained pastor, whom he regarded as an employee of the state. Because his friend Emil Boesen, a pastor, insisted that a lay person could not administer the sacrament, he died without it. To the day of his death, November 11, 1855, he was incarnating his protest.

Many will think Kierkegaard antisocial, but that charge is unfair. He opposed the mob with its careless convention and collective irrationality. He did not oppose humanity. Rather, he poured himself out as a libation in order that Christianity might come to itself by way of true reform. That reform would occur, he was convinced, only when each of us becomes that solitary individual, ready to will one thing. This is a powerful challenge for any age.

—E. GLENN HINSON

NOTES

1. *The Journals of Kierkegaard,* tr. and selected by Alexander Dru (New York and Evanston: Harper & Row, Publishers, 1958), p. 96.

2. Ibid., p. 112.

3. Ibid., p. 116.

4. Ibid., p. 102.

5. Ibid., p. 103.

6. Ibid., pp. 106–8.

7. Ibid., p. 107.

8. Ibid., p. 175.

9. Ibid., pp. 80–81.

10. Ibid., pp. 81–82.

11. Ibid., p. 39.

12. Johannes Hohlenberg, *Sören Kierkegaard,* tr. T. H. Croxall (London: Routledge & Kegan Paul, Ltd., 1954), pp. 59–64.

13. *Journals,* p. 50.

14. Ibid., pp. 50–51.

15. Ibid., p. 59.

16. Ibid.

17. Walter Lowrie, *Kierkegaard* (London, New York, Toronto: Oxford University Press, 1938), p. 182.

18. *Journals,* pp. 71–72.

19. Ibid., p. 87.

20. Ibid., p. 73.

21. Ibid., p. 95.

22. Ibid., p. 128.

23. Ibid., p. 137.

24. Ibid., pp. 139–40.

25. Ibid., p. 140.

26. Ibid., p. 142.

27. Ibid., p. 164.

28. Ibid., p. 233.

29. Ibid., p. 213.

30. Ibid., p. 241.

1. INTRODUCTION:

MAN AND THE ETERNAL

Father in Heaven! What is a man without Thee! What is all that he knows, vast accumulation though it be, but a chipped fragment if he does not know Thee! What is all his striving, could it even encompass a world, but a half-finished work if he does not know Thee: Thee the One, who art one thing and who art all! So may Thou give to the intellect, wisdom to comprehend that one thing; to the heart, sincerity to receive this understanding; to the will, purity that wills only one thing. In prosperity may Thou grant perseverance to will one thing; amid distractions, collectedness to will one thing; in suffering, patience to will one thing. Oh, Thou that givest both the beginning and the completion, may Thou early, at the dawn of day, give to the young man the resolution to will one thing. As the day wanes, may Thou give to the old man a renewed remembrance of his first resolution, that the first may be like the last, the last like the first, in possession of a life that has willed only one thing. Alas, but this has indeed not come to pass. Something has come in between. The separation of sin lies in between. Each day, and day after day something is being placed in between: delay, blockage, interruption, delusion, corruption. So in this time of repentance may Thou give the courage once again to will one thing. True, it is an interruption of our ordinary tasks; we do lay down our work as though it were a day of rest, when the penitent (and it is only in a time of repentance that the heavy-laden worker may be quiet in the confession of sin) is alone before Thee in self-accusation. This is indeed an interruption. But it is an interruption that searches back into its very beginnings that it might bind up anew that which sin has separated, that in its grief it might atone for lost time, that in its anxiety it might bring to completion that which lies before it. Oh, Thou that givest both the beginning and the completion, give Thou victory in the day of need so that what neither a man's burning wish nor his determined resolution may attain to, may be granted unto him in the sorrowing of repentance: to will only one thing.

"To everything there is a season," says Solomon.[1] And in these words he voices the experience of the past and of that which lies behind us. For when an old man relives his life, he lives it only by dwelling upon his memories; and when wisdom in an old man has outgrown the immediate impressions of life, the past viewed from the quiet of memory is something different from the present in all its bustle. The time of work and of strain, of merrymaking and of dancing is over. Life requires nothing more of the old man and he claims nothing more of it. By being present, one thing is no nearer to him than another. Expectation, decision, repentance in regard to a thing do not affect his judgment. By being a part of the past, these distinctions all become meaningless, for that which is completely past has no present to which it may attach itself. Oh, the desolation of old age, if to be an old man means this: means that at any given moment a living person could look at life as if he himself did not exist, as if life were merely a past event that held no more present tasks for him as a living person, as if he, as a living person, and life were cut off from each other within life, so that life was past and gone, and he had become a stranger to it. Oh, tragic wisdom, if it were of everything human that Solomon spoke, and if the speech must ever end in the same manner, insisting that everything has its time, in the well-known words: "What profit hath he that worketh in that wherein he laboureth" (Ecclesiastes iii. 9)? Perhaps the meaning would have been clearer if Solomon had said, "There was a time for all, all had its time," in order to show that, as an old man, he is speaking of the past and that in fact he is not speaking to someone but is talking to himself. For the person who talks about human life, which changes with the years, must be careful to state his own age to his listeners. And that wisdom which is related to such a changeable and temporal element in a man must, as with every frailty, be treated with caution in order that it shall not work harm.

Only the Eternal is always appropriate and always present, is always true. Only the Eternal applies to each human being, whatever his age may be. The changeable exists, and when its time has passed it is changed. Therefore any statement about it is subject to change. That which may be wisdom when spoken by an old man about past events may be folly in the mouth of a youth or of a grown man when spoken of the present. The youth would not be able to understand it and the grown man would not want to understand it. Even one who is a little advanced in age may fully agree with Solomon in saying, "There is a time to dance from sheer joy." And yet how can he agree with him? For his dancing time is past, and therefore he speaks of it as of something past. And it does not matter whether, in that day when both youth and the longing to dance were his, he grieved at its being denied him, or whether in joyous abandon he yielded to the invitation to dance: one who is a little advanced in age will still say quietly, "There is a time to dance." But for the youth, to be allowed to hurry off to the dance and to sit shut in at home are two such different things that it does not occur to him to consider them on the same level and to say, "There is a time for the one and a time for the other." A man is changed in the course of the years, and each time some portion of life lies behind him he tends to talk of its varied content as if it were all on the same level. But it does not follow from this that he has become any wiser. For by this, one has only said that he has changed. Perhaps even now there is something that makes him restless in the same way that the dance disturbs the youth, something that absorbs his attention in the same way that a toy absorbs a child. It is in this manner that a man changes, over the years. Old age is the final change. The old man speaks in the same vein of it all, of all the changeable that is now past.

But is this all of the story? Has all been heard that may be said about being a man, and about man's temporal life? The most important and decisive thing of all is certainly left out. For the talk about the natural changes of human life over the years, together with what externally happened there, is not in essence any different from talking of plant or of animal life. The animal also changes with the years. When it is older it has other desires than it had at an earlier age. At certain times it, too, has its happiness in life, and at other times it must endure hardship. Yes, when late autumn comes, even the flower can speak the wisdom of the years and say with truthfulness, "All has its time, there is 'a time to be born and a time to die'; there is a time to jest lightheartedly in the spring breeze, and a time to break under the autumn storm; there is a time to burst forth into blossom, beside the running water, beloved by the stream, and a time to wither and be forgotten; a time to be sought out for one's beauty, and a time to be unnoticed in one's wretchedness; there is a time to be nursed with care, and a time to be cast out with contempt; there is a time to delight in the warmth of the morning sun and a time to perish in the night's cold. All has its time; 'what profit hath he that worketh in that wherein he laboureth?'"

Yes, the animal, too, when it has lived its time may speak the wisdom of the years and say with truth, "All has its time. There is a time to leap with joy, and a time to drag oneself along the earth; there is a time to waken early, and a time to sleep long; there is a time to run with the herd, and a time to go apart to die; there is a time to build nests with one's beloved, and there is a time to sit alone on the roof; there is a time to soar freely among the clouds, and a time to sink heavily to the earth. All has its time: 'what profit hath he that worketh in that wherein he laboureth?'" And, in case you should say to the flower, "Is there, then, nothing more to tell?" then it will answer you, "No, when the flower is dead, the story is over." Otherwise the story must have been different from the beginning and been different as it went along, not merely becoming different at the end. For let us assume that the flower concluded its story in another fashion and added, "The story is not over, for when I am dead, I am immortal." Would this not be a strange story? If the flower were really immortal, then immortality must be just that which prevented it from dying, and therefore immortality must have been present in each instant of its life. And the story of its life must once again have been wholly different in order to express continually immortality's difference from all the changeableness and the different kinds of variations of the perishable. Immortality cannot be a final alteration that crept in, so to speak, at the moment of death as the final stage. On the contrary, it is a changelessness that is not altered by the passage of the years. Therefore, to the old man's words that "all has its time," the wise Solomon adds, "God made all things beautiful in his time; also he hath set eternity within man's heart" (Ecclesiastes iii. 11).[2] Thus says the sage. For the talk about change, and the varied way of talking about change is indeed confusing even when it comes from the mouth of an old man. Only the Eternal is constructive.

The wisdom of the years is confusing. Only the Wisdom of eternity is edifying.

If there is, then, something eternal in a man, it must be able to exist and to be grasped within every change. Nor can it be wisdom to say, indiscriminately, that this something eternal has its time like the perishable, that it makes its circle like the wind that never gets further; that it has its course like the river that never fills up the sea. Nor can it be wisdom to talk of this eternal element in the same vein as if one were speaking of the past, as if it is past and past in the sense that it can never, not even in repentance, relate itself to a present person but only to an absent one. For repentance is precisely the relation between something past and someone that has his life in the present time. It was unwise of the youth to wish to talk in the same terms of the pleasure of dancing and of its opposite. For this clear act of folly betrayed that the youth, in his youth, would like to have outgrown youth. But as for the Eternal, the time never comes when a man has grown away from it, or has become older—than the Eternal.

If there is, then, something eternal in a man the discussion of it must have a different ring. It must be said that there is something that shall always have its time, something that a man shall always do, just as one Apostle says that we should always give thanks to God.[3] For that which has its time must properly be looked upon as an associate and an equal with other temporal things that in their turn shall pass away. But the Eternal is that which is set over all. The Eternal will not have its time, but will fashion time to its own desire, and then give its consent that the temporal should also be given its time. So the Scriptures say, "The one shall be done, the other shall not be neglected."[4] But that which shall not be neglected is just that which cannot come into consideration until that is done which ought to be done. In like fashion with the Eternal. If the wisdom of life should ever alter that which concerns the eternal in a man to the point of changing it into something temporal, then this would be folly whether it be spoken by an old man or by a youth. For in relation to the Eternal, age gives no justification for speaking absurdly, and youth does not exclude one from being able to grasp what is true. Should someone explain that the fear of God, in the sense of that felt in this world of time, should belong to childhood and therefore disappear with the years as does childhood itself, or should be like a happy state of mind that cannot be maintained, but only remembered; should someone explain that penitence comes like the weakness of old age, with the wasting away of strength, when the senses are blunted, when sleep no longer strengthens but weakens; then this would be impiety and folly. Yes, to be sure, it is a fact that there was a man who with the years forgot his childish fear of God, was swindled out of the best, and was taken in by that which was most insolent. Yes, to be sure, it is a fact that there was a man whom repentance first overtook in the painfulness of old age, when he no longer had the strength to sin, so that the repentance not only came late, but the despair of late repentance became the final stage. But this is no story of an event that calls for an ingenious explanation or that would even of itself explain life. When it happens, it is a horrible thing. And even if a man should become a thousand years old, he would not have become so old that he dares speak otherwise of it than the youth— with fear and trembling. For in relation to the Eternal, a man ages neither in the sense of time nor in the sense of an accumulation of past events. No, when an old person has outgrown the childish and the youthful, ordinary language calls this, maturity and a gain. But willfully ever to have outgrown the Eternal is spoken of as falling away from God and as perdition; and only the life of the ungodly "shall be as the snail that melts, as it goes" (Psalm lviii. 8).

2. REMORSE, REPENTANCE, CONFESSION:

ETERNITY'S EMISSARIES TO MAN

There is, then, something which should at all times be done. There is something which in no temporal sense shall have its time. Alas, and when this is not done, when it is omitted, or when just the opposite is done, then once again, there is something (or more correctly it is the same thing, that reappears, changed, but not changed in its essence) which should at all times be done. There is something which in no temporal sense shall have its time. There must be repentance and remorse.

One dare not say of repentance and remorse that it has its time; that there is a time to be carefree and a time to be prostrated in repentance. Such talk would be: to the anxious urgency of repentance—unpardonably slow; to the grieving after God—sacrilege; to what should be done this very day, in this instant, in this moment of danger—senseless delay. For there is indeed danger. There is a danger that is called delusion. It is unable to check itself. It goes on and on: then it is called perdition. But there is a concerned guide, a knowing one, who attracts the attention of the wanderer, who calls out to him that he should take care. That guide is remorse. He is not so quick of foot as the indulgent imagination, which is the servant of desire. He is not so strongly built as the victorious intention. He comes on slowly afterwards. He grieves. But he is a sincere and faithful friend. If that guide's voice is never heard, then it is just because one is wandering along the way of perdition. For when the sick man who is wasting away from consumption believes himself to be in the best of health, his disease is at the most terrible point. If there were someone who early in life steeled his mind against all remorse and who actually carried it out, nevertheless remorse would come again if he were willing to repent even of this decision. So wonderful a power is remorse, so sincere is its friendship that to escape it entirely is the most terrible thing of all. A man can wish to slink away from many things in life, and he may even succeed, so that life's favored one can say in the last moment, "I slipped away from all the cares under which other men suffered." But if such a person wishes to bluster out of, to defy, or to slink away from remorse, alas, which is indeed the most terrible to say of him, that he failed, or—that he succeeded?

A Providence watches over each man's wandering through life. It provides him with two guides. The one calls him forward. The other calls him back. They are, however, not in opposition to each other, these two guides, nor do they leave the wanderer standing there in doubt, confused by the double call. Rather the two are in eternal understanding with each other. For the one beckons forward to the Good, the other calls man back from evil. Nor are they blind guides. Just for that reason there are two of them. For in order to make the journey secure, they must look both forward and backward. Alas, there was perhaps many a one who went astray through not understanding how to continue a good beginning. For his course was along a false way, and he pressed on so continuously that remorse could not call him back onto the old way. There was perhaps someone who went astray because, in the exhaustion of repentance, he could go no further, so that the guide could not help him to find the way forward. When a long procession is about to move, a call is heard first from the one who is furthest forward. But he waits until the last has answered. The two guides call out to a man early and late, and when he listens to their call, then he finds his way, then he can know where he is, on the way. Because these two calls designate the place and show the way. Of these two, the call of remorse is perhaps the best. For the eager traveler who travels lightly along the way does not, in this fashion, learn to know it as well as a wayfarer with a heavy burden. The one who merely strives to get on does not learn to know the way as well as the remorseful man. The eager traveler hurries forward to the new, to the novel, and, indeed, away from experience. But the remorseful one, who comes behind, laboriously gathers up experience.

The two guides call out to a man early and late. And yet, no, for when remorse calls to a man it is always late. The call to find the way again by seeking out God in the confession of sins is always at the eleventh hour. Whether you are young or old, whether you have sinned much or little, whether you have offended much or neglected much, the guilt makes this call come at the eleventh hour. The inner agitation of the heart understands what remorse insists upon, that the eleventh hour has come. For in the sense of time, the old man's age is the eleventh hour; and the instant of death, the final moment in the eleventh hour. The indolent youth speaks of a long life that lies before him. The indolent old man hopes that his death is still a long way off. But repentance and remorse belong to the eternal in a man. And in this way each time that repentance comprehends guilt it understands that the eleventh hour has come: that hour which human indolence knows well enough exists and will come, when it is talked about in generalities, but not when it actually applies to the indolent one himself. For even the old man thinks that there is some time left and the indolent youth deceives himself when he thinks that difference in age is the determining factor in regard to the nearness of the eleventh hour. See, then, how good and how necessary it is that there are two guides. For whether it be the lightly armed desire of youth which it is presumed will press forward to victory, or whether it be the mature man's determination that will fight its way through life, they both count on having a long time at their disposal. They presuppose, in the plans for their efforts, a generation or at least a number of years, and therefore they waste a great deal of time and on that account the whole thing so readily ends in delusion.

But repentance and remorse know how to make use of time in fear and trembling. When remorse awakens concern, whether it be in the youth, or in the old man, it awakens it always at the eleventh hour. It does not have much time at its disposal, for it is at the eleventh hour. It is not deceived by a false notion of a long life, for it is at the eleventh hour. And in the eleventh hour one understands life in a wholly different way than in the days of youth or in the busy time of manhood or in the final moment of old age. He who repents at any other hour of the day repents in the temporal sense. He fortifies himself by a false and hasty conception of the insignificance of his guilt. He braces himself with a false and hasty notion of life's length. His remorse is not in true inwardness of spirit. Oh, eleventh hour, wherever thou art present, how all is changed! How still everything is, as if it were the midnight hour; how sober, as if it were the hour of death; how lonely, as if it were among the tombs; how solemn, as if it were within eternity. Oh, heavy hour of labor (although labor is at rest), when the account is rendered, yet there is no accuser there; when all is called by its own name, yet there is nothing said; when each improper word must be repeated, in the light of eternity! Oh, costly bargain, where remorse must pay so dearly for what seemed in the eyes of light-heartedness and busyness and proud struggling and impatient passion and the judgment of the world to be reckoned as nothing! Oh, eleventh hour, how terrible if Thou shouldst remain, how much more terrible than if death should continue through a whole life!

So repentance must have its time if all is not to be confused. For there are two guides. The one beckons forward. The other calls back. But repentance shall not have its time in a temporal sense. It will not belong to a certain section of life as fun and play belong to childhood, or as the excitement of love belongs to youth. It will not come and disappear as a whim or as a surprise. No, remorse should be an action with a collected mind, so that it may be spoken of to the edification of the hearer and so that new life may be born of it, so that it does not become an event whose sorrowful heritage is a feeling of sadness. In a setting of freedom, bearing the impress of eternity, repentance should have its time, yes, even its time of preparation. For in proportion to what should be done there, the time of collection and preparation is not a drawn-out affair. On the contrary there is a sense of reverence, a holy fear, a humility, that that which is to be done in the pure sincerity of this act of repentance may not become vain and overhasty. That a man wishes to prepare himself is no torpid delay. On the contrary, it is an intense agitation of heart that is already in alliance with what is to be done there. From the point of view of the Eternal, repentance must come instantaneously, indeed there is not even time to utter the words. But man is in the temporal dimension and moves along in time. Thus the Eternal and the temporal seek to make themselves intelligible to each other. Just as the temporal does not wish for delay simply in order to withdraw itself, but, conscious of its weakness, asks time to prepare itself; so the Eternal yields not because it gives up its claim, but in order by tender treatment to give frail man a little time.

The Eternal with its "obey at once" must not become a sudden shock which merely confuses the temporal. It should, on the contrary, be of assistance to the temporal throughout life. As the superior in relation to its mental inferior, or as an older person in relation to a child, can press its claim to such an extreme that it ends by actually weakening the mind of the mentally inferior or the child, so also the Eternal can in the imagination of an excitable person make an attempt to push the temporal into madness. But the grieving of repentance after God and the heartfelt anxiety must not, above all, be confused with impatience. Experience teaches that the right moment to repent is not always the one that is immediately present. For repentance in this precipitate moment when labored thoughts and various passions are acutely active or at least are strained by this unburdening may so easily be mistaken about that which is really to be repented. It can so easily be confused with its opposite, with the momentary feeling of contrition, that is, with impatience. It can so easily be confused with a painful agonizing sorrow after the world, that is, with impatience; with a desperate feeling of grief in itself, that is, with impatience. But impatience, no matter how long it continues to rage, never becomes repentance. However clouded, then, the mind becomes, the sobs of impatience, no matter how violent they are, never become sobs of repentance. The tears of impatience lack the blessed fruitfulness. They are like empty clouds that bear no water, or like convulsive puffs of wind. On the other hand, if a man assumed an even heavier guilt, but at the same time improved and year after year went steadily forward in the good, it is certain that from year to year, as he advanced in the good, he would with greater intensity repent of his guilt, the guilt which year by year in a temporal sense he would be leaving further and further behind. For it is indeed the case that guilt must be alive for a man if he is honestly to repent. But just for that reason, precipitate repentance is false and is never to be sought after. For it may not be the inner anxiety of heart but only the momentary feeling that presents the guilt so actively. This kind of repentance is selfish, a matter of the senses, sensually powerful for the moment, excited in expression, impatient in the most diverse exaggerations—and, just on this account, is not real repentance. Sudden repentance would drink down all the bitterness of sorrow in a single draught and then hurry on. It wants to get away from guilt. It wants to banish all recollection of it, fortifying itself by imagining that it does this in order not to be held back in the pursuit of the Good. It is its wish that guilt, after a time, might be wholly forgotten. And once again, this is impatience. Perhaps a later sudden repentance may make it apparent that the former sudden repentance lacked true inwardness.

It is told that there was once a man who through his misdeeds deserved the punishment which the law meted out to him. After he had suffered for his wrong acts he went back into ordinary society, improved. Then he went to a strange land, where he was not known, and where he became known for his worthy conduct. All was forgotten. Then one day there appeared a fugitive that recognized the distinguished person as his equal back in those miserable days. This was a terrifying memory to meet. A deathlike fear shook him each time this man passed. Although silent, this memory shouted in a high voice until through the voice of this vile fugitive it took on words. Then suddenly despair seized this man, who seemed to have been saved. And it seized him just because repentance was forgotten, because the improvement toward society was not the resigning of himself to God, so that in the humility of repentance he might remember what he had been. For in the temporal, and sensual, and social sense, repentance is in fact something that comes and goes during the years. But in the eternal sense, it is a silent daily anxiety. It is eternally false, that guilt is changed by the passage of a century. To assert anything of this sort is to confuse the Eternal with what the Eternal is least like—with human forgetfulness.

If anyone in a brazen and impious mood should pronounce absolution from the Good, on the ground that all is lost, then this is sacrilege and this will only add to the guilt by piling up more and more fresh guilt. Now let us indeed consider this. Guilt is not increased for the reason that it seems more and more tragic to the improved individual. It is not a gain that guilt should be wholly forgotten. On the contrary, it is loss and perdition. But it is a gain to win an inner intensity of heart through a deeper and deeper inner sorrowing over guilt. It is not a gain to notice, because of a man's forgetfulness, that he is growing older. But it is a gain to notice that a man has grown older by the deeper and deeper penetration into his heart of the transformation wrought by remorse. One should be able to tell the age of a tree from its bark; in truth one can also tell a man's age in the Good by the intensity of his repentance. There is a battle of despair that struggles—with the consequences. The enemy attacks constantly from behind, and yet the fighter shall continue to advance. When this is so, the repentance is still young and weak. There is a suffering of repentance, that is not impatient in bearing the punishment, but yet each moment cringes under it. When this is so, the repentance is still young and weak. There is a silent, sleepless sorrow at the picturing of what has been wasted. It does not despair, but in its daily grieving, it is always restless. When this is so, the repentance is still young and weak. There is a laborious moving forward in the Good that is like the gait of one whose feet are without skin. He is willing enough, he will gladly walk swiftly, but he has suffered a loss of courage. The pains make his going uncertain and agonizing. When this is so, the repentance is still young and weak.

But when, in spite of this, more confident steps are made along the way, when punishment itself becomes a blessing, when consequences even become redemptive, when progress in the Good is apparent; then is there a milder but deep sorrow that remembers the guilt. It has wearied out and overcome what could deceive and confuse the sight. Therefore it does not see falsely, but sees only the one sorrowful thing. This is the older, the strong and the powerful repentance. When it is a matter of the senses, it is true that they deteriorate and decline in the course of the years. Of a dancer one must say that her time is past when her youth is gone. But it is otherwise with a penitent. And it must be said of repentance that, if it is forgotten, then its strength was only an immaturity; but the longer and the more deeply one treasures it, the better it becomes. For guilt looks most terrifying the nearer at hand one sees it. But repentance is most acceptable to God, the further away repentance views the guilt, along the way of the Good.

So, then, repentance should not merely have its time, but even its time of preparation. Although it should be a silent daily concern, it should also be able to collect itself and be well prepared for the solemn occasion. One such an occasion is the office of Confession, the holy act for which preparation should be made in advance. As a man changes his raiment for a feast, so is a man changed in his heart who prepares himself for the holy act of confession. It is indeed like a changing of raiment to lay off manyness, in order rightly to center down upon one thing; to interrupt the busy course of activity, in order to put on the quiet of contemplation and be at one with oneself. And this being at one with oneself is the simple festival garment of the feast that is the condition of admittance. The manyness, one may see with a dispersed mind, see something of it, see it in passing, see it with half-closed eyes, with a divided mind, see it and indeed not see it. In the rush of busyness, one may be anxious over many things, begin many things, do many things at once, and only half do them all. But one cannot confess without this at-oneness with oneself. He that is not truly at one with himself during the hour of the office of Confession is merely dispersed. If he remains silent, he is not collected; if he speaks, it is only in a chatty vein, not in confession.

But he that in truth becomes at one with himself, he is in the silence. And this is indeed like a changing of raiment: to strip oneself of all that is as full of noise as it is empty, in order to be hidden in the silence, to become open. This silence is the simple festivity of the holy act of confession. For at dancing and festive occasions worldly judgment holds that the more musicians, the better. But when we are thinking of divine things, the deeper the stillness the better. When the wanderer comes away from the much-traveled noisy highway into places of quiet, then it seems to him (for stillness is impressive) as if he must examine himself, as if he must speak out what lies hidden in the depths of his soul. It seems to him, according to the poets' explanation, as if something inexpressible thrusts itself forward from his innermost being, the unspeakable, for which indeed language has no vessel of expression. Even the longing is not the unspeakable itself. It is only a hastening after it. But what silence means, what the surroundings will say in this stillness, is just the unspeakable.

Now the surprise expressed by the trees, if it can be said that the trees looked down in surprise upon the wanderer, explains nothing. And the wood's echo makes very clear indeed that it explains nothing. No, as an impregnable fortress throws back the attack of the enemy, so the echo throws back the voice, no matter how loudly the wanderer shouts. And the clouds hang as they please, and dream only of themselves. Whether seeming to be in restful revery, or enjoying voluptuous soft movements; whether in their transparence running swiftly off, driven by the wind, or gathering in a dark mass to battle with the wind, at least they do not trouble themselves over the wanderer.

And the sea, like a wise man, is sufficient unto itself. Whether it lies like a child and amuses itself with its soft ripples as a child that plays with its mouth, or at noon lies like a drowsy thinker in carefree enjoyment and allows its gaze to wander over all, or in the night ponders deeply over its own being; whether in order to see what is going on, it cunningly conceals itself as though it no longer existed, or whether it rages in its own passion: the sea has a deep ground, it knows well enough what it knows. That which has that deep ground always knows this; but there is no sharing of this knowledge.

And what a puzzling arrangement the army of stars presents! Yet there seems to be an agreement between them that they shall arrange themselves in this fashion. But the stars are so far away that they cannot see the wanderer. It is only the wanderer who can see the stars, hence there may come no agreement between him and the stars. So this melancholy of poetical longing is grounded in a deep misunderstanding, because the lonely wanderer is everywhere surrounded in nature by that which does not understand him, even though it always seems as if an understanding must be arrived at.

Now the unspeakable is like the murmuring of a brook. If you go buried in your own thoughts, if you are busy, then you do not notice it at all in passing. You are not aware that this murmuring exists. But if you stand still, then you discover it. And if you have discovered it, then you must stand still. And when you stand still, then it persuades you. And when it has persuaded you, then you must stoop and listen attentively to it. And when you have stooped to listen to it, then it captures you. And when it has captured you, then you cannot break away from it, then you are overpowered. Infatuated, you sink down at its side. At each moment it is as if in the next moment it must offer an explanation. But the brook goes on murmuring, and the wanderer at its side grows older.

It is otherwise with one who confesses. The stillness also impresses him, yet not in the melancholy mood of misunderstanding, but rather with the seriousness of eternity. He is not, like the wanderer, uncertain about how he came upon the still places. Nor is he like the poet who wishes to seek out loneliness and its mood. No, to confess is a holy act, for which purpose, the mind is collected in preparation. That which environs you knows well enough what this stillness means and that it calls for earnestness. It knows that it is its wish to be understood. It knows that fresh guilt is incurred if it be misunderstood. And the One that is present at this confession is an omniscient One. He knows and remembers all that this man has ever confided to Him, or that this man has ever withdrawn from His confidence. He is an omniscient One that again at the final moment of this man's life will remember this hour, will remember what this man confided to Him and what this man withdrew from His confidence. He is an omniscient One who knows every thought from a distance, who knows plainly the very path of each thought, even when it eludes a man's own consciousness. He is an omniscient One "who seeth in secret," with whom a man speaks even in silence, so that no one shall venture to deceive Him either by talk, or by silence, as in this world where one man can conceal much from the other now by being silent, and again even more by talking.

The person making the confession is not like a servant that gives account to his lord for the management which is given over to him because the lord could not manage all or be present in all places. The all-knowing One was present at each instant for which reckoning shall be made in the account. The account of what is done is not made for the lord's sake but for the servant's sake, who must even render account of how he used the very moment of rendering the account. Nor is the person confessing like one that confides in a friend to whom sooner or later he reveals things that the friend did not previously know. The all-knowing One does not get to know something about the maker of the confession, rather the maker of confession gets to know about himself. Therefore, do not raise the objection against the confession that there is no point in confiding to the all-knowing One that which He already knows. Reply first to the question whether it is not conferring a benefit when a man gets to know something about himself which he did not know before. A hasty explanation could assert that to pray is a useless act, because a man's prayer does not alter the unalterable. But would this be desirable in the long run? Could not fickle man easily come to regret that he had gotten God changed? The true explanation is therefore at the same time the one most to be desired. The prayer does not change God, but it changes the one who offers it. It is the same with the substance of what is spoken. Not God, but you, the maker of the confession, get to know something by your act of confession.

Much that you are able to keep hidden in darkness, you first get to know by your opening it to the knowledge of the all-knowing One. Even the most atrocious misdeeds are committed, even blood is spilt, and many times it must in truth be said of the guilty one: he knew not what he did. Perhaps he died, without ever in repentance really getting to know what it was he had done. For does passion ever properly know what it does? Does not passion's insidious temptation and its apparent excuse center in that deceptive ignorance about itself because, in the instant, it has forgotten the Eternal? For if passion continues in a man, it changes his life into nothing but instants and as passion cunningly serves its deluded master, it gradually gains the ascendancy until the master serves it like a blind serf!

For when hate, and anger, and revenge, and despondency, and melancholy, and despair, and fear of the future, and reliance on the world, and trust in oneself, and pride that infuses itself even into sympathy, and envy that even mingles itself with friendship, and that inclination that may have changed but not for the better: when these dwell in a man—when was it without the deceptive excuse of ignorance? And when a man remained ignorant of them, was it not precisely because he at the same time remained ignorant of the fact that there is an all-knowing One?

Yes, there is an ignorance which no one needs be troubled over if he was deprived either of the opportunity or the capacity to learn. But there is an ignorance about one's own life that is equally tragic for the learned and for the simple, for both are bound by the same responsibility. This ignorance is called self-deceit. There is an ignorance that by degrees, as more and more is learned, gradually changes into knowledge. But there is only one thing that can remove that other ignorance which is self-deception. And to be ignorant of the fact that there is one thing and only one thing, and that only one thing is necessary, is still to be in self-deception.

The ignorant one may have been ignorant of much. He can increase his knowledge, and still there is much that he does not know. But if the self-deluded one speaks of quantity, and of variety, then he is still in self-deception, still deeply ensnared by and in the grip of multiplicity. The ignorant man can gradually acquire wisdom and knowledge, but the self-deluded one if he won "the one thing needful" would have won purity of heart.

3.   BARRIERS TO WILLING ONE THING:

VARIETY AND GREAT MOMENTS
ARE NOT ONE THING

So let us, then, upon the occasion of a time of Confession speak about this sentence: PURITY OF HEART IS TO WILL ONE THING as we base our meditation on the Apostle James' words in his Epistle, chapter 4, verse 8:

"*Draw nigh to God, and he will draw nigh to you. Cleanse your*

hands, ye sinners; and purify your hearts, ye double-minded." For
only the pure in heart can see God, and therefore, draw nigh to
Him; and only by God's drawing nigh to them can they maintain
this purity. And he who in truth wills only one thing can will only
the Good, and he who only wills one thing when he wills the Good
can only will the Good in truth.

Let us speak of this, but let us first put out of our minds the occasion of the office of Confession in order to come to an agreement on
an understanding of this verse, and on what the apostolic word of
admonition "purify your hearts, ye double-minded" is condemning,
namely *double-mindedness*. Then at the close of the talk we may
return more specifically to a treatment of the occasion.

1. IF IT IS TO BE POSSIBLE THAT A MAN CAN WILL ONLY ONE
    THING, THEN HE MUST WILL THE GOOD.

To will only one thing: but will this not inevitably become a
long-drawn-out talk? If one should consider this matter properly
must he not first consider, one by one, each goal in life that a man
could conceivably set up for himself, mentioning separately all of
the many things that a man might will? And not only this; since
each of these considerations readily becomes too abstract in character, is he not obliged as the next step to attempt to will, one after
the other, each of these goals in order to find out what is the single
thing he is to will, if it is a matter of willing only one thing? Yes, if
someone should begin in this fashion, then he would never come to
an end. Or more accurately, how could he ever arrive at the end
since at the outset he took the wrong way and then continued to go
on further and further along this false way? It is only by a painful
route that this way leads to the Good, namely, when the wanderer
turns around and goes back. For as the Good is only a single thing,
so all ways lead to the Good, even the false ones: when the repent-
ant one follows the same way back. Oh, Thou the unfathomable
trustworthiness of the Good! Wherever a man may be in the world,
whichever road he travels, when he wills one thing, he is on a road
that leads him to Thee! Here such a far-flung enumeration would
only work harm. Instead of wasting many moments on naming the
vast multitude of goals or squandering life's costly years in per-

sonal experiments upon them, can the talk do as life ought to do—with a commendable brevity stick to the point?

In a certain sense nothing can be spoken of so briefly as the Good, when it is well described. For the Good without condition and without qualification, without preface and without compromise, is absolutely the only thing that a man may and should will, and is only one thing. Oh, blessed brevity, oh, blessed simplicity, that seizes swiftly what cleverness, tired out in the service of vanity, may grasp but slowly! That which a simple soul, in the happy impulse of a pious heart, feels no need of understanding in an elaborate way, since he simply seizes the Good immediately, is grasped by the clever one only at the cost of much time and much grief. The way this one thing is willed is not such that: one man wills one thing but that which he wills is not the Good; another wills one thing nor is what he wills the Good; a third wills one thing and what he wills *is* the Good. No, it is not done in that way. The person who wills one thing that is not the Good, he does not truly will one thing. It is a delusion, an illusion, a deception, a self-deception that he wills only one thing. For in his innermost being he is, he is bound to be, double-minded. Therefore, the Apostle says, "Purify your hearts, ye double-minded," that is, purify your hearts of double-mindedness; in other words, let you heart in truth will only one thing, for therein is the heart's purity.

And again it is of this same purity of heart that the Apostle is speaking when he says, "If someone lacks wisdom, then let him pray . . . but in faith, not like a double-minded man" (James i. 5, 6, 8). For purity of heart is the very wisdom that is acquired through prayer. A man of prayer does not pore over learned books, for he is the wise man "whose eyes are opened"—when he kneels down (Numbers xxiv. 16).

In a word, then, there is a man whose mind remains piously ignorant of the multitude of things, for the Good is one thing. The more difficult part of the talk is directed to the man whose mind in its double-mindedness has made the doubtful acquaintance of the multitude of things, and of knowledge. If it is certain that a man in truth wills one thing, then he wills the Good, for this alone can be willed in this manner. But both of these assertions speak of identical things, or they speak of different things. The one assertion plainly designates the name of the Good, declaring it to be that one thing. The other assertion cunningly conceals this name. It appears almost as if it spoke of something else. But just on that account it forces its way, searchingly, into a man's innermost being. And no matter how much he may protest, or defy, or boast that he wills only one thing, it searches him through and through in order to show the double-mindedness in him if the one thing he wills is not the Good.

For in truth there was a man on earth who seemed to will only one thing. It was unnecessary for him to insist upon it. Even if he had been silent about it, there were witnesses enough against him who testified how inhumanly he steeled his mind, how nothing touched him, neither tenderness, nor innocence, nor misery; how his blinded soul had eyes for nothing, and how the senses in him had only eyes for the one thing that he willed. And yet it was certainly a delusion, a terrible delusion, that he willed one thing. For pleasure and honor and riches and power and all that this world has to offer only appear to be one thing. It is not, nor does it remain one thing, while everything else is in change or while he himself is in change. It is not in all circumstances the same. On the contrary, it is subject to continual alteration. Hence even if this man named but one thing whether it be pleasure, or honor or riches, actually he did not will one thing. Neither can he be said to will one thing when that one thing which he wills is not in itself one: is in itself a multitude of things, a dispersion, the toy of changeableness, and the prey of corruption! In the time of pleasure see how he longed for one gratification after another. Variety was his watchword. Is variety, then, to will one thing that shall ever remain the same? On the contrary, it is to will one thing that must never be the same. It is to will a multitude of things. And a person who wills in this fashion is not only double-minded but is at odds with himself. For such a man wills first one thing and then immediately wills the opposite, because the oneness of pleasure is the snare and a delusion. It is the diversity of pleasures that he wills. So when the man of whom we are speaking had gratified himself up to the point of disgust, he became weary and sated. Even if he still desired one thing—what was it that he desired? He desired new pleasures; his enfeebled soul raged so that no ingenuity was sufficient to discover something new —something new! It was change he cried out for as pleasure served him, change! change! And it was change that he cried out for as he came to pleasure's limit, as his servants were worn out—change! change!

Now it is to be understood that there are also changes in life that can prove to a man whether he wills one thing. There is the change of the perishable nature when the sensual man must step aside, when dancing and the tumult of the whirling senses are over, when all becomes soberly quiet. That is the change of death. If, for once, the perishable nature should seem to forget to close in, if it should seem as if the sensual one had succeeded in slipping by: death does not forget. The sensual one will not slip past death, who has dominion over what belongs to the earth and who will change into nothing the one thing which the sensual person desires.

And last of all, there is the change of eternity, which changes all. Then only the Good remains and it remains the blessed possession of the man that has willed only one thing. But that rich man whom no misery could touch, that rich man who even in eternity to his own damnation must continue to will one thing, ask him now whether he really wills one thing. So, too, with honor and riches and power. For in the time of strength as he aspired to honor, did he really discover some limit, or was that not simply the striver's restless passion to climb higher and higher? Did he find some rest amid his sleeplessness in which he sought to capture honor and to hold it fast? Did he find some refreshment in the cold fire of his passion? And if he really won honor's highest prize, then is earthly honor in itself one thing? Or in its diversity when the thousands and thousands braid the wreath, is honor to be likened to the gorgeous carpet of the field—created by a single hand? No, like worldly contempt, worldly honor is a whirlpool, a play of confused forces, an illusory moment in the flux of opinions. It is a sense-deception, as when a swarm of insects at a distance seem to the eye like one body; a sense-deception, as when the noise of the many at a distance seems to the ear like a single voice.

Even if honor were unanimous it would still be meaningless, and the more so, the more thousands that create the unanimity. And the greater the multitude that created unanimity, the sooner will it show itself to be meaningless. And indeed it was this unanimity of the thousands that he desired. It was not the approbation of the good men. They are soon counted. No, it was rather the approbation of the thousands. Is, then, this desire for counting, is this to will one thing? To count and count until it suffices, to count and count until a mistake is made; is this to will one thing? Whoever, therefore, wills this honor or fears this contempt, whether or not he is said to will one thing in his innermost being, is not merely double-minded but thousand-minded, and at variance with himself. So is his life when he must grovel—in order to attain honor; when he must flatter his enemies—in order to attain honor; when he must woo the favor of those he despises—in order to attain honor; when he must betray the one whom he respects—in order to attain honor. For to attain honor means to despise oneself after one has attained the pinnacle of honor—and yet to tremble before any change. Change, yes, where does change rage more unchecked than here? What desertion is more swift and sudden, like a mistake in foolery, like a hit by a blind man, when the seeker for honor has not even time to take off the garb of honor before insult seizes him in it? Change, the final change, the absolute certainty among the range of unpredictables: no matter how loud the thunder of honor may sound over his grave, even if it could be heard over the whole earth, there is one who cannot hear it: the dead man, he who died with honor, the single thing he had desired. But also in dying he lost the honor, for it remains outside, it marches home again, it dies away like an echo. Change, the true change, when eternity exists: I should like to know if honor's crown is offered to the much-honored one there! And yet eternity is more just than the earth and the world; for in eternity there is a crown of honor laid aside for each of those that have in truth willed only one thing. So also with riches and power and the world that passes away and the lust thereof. The one who has willed either of them, even if he only willed one thing, must, to his own agony, continue to will it when it has passed, and learn by the agony of contradiction that it is not one thing. But the one who in truth willed one thing and therefore willed the Good, even if he be sacrificed for it, why should he not go on willing the same in eternity, the same thing that he was willing to die for? Why should he not will the same, when it has triumphed in eternity?

To will one thing, therefore, cannot mean to will that which only appears to be one thing. The fact is that the worldly goal is not one thing in its essence because it is unreal. Its so-called unity is actually nothing but emptiness which is hidden beneath the manyness.

In the short-lived moment of delusion the worldly goal is therefore a multitude of things, and thus not one thing. So far is it from a state of being and remaining one thing, that in the next moment it changes itself into its opposite. Carried to its extreme limit, what is pleasure other than disgust? What is earthly honor at its dizzy pinnacle other than contempt for existence? What are riches, the highest superabundance of riches, other than poverty? For no matter how much all the earth's gold hidden in covetousness may amount to, is it not infinitely less than the smallest mite hidden in the contentment of the poor! What is worldly omnipotence other than dependence? What slave in chains is as unfree as a tyrant! No, the worldly goal is not one thing. Diverse as it is, in life it is changed into its opposite, in death into nothing, in eternity into damnation: for the one who has willed this goal. Only the Good is one thing in its essence and the same in each of its expressions. Take love as an illustration. The one who truly loves does not love once and for all. Nor does he use a part of his love, and then again another part. For to change it into small coins is not to use it rightly. No, he loves with all of his love. It is wholly present in each expression. He continues to give it away as a whole, and yet he keeps it intact as a whole, in his heart. Wonderful riches! When the miser has gathered all the world's gold in sordidness—then he has become poor. When the lover gives away his whole love, he keeps it entire—in purity of the heart. Shall a man in truth will one thing, then this one thing that he wills must be such that it remains unaltered in all changes, so that by willing it he can win immutability. If it changes continually, then he himself becomes changeable, double-minded, and unstable. And this continual change is nothing else than impurity.

Now, willing one thing does not mean to commit the grave mistake of a brazen, unholy enthusiasm, namely, to will the big, no matter whether it be good or bad. Also one who wills in this fashion no matter how desperately he does it, is indeed double-minded. Is not despair simply double-mindedness? For what is despairing other than to have two wills? For whether the weakling despairs over not being able to wrench himself away from the bad, or whether the brazen one despairs over not being able to tear himself completely away from the Good: they are both double-minded, they both have two wills. Neither of them honestly wills one thing, however desperately they may seem to will it. Whether it was a woman whom desire brought to desperation, or whether it was a man who despaired in defiance; whether a man despaired because he got his will, or despaired because he did not get his will: each one in despairing has two wills, one that he fruitlessly tries wholly to follow and one that he fruitlessly tries wholly to avoid. In this fashion has God, better than any king, insured himself against every rebellion. For it has indeed happened that a king has been dethroned by a rebellion. But each rebel against God, in the last instance, is himself reduced to despair. Despair is the limit—"here and no further!" Despair is the limit. Here are met the cowardly timorous ill-temper of self-love, and the proud defiant presumption of the mind—here they are met in equal impotence.

Only too soon personal experience and the experience of others teaches how far most men's lives are from being what a man's life ought to be. All have great moments. They see themselves in the magic mirror of possibility which hope holds before them while the wish flatters them. But they swiftly forget this sight in the daily round of things. Or perhaps they talk enthusiastic words, for "the tongue is a little member, and boasteth great things."[5] But talk takes the name of enthusiasm in vain by proclaiming loudly from the housetop what it should work out in silence. And in the midst of the trivial details of life these enthusiastic words are quickly forgotten. It is forgotten that such a thing was said of this man. It is forgotten that it was he himself who said it. Now and then, perhaps memory wakens with horror, and remorse seems to promise new strength. But, alas, this, too, lasts only for a good-sized moment. All of them have intentions, plans, resolutions for life, yes, for eternity. But the intention soon loses its youthful strength and fades away. The resolution is not firmly grounded and is unable to withstand opposition. It totters before circumstances and is altered by them. Memory, too, has a way of failing, until by common practice and habit they learn to draw sympathy from one another. If someone proclaims the slender comfort that excuses yield, instead of realizing how treacherous is such sympathy, they finally come to regard it as edifying, because it encourages and strengthens indolence. Now there are men who find it edifying that the demand to will one thing be asserted in all its sublimity, in all its severity, so that it may press its claim into the innermost fastness of the soul. Others find it edifying that a wretched compromise should be made between God, the claim, and the language used. There are men who find it edifying if only someone will challenge them. But there are also the sleepy souls who regard it as not only pleasing, but even edifying, to be lulled to sleep.

This is indeed a lamentable fact; but there is a wisdom which is not from above, but is earthly and fleshly and devilish. It has discovered this common human weakness and indolence; it wants to be helpful. It perceives that all depends upon the will and so it proclaims loudly, "Unless it wills one thing, a man's life is sure to become one of wretched mediocrity, of pitiful misery. He must will one thing regardless of whether it be good or bad. He must will one thing, for therein lies a man's greatness." Yet it is not difficult to see through this powerful error. As to the working out of salvation, the holy Scripture teaches that sin is the corruption of man. Salvation, therefore, lies only in the purity with which a man wills the Good. That very earthly and devilish cleverness distorts this into a temptation to perdition; weakness is a man's misfortune; strength the sole salvation: "When the unclean spirit is gone out of a man, he walketh through dry and empty places but finds no rest. Then he turns back again and now he brings with him" that unclean cleverness, the wisdom of the desert and the empty places, that unclean cleverness—that now drives out the spirit of indolence and of mediocrity "so that the last stage becomes worse than the first."[6] How shall one describe the nature of such a man? It is said of a singer that by overscreeching he can crack his voice. In like fashion, such a man's nature by overscreeching itself and the voice of conscience, has cracked. It is said of a man who stands dizzily upon a high place, that all things run together before his eyes. Such a man has made himself giddy in the infinite, where those things which are forever separate run together into one thing, so that only the vast remains.

It is this dryness and emptiness that always gives birth to giddiness. But no matter how desperately such a man may seem to will one thing, he is double-minded. If he, the self-willed one, had his way, then there would be only this one thing: he would be the only one that was not double-minded, he the only one that had cast off every chain, he the only one that was free. But the slave of sin is not yet free; nor has he cast off the chain, "because he scoffs at it."[7]

He is in bonds, and therefore double-minded, and for once he may not have his own way. There is a power that binds him. He cannot tear himself loose from it. Nay, he cannot even wholly will it. For this power, too, is denied him. If you, my listener, should see such a man, although it is unlikely, for without a doubt weakness and mediocrity are the more common, if you should meet him in what he himself would call a weak moment, but which, alas, you would have to call a better moment; if you should meet him when he had found no rest in the desert, when the giddiness passes away for a moment and he feels an agonizing longing for the Good; if you should meet him when, shaken in his innermost being, and not without sadness, he was thinking of that man of single purpose who even in all his frailty still wills the Good: then you would discover that he had two wills, and you would discover his painful double-mindedness.

Desperate as he was, he thought: lost is lost. But he could not help turning around once more in his longing for the Good. How terribly embittered he had become against this very longing, a longing that reveals that, just as a man in all his defiance has not power enough wholly to loose himself from the Good, because it is the stronger, so he has not even the power wholly to will it.

Perhaps you may even have heard that desperate one say, "Some good went down with me." When a man meets his death by drowning, as he sinks, without being quite dead he comes to the surface again. At last a bubble comes out of his mouth. When this has happened, then he sinks, dead. That bubble was the last breath, the last supply of air, that could make him lighter than the sea. So with that remark. In that remark the last hope of salvation expired. In that remark he gave himself up. Was there still concealed in this thought a hope of salvation? Hidden in the soul, was there still in this thought a possible link with salvation? When a remark is pronounced in confidence to another man (oh, terrible misuse of confidence, even if the desperate one only misused it against himself!), when this word is heard, then he sinks forever.

Alas, it is horrible to see a man rush toward his own destruction. It is horrible to see him dance on the rim of the abyss without any intimation of it. But this clarity about himself and about his own destruction is even more horrible. It is horrible to see a man seek comfort by hurling himself into the whirlpool of despair. But this coolness is still more horrible: that, in the anxiety of death, a man should not cry out for help, "I am going under, save me"; but that he should quietly choose to be a witness to his own destruction! Oh, most extreme vanity, not to wish to draw man's eyes to himself by beauty, by riches, by ability, by power, by honor, but to wish to get his attention by his own destruction, by choosing to say of himself what at most pity in all sadness may venture to say of such a person at his grave, "Yet, some good went down with him." Oh, horrible doubleness of mind in a man's destruction, to wish to draw a sort of advantage out of the fact that the Good remains the only thing that a man has not willed. For now the other will becomes apparent to him, even if it were so weak as to be but a feeble dallying in the moment of destruction, an attempt to be exceptional by means of his own destruction.

To will one thing cannot, then, mean to will what in its essence is not one thing, but only seems to be so by means of a horrible falsehood. Only through a lie is it one thing. Now just as he that only wills this one thing is a liar, so he that conjures up this one thing is the father of lies. That dryness and emptiness is not in truth one thing, but is in truth nothing at all. And it is destruction for the man that only wills that one. If, on the contrary, a man should in truth will only one thing, then this thing must, in the truth of its innermost being, be one thing. It must, by an eternal separation, cut off the heterogeneous from itself in order that it may in truth continue to be one and the same thing and thereby fashion that man who only wills one thing into conformity with itself.

In truth to will one thing, then, can only mean to will the Good, because every other object is not a unity; and the will that only wills that object, therefore, must become double-minded. For as the coveted object is, so becomes the coveter. Or would it be possible that a man by willing the evil could will one thing, provided that it was possible for a man so to harden himself as to will nothing but the evil? Is not this evil, like evil persons, in disagreement with itself, divided against itself? Take one such man, separate him from society, shut him up in solitary confinement. Is he not at odds with himself there, just as a poor union between persons of his sort is an association that is ridden with dissension? But a good man, even if he lived in an out-of-the-way corner of the world and never saw any human being, would be at one with himself and at one with all about him because he wills one thing, and because the Good is one thing. *Each one who in truth would will one thing must be led to will the Good,* even though now and then it happens that a man begins by willing one thing that is not in its deepest sense the Good although it may be something quite innocent; and then, little by little, he is changed really in truth to will one thing by willing the Good. Love, from time to time, has in this way helped a man along the right path. Faithfully he only willed one thing, his love. For it, he would live and die. For it, he would sacrifice all and in it alone he would have his eternal reward. Yet the act of being in love is still not in the deepest sense the Good. But it may possibly become for him a helpful educator, who will finally lead him by the possession of his beloved one or perhaps by her loss, in truth to will one thing and to will the Good. In this fashion a man is educated by many means; and true love is also an education toward the Good.

Perhaps there was a man whose enthusiasm reached out toward a definite cause. In his enthusiasm he desired only one thing. He would live and die for that cause. He would sacrifice all for that in which alone he would have his happiness, for love and enthusiasm are not satisfied with a divided heart. Yet his endeavor was perhaps still not in the deepest sense the Good. Thus enthusiasm became for him a teacher, whom he outgrew, but to whom also he owed much. For, as it is said, all ways lead to the Good, when a man in truth only wills one thing. And where there is some truth in the fact that he wills one thing, this is all for the best. But there is danger that the lover and the enthusiast may swerve out of the true course and aim perhaps for the impressive instead of being led to the Good. The Good is certainly also in truth the impressive, but the impressive is not always the Good. And one can bid for a woman's favor by willing something when it is merely impressive. This can flatter the girl's pride and she can repay it with her adoration. But God in heaven is not as a young girl's folly. He does not reward the impressive with admiration. The reward of the good man is to be allowed to worship in truth.

4. BARRIERS TO WILLING ONE THING:

THE REWARD-DISEASE

2. IF IT BE POSSIBLE FOR A MAN REALLY IN TRUTH TO WILL
    ONE THING, THEN HE MUST WILL THE GOOD IN TRUTH.

A. IF IT BE POSSIBLE FOR A MAN TO WILL THE GOOD IN
    TRUTH, THEN HE MUST BE AT ONE WITH HIMSELF IN WILL-
    ING TO RENOUNCE ALL DOUBLE-MINDEDNESS.

*Therefore, if it be possible for a man to will one thing,
then he must will the Good, for only the Good is one.
Thus if it becomes a fact that he wills one thing, he must
will the Good in truth.*

Oh, that one might be able, at this point, to speak rightly! For at
this point what the talk is concerned with is the life that most men
lead: they desire the Good, and yet the world is still so filled with
double-mindedness. Here, too, the speaker has his own life, his own
frailties, his own share of doubleness of mind. Oh, that the talk
might not seem to wish to judge or accuse others. For to wish to
judge others instead of one's self would also be double-mindedness.
Oh, that the talk might not seem to press demands that are binding
upon others but that exempt the speaker, as if he had only the task
of talking. For this, too, is double-mindedness, just as it is hidden
pride to wish to offer comfort to others but not to be willing to let
oneself be comforted. No matter how adroitly, by means of a sad or
cheerful mood, he knows how in sympathy to console others, if at
the same time he believes that for himself there is no consolation,
this is hidden pride and so double-mindedness. Oh, that one might
wound no one except to his healing; that the talk might embitter no
one and yet be the truth, that the talk along with truth might be
sufficiently penetrating to reveal that which is hidden! Oh, that the
talk might wipe out double-mindedness and win hearts for the
Good! Yet not by persuasion. For this also readily becomes double-

minded, to wish to enjoy the pleasure of persuading, to treasure the
longing for it, to quiet oneself by it—and thereby forget what is to
be done. Oh, that the talk might repel the listeners from the
speaker and attract them only to the Good!

1.   *In the first place a statement must be made which is easy
     to grasp: that the man who desires the Good for the sake
     of the reward does not will one thing, but is double-
     minded.*

The Good is one thing; the reward is another that may be present
and may be absent for the time being, or until the very last. When
he, then, wills the Good for the sake of the reward, he does not will
one thing but two. It is now certain that he will not in this way
make much progress along the pathway of the Good. For in truth it
is as if a man, instead of naturally using both eyes to see one thing,
should use one eye to see one side and the other eye to see the
other side. This does not succeed. It only confuses sight. However,
we are not speaking about this here, except to note that it is double-mindedness. In ancient times this problem was also frequently
an object of consideration. There were shameless teachers of impu-
dence[8] who thought it right to do wrong on a large scale and then to
make it appear as if one willed the Good. In this way they thought
one had a double advantage: the pitiful advantage of being able to
do wrong, to be able to get one's own way, to let one's passions
rage, and the hypocritical advantage of seeming to be good. But in
ancient times there was also a simple sage, whose simplicity became a snare for the impudent ones' sophistry. He taught that in
order really to be certain that it was the Good that man willed, one
ought even to shun seeming good, presumably in order that the reward should not become tempting. For so different is the Good and
the reward, when the reward is separately striven after, that the
Good is the ennobling and the sanctifying; the reward is the tempting. But the tempting is never the Good. This reward, that we are
talking about here, is the world's reward. For the reward which
God for eternity has joined with the Good has nothing bad in it. It
is also quite certain. Neither things present nor things to come, nor
height nor depth, can separate it from the Good.[9] Angels cannot
will such separation and all the devils are not strong enough to ac-

complish it. But if the world itself is not Good in its innermost being; if, as the Scripture says, it still "lieth in wickedness,"[10] or if it is far from being as one for whom it is a rare exception not to will the Good; if this be so, then earthly reward is of a doubtful character. And hence it is all the more likely that the world will reward what it takes for the Good, what to a certain degree resembles the Good, what, as those impudent ones taught, has the Good's appearance—and those impudent ones were not lacking in intimate knowledge of the world. Hence reward is indeed that which tempts.

The question is not difficult. If a man loves a girl for the sake of her money, who will call him a lover? He does not love the girl, but the money. He is not a lover but a money-seeker. But if a man said, "It is the girl I love and she has money," and he should ask us for our judgment, for we have no particular call to judge, then a good answer would be, "It is a difficult matter with this money. Money may have a great influence, one can easily be deceived, and it is very difficult to know oneself." If he were really very intent on this matter he could even wish that the money were not there, just to test his love. For a true lover would say, "The girl has only one fault, she has money."

And what now may the girl say! If she said, "The advantage I wish to have is that it is I that have made him rich." I wonder if she could be called a real lover? For she did not really love him, but the money. If, on the contrary, the two in their love agreed to do a good act with this money which was a hindrance to them, then it would be made possible for them to desire love alone. Let us hope that no one would set about to disturb the innocent fancy of this beautiful thought by telling us, "What life will surely teach that pair!" Alas, there is a wretched knowledge, a shabby acquaintance with the real, that is not merely wretched and shabby but also on all occasions puts on an important front. As though that knowledge were anything but infamy in any person who in a cowardly and traitorous and envious and empty puffed-up manner dares to make such a comment! As if that knowledge were other than contemptible double-mindedness that both wills and does not will, and therefore will only lie, lie about the Good, and lie about the man who is good. Yes, what was once said of memory is applicable to that sort of knowledge, namely, that one might prefer to learn the art of forgetting.[11] Indeed it is easy enough for one to become schooled in that sort of knowledge. It may be learned readily enough from all the wretched ones, so that one might rather wish and pray that there was an art that one could learn that would teach him to remain ignorant of such knowledge.

Now about desiring the girl without the money. Let us consider the Good, where all is on a more perfect plane, where earnestness and truth are the innocent fancy of beautiful thought. To will the Good for the sake of reward is double-mindedness. To will one thing is, therefore, to will the Good without considering the reward. In truth to will one thing is to will the Good, but not, therefore, to desire reward in the world. The reward can of course come without a man's willing it. Even though it is in the outward realms, the reward may come from God. But when a man considers that all reward in the outer realm can become what the world's reward always is—a temptation for him, then he must guard himself even against true reward just in order rightly to be able to will the Good. Oh, that he might not forget, that this, even such a desire to guard himself, may once more be a temptation to pride.

But if it be true of the reward for Good in the world, that the reward the world gives is so dangerous, then the Good has almost an edifying quality here in this world (even if this edification is somewhat softened in the blessed smile of eternity). For here the man who in truth wills the Good, by willing one thing, is very rarely led into the difficulty of being tempted by reward. Now, that the Good has its own reward is indeed forever certain. There is nothing so certain. It is not even more certain that God exists, for that is one and the same thing. But here on earth, Good is often temporarily rewarded by ingratitude, by lack of appreciation, by poverty, by contempt, by many sufferings, and now and then by death. It is not this reward to which we refer when we say that the Good has its reward. Yet this is the reward that comes in the external world and that comes first of all. And it is precisely this reward which the man is anxious about, who wills the Good for the sake of the reward. For he has no time to wait, no time, no years, no life to give away— for an eternity. Hence that reward which comes in the external world is so far from being desirable, that, on the contrary, it is both valuable and encouraging when it does not come in the outer world, so that the double-mindedness in the inner realm may perish, and so that the reward in heaven may be all the greater.

To will the Good for the sake of the reward is, as it were, a symbol of double-mindedness. And a double-minded man, according to the Apostle James' words, is "unsteady in all his ways." Nor does he accomplish anything. For a double-minded man, says the same Apostle, may not expect to receive that for which he prays. Even if such a double-minded one, who wills the Good for the sake of the reward, may puff himself up, appear defiant, and fancy that he has won his goal, even if many blind ones foolishly think the same; yet let us not deceive each other, my listener, or allow a sense-deception to do so. It is quite possible that he will win good things, that are called reward. Still he does not get them as reward, at least not in truth, if it be true that to will the Good in truth is recognizable by one's willing it without reward. Oh, Thou the Good's wonderful at-oneness with thyself that protects thee from being deceived! When, for the sake of the reward, a double-minded person only pretends to will the Good, and he seems to get the reward, nevertheless he does not get it. For that which he gets, he does not get as reward—for the Good. So far is he from getting it as reward that rather at the very moment that he receives the Good, he discovers that the reward has vanished.

Look at the girl who has money. A false lover can perhaps deceive her, so that it appears as if he loved her, although what he really loves is the money. She may joyfully, perhaps even gratefully, continue to live in the fantasy that she is loved. But no one can deceive the Good, nay, not in all eternity! Not in all eternity! Yes, it is just there that one has the least chance of deceiving it. Perhaps here on earth it can be accomplished; not that the Good is deceived, but men may be deceived by the likeness of the Good. Such does not escape the attention of the Good. From time to time it focuses its wrath on such a man and reveals his deception. But often the Good lets the deceiver go his way because the Good knows, in itself, that it is the stronger. Only a weak and effeminate man demands immediate justification, demands immediate success in the outer world, just because he is weak, and therefore must have an outward proof—that he is the strongest. The one who is really strong and is really the more powerful, quietly concedes a domain to the weakling and readily allows him to give the impression

of being the stronger. So with the Good, when it tolerates such a
deceiver, it is as if it said to him secretly, "Yes, enjoy yourself with
your false appearance, but remember, we two, we shall talk together again."

The double-minded one stands at a parting of the ways. Two visions appear: the Good and the reward. It is not in his power to
bring them into agreement, for they are fundamentally different
from each other. Only that reward which God for all eternity adds
to the Good in the inner realm, only that is in truth homogeneous
with the Good. So he stands pondering and reflecting. If he is
wholly absorbed in his pondering, then he continues to stand—a
symbol of double-mindedness. But suppose he should tear himself
free from the deliberation and should now go forward. Along
which way? Ah, do not ask him about that. Perhaps he is able to
answer learned questions and to betray extensive knowledge. But
one thing he cannot do, one and only one thing he is not able to do:
he cannot answer the question about which of the two ways he is
taking. By repeated thoughtful pondering in an attempt to see the
heterogeneous together, he has somewhat confused his sight. He
believes he has found that there is a third way and that it is this
third way along which he is going. This third way has no name. For
it does not really exist, and so it is obvious that he, if he is sincere,
cannot say which way he is taking. If he is sincere, for otherwise he
would indeed declare that he is going along the way of the Good, it
may even be important to convince men of that—in order that they
may honor him. For honor belongs to the reward which he is seeking after. The third way is the secret which he keeps to himself.
And now how does he go along this third way which is narrower
than any rope-dancer's rope, for it simply does not exist? Does he
go steadily and firmly like one that has a definite goal before his
eyes; like one that scarcely looks at anything around him in order
not to be disturbed; like one that looks for one thing alone—for the
goal? No, only a person upon the path of the Good walks in this
fashion with only the Good before his eyes.

Does he, then, go like the one that is hunting for every sensation
along the broad way of pleasure? No, that he does not do. Does he
go like a carefree youth who lightheartedly lets his gaze wander
over everything about him on his way? Alas, he is too old for that.
How does he go, then? He walks so slowly under the circum-

stances, because of the difficulty of the way. He feels his way forward with his foot and as he finally plants his foot and takes a step, he immediately looks about at the clouds, notes the way the wind blows, and whether the smoke goes straight up from the chimney. It is, namely, the reward—earth's reward—that he is looking for. And that reward is like the clouds and like the wind and like the smoke of the chimney. And so he asks his way continually. He gives minute attention to the faces of the passing people in order to learn how the reward stands, what the prices are, what demands the time and the people would place upon the Good if they were to give the reward.

What is he really after? Nay, do not ask him about that. Perhaps he would be able to answer every other question with the exception of that one about the way. But this question he cannot answer in definite terms, if he is to answer it sincerely, for the reason that the answer is all too readily at hand: that he wills the Good and detests vice—when vice seems to be loathsome; that he wills the approbation of good people—when they are in the majority and possess the power; that he will benefit the good cause—when it is so good as to confer some advantage upon him. Yet in sincerity he dares not say definitely what he wills. He dares not say loudly and decisively with the full voice of conviction that he wills the Good. He utters it with the dull caution of double-mindedness. For he knows well enough that the Good and the reward are not rationed out together. Let us assume that by such a careless utterance the Good and the reward came into conflict, and let us assume that he be considered as willing the Good in this manner. Now suppose that the reward is missing, which has previously happened in this world. What would he do then? Would he will the Good and even be willing to forego the appearance of willing the Good? No, definitely not. Does he, then, will the reward? Yes, but he will not plainly admit it. Does he, then, will the Good? Yes, now and then, perhaps, for decency's sake, as it is called. He pretends, therefore, to will the Good—for the sake of honor and reward. As a matter of fact he does occasionally will the Good—to save his face.

This is what happens to the man who hankers after a reward. He is so double-minded that one hardly knows whether to laugh or to weep over him, if one does not know that all double-mindedness is destruction. But if one knows this, he knows well enough what to do, especially when he has his own share of this double-mindedness.

Now this matter of willing the Good for the sake of reward may take a somewhat different form. Perhaps there was a man who really in all sincerity willed the Good. Humbly before God, and quickened in his enthusiasm, he cheerfully understood when the world and when men worked against him. He cheerfully understood that this opposition was the reward, and that there was nothing further to be said about it. Strengthened by God, bracing himself only by his confidence, he almost never desired to be rewarded in any other way by this world. But then he became weary. He clutched after the reward in the narrower sense, and after an easier understanding of the reward. For in general the closer the understanding lies to misunderstanding, the easier it becomes. He could not bear with the Eternal. He could not endure the opposition of the world and of the people. So first he claimed the reward, under the interpretation that there ought to be an agreement between the Good and the world. Finally, he demanded the reward alone. In this fashion he slipped backwards. Oh, sad end to a good beginning! Oh, Thou the Good's stern zeal for thyself, that Thou perhaps permittest him to get the reward in the world, just when Thou hast rejected him; that Thou lettest him get the reward of the world, while he has ungratefully forgotten what a blessedness it is to have Thy reward, while earth withholds her reward from him!

Or he did not begin so high, but simply with willing the Good in truth. Without knowledge of the world, without having conceived in his heart the possibility of what may happen to a man, he piously hoped that the Good would not withhold its reward. Now understood in the light of eternity, this is an eternal and sacred truth. But in the sense of temporal existence, it is foolish and fruitless cleverness. So he went out into the school of experience, for we all go to school as long as we live. Life's school is for adults and therefore is somewhat more stern than the children's school, where the attentive and industrious ones come to the fore among those of the same age. So life took him into its stern school. But he resisted. He reduced his demands. He did not wish to deceive the Good. Alas, neither would that help. He believed that as long as he clung to the Good, he possessed a claim upon life. Now it seemed to him as though the Good alone had claims upon him. At this his courage slackened. He looked about him where so many others helped themselves to the reward. The tempter began to frighten him into a feeling of faint-heartedness as to why he did not wish to be like the others and as to why he insisted upon running after the vagaries of imagination instead of laying hold of that which is certain. Then his mind was changed. In life it happened to him just as in school it might happen to the superior pupil if there were no teacher. The mediocre would gain the dominance and gain power to seduce the superior pupils, because the good pupil had no teacher in whom to seek protection. And in life there is no visible teacher who encourages the good pupil, for we are all pupils. If the good pupil keeps on, he must find the encouragement in himself. This he did not find. His courage was shattered. Perhaps he did not find what he now sought in the world. And so he went down, he the deceived one, whom the world deceived as to the reward, when he willed the Good, and whom the world betrayed most terribly, when it got him to forsake the Good.

5. BARRIERS TO WILLING ONE THING:

WILLING OUT OF FEAR OF PUNISHMENT

2. *Next, it must be said that the man who only wills the Good out of fear of punishment does not will one thing. He is double-minded.*

The other aspect of the reward-centered man is willing the good only out of fear of punishment. For in essence, this is the same as to will the Good for the sake of the reward, to the extent that avoiding an evil is an advantage of the same sort as that of attaining a benefit. The Good is one thing. Punishment is something else. Therefore the double-minded person does not desire one thing when he desires the Good under the condition that he shall avoid punishment. The condition lays its finger upon just the double-mindedness. If that condition were not there, he would not fear the punishment, for punishment is indeed not what a man should fear.

He should fear to do wrong. But if he has done wrong, then he must, if he really wills one thing and sincerely wills the Good, desire to be punished, that the punishment may heal him just as medicine heals the sick. If one who is sick fears the bitterness of the medicine, or fears "to let himself be cut and cauterized by the physician," then what he really fears is—to get well, even though in delirium he swears most positively that this is not the case, and that, on the contrary, he all too eagerly longs for his health. As for this assurance, the more zealously it is made, the more clearly is its double-mindedness revealed: that he desires his health and yet does not will it, although he has it in his power. To desire what one cannot carry out is not such double-mindedness because the hindrance is not within the control of the one who desires it. But when the person who desires is himself the obstacle that keeps himself from getting his desire fulfilled, not by giving it up, for then he would be at one with himself, but both by not willing and yet by willing to continue to desire: then the double-mindedness is clear—if it can be made clear—or at least the fact is clear that it is double-mindedness. If what a man fears is not the mistake itself, but the reproach at being caught in the mistake, then that fear so far from helping him out of the error may even lead him into that which is still more ruinous, even if apart from this he had made no mistake.

So, too, with one who wishes to do good out of fear of punishment, if indeed it can be done in that fashion, if it is not as when the fear-ridden person turns his whole life into nothing but illness, out of fear of becoming ill. Fear of the punishment is so far from helping him to do the Good in truth, that it ruins him, just because punishment is a medicine. But everyone, even a child knows that nothing is so dangerous as a medicine—when it is used in the wrong way. Even if it does not end in death, it may bring on critical illness. And spiritually understood there is a ruinous illness, namely, *not to fear what a man should fear;* the sacredness of modesty, God in the heavens, the command of duty, the voice of conscience, the accountability to eternity. In order to be insured against or of being saved from this illness, it is profitable to a man that he should punish himself, "that he beat his breast and chastise his heart." It is still more fruitful that he be punished in order that the punishment may keep him awake and sober, for in whatever way this may be more precisely understood, it will be to his profit and his advantage; yes, truly to his advantage, if he voluntarily allows himself to be punished.

But then in a spiritual sense, there is another illness, a still more destructive one: *To fear what a man should not and ought not to fear*. The first illness is defiance and obstinacy and willfulness. The second is cowardice and servility and hypocrisy. And this last is terrible just because it is an illness where the physician sees to his horror that the sick person has used the medicine—in the wrong way. It may indeed seem that the one that wills the Good out of fear of punishment may still not be called ill, for he really wills the Good. For surely punishment is not an illness? Yet he is none the less ill and his illness is just this: the confusing of the illness and the medicine. It might seem that the one who wills the Good out of fear of punishment cannot be said to have used the medicine, and therefore cannot be said to have used it wrongly. For he indeed wills the Good. He wishes to be healthy—out of his fear of having to use the medicine. But spiritually understood, where illness is not in the material body as the fever is in the blood, and where medicine is not something external, like drops in a bottle, then fear means: to use and to have used, to have taken the medicine—in the wrong way. This shows itself clearly in the terrible and fatal manifestations of that other illness.

It has been noted that fear of poverty suddenly makes the extravagant person miserly; but it is never observed that it makes him thrifty, and why not? Because the fear of the medicine lay in taking it in the wrong way. Indeed, fear of the body's infirmities has taught the voluptuary to observe moderation in debauchery (for the fear was to take the medicine in the wrong way) but it has never made him chaste. It taught him, instead of forgetting God in the whirlpool of vice (and distraction of mind!), daily to mock God by moderation—in debauchery (abominable discretion!). And indeed, fear of punishment has made the sinner into a hypocrite, who in hypocrisy's loathsome doubleness of mind pretended to love God (for the fear was to take the medicine in the wrong way), but it has never made him pure of heart. This is firmly established: that punishment is not illness, but medicine. Thus it may be a punishment for the frivolous person to be confined to a sick bed, but suppose in truth he understands it as punishment, then the illness, the fever or whatever other disorder it now may be, then it is a medicine. On the other hand, all double-mindedness that wills the Good only out of fear of punishment can always be known in the end, because it considers punishment as an illness. If double-mindedness, then, which one may inwardly pity, is an overtense anxiety, as when the horrified imagination of the sick person alters the effect of the medicine: then the mark is that punishment is confused with illness and one who suffers from it simply does not in truth desire to be released from the illness, but in falsity desires to be rid of the medicine.

Now which is the punishment that is to be feared; what, more precisely, is understood by it? When we reflect upon that, double-mindedness becomes more obvious. For one and the same illness may be regarded very differently and its danger varies according to the different wrong conceptions of punishment that are present. *Someone may think that by punishment is meant what is now seldom mentioned—the punishment of eternity.* And it might seem that the person was not double-minded who wills the Good out of fear of that punishment, since he refers the punishment to eternity, therefore to the same place where the Good has its home. And yet, he does not will the Good, he wills it only out of fear of punishment. Therefore—if there were no punishment! In that "if" lurks double-mindedness. If there were no punishment! In that "if" hisses double-mindedness. If there were no punishment, or if indeed there was a man who could convince him that eternity's punishment was a fantasy; or if it became common practice to think in this fashion; or if he could travel to a foreign country where it was common practice; or if cowardly and hypocritical superstition could discover a cheap means of propitiation!!! Look at the double-mindedness! Note that it can just as easily seek its consolation in unbelief as in superstition. And if double-mindedness does not seek them out, then it is they that try to capture double-mindedness until the matter becomes obvious. If one were briefly to characterize double-mindedness by a single appropriate expression, what would be more characteristic than that—"if," "in case that"! For when the will in a man gets command so that he keeps on willing the Good and in truth willing only that one thing, then there is no "in case that." But double-mindedness brings itself to a stop continually by its "in case that." It does not contain the impetus of eternity and does not have the infinite's open road before it. It passes itself and meets itself as it is coming to a stop. It is said that by the holy sign of the cross one can halt the evil Spirit, so that it cannot go on. In this fashion, double-mindedness brings itself to a halt by its pitiful sign, by its "in case that." For a moment it may seem as if double-mindedness did not exist. Double-mindedness can perhaps speak in such a fashion that it deceives. But when a man begins to act and there is double-mindedness in him, then he is plunged immediately into this paralyzing "in case that." It is true that a man may fill up the temporal order with his talk, but eternity will reveal the nature of his deeds. Only for him who wills the Good in truth, only for him can what is taught about the punishments of eternity be eternally true. The one that merely fears the punishment, for him it cannot remain eternally true, for there is nothing eternal in him, since the Eternal can only be in him if he wills the Good in truth. There is only one proof that the Eternal exists: faith in it.

Fear is a tottering proof, that proves that the fearful one does not believe or does so as when the devil believes, but trembles because he does not believe. Only one thing can help a man to will the Good in truth: the Good itself. Fear is a deceitful aid. It can embitter one's pleasure, make life laborious and miserable, make one old and decrepit; but it cannot help one to the Good since fear itself has a false conception of the Good—and the Good does not allow itself to be deceived. Or does not this also belong to the true nature of the Good, this zeal for itself, that will not tolerate anyone else, any strange helper, any interference by some contentious one who might only create confusion. For, when the Good took up its place at the goal where the reward beckons or where the Good itself beckons to a man, the Good against its will would then be forced to see and to put up with the fact that there were two paths, and two men bent on them; the one because he willed the Good in truth, and humbly but gladly followed its beckoning; the other because fear drove him thence. Spiritually understood, is it conceivable that two such different men could possibly be able to come to the same place! For in a spiritual sense, place is not something external, to which a slave might come against his will when the overseer uses his scourge. And the path is not something that does not matter whether one rides forward or backwards. But the place and the path are within a man and just as the place is the blessed state of the striving soul, so the path is the striving soul's continual transformation. Nay, as the Good is only one thing, so it wishes also to be the only thing that aids a man. The Good suckles and nurses the infant, rears and nourishes the youth, strengthens the adult, supports the aged. The Good teaches the striving one. It helps him. But only in the way that the loving mother teaches a child to walk alone. The mother is far enough away from the child so that she cannot actually support the child, but she holds out her arms. She imitates the child's movements. If it totters she swiftly bends as if she would seize it—so the child believes that it is not walking alone. The most loving mother can do no more, if it be truly intended that the child shall walk alone. And yet she does more; for her face, her face, yes, it is beckoning like the reward of the Good and like the encouragement of Eternal Blessedness. So the child walks alone, with eyes fixed upon the mother's face, not on the difficulties of the way; supporting himself by the arms that do not hold on to him, striving after refuge in the mother's embrace, hardly suspecting that in the same moment he is proving that he can do without her, for now the child is walking alone. Fear, on the other hand, is a dry nurse for the child: it has no milk; a bloodless corrector for the youth: it has no beckoning encouragement; a niggardly disease for the adult: it has no blessing; a horror for the aged: when fear has to admit that the long painful time of schooling did not bring Eternal Blessedness.

Fear also wishes to help a man. It desires to teach him to walk alone, but not as a loving mother does it. For it is fear itself that continually upsets the child. It desires to help him forward, but not as a loving mother's beckoning. For it is fear itself that weighs him down so that he cannot move from the spot. It desires to lead him to the goal, and yet it is the fear itself that makes the goal terrifying. It desires to help him to the Good, and yet that kind of learner never wins the favor of the Good. Nor does he ever become God's friend. For, as the Scriptures teach, not only thieves and robbers, but also the fearful may not enter into the kingdom of Heaven. The fearful one desires Heaven not for itself. He desires it only out of fear of punishment. Is not such a man double-minded even though he was not one of those who would appear wholly other than he was? Would not such a man be double-minded if you saw him in his dreams, when in sleep he has cast off the yoke of fear, when all is as he would really have it be, and he is as he really is, as he would be upon waking if fear did not exist? For it is said of old that one learns to know a man's soul by his dreams.[12]

If by the word punishment, one thinks of eternity's punishment, it gives a false impression, as if indeed it were not double-mindedness to will the Good only out of fear of punishment. But yet this *is* double-mindedness. Even if it happened to be a good man who in the agony of fear preserved a certain slavish blamelessness out of fear of punishment: still he is double-minded. *He does continually what he really would rather not do*, or at least what he has no pleasure in doing, for this pleasure is only a low sensual pleasure, in fact of all sensual pleasures it is the lowest. It is the one whose miserable glory consists solely in avoiding something, hence the pleasure is not a pleasure in itself, but only by contrast. *Nor does he attribute the punishment to God and to the Good.* On the contrary, as he pictures it, the Good is one thing, the punishment is an entirely different matter. But in that case the Good is not one thing. Thus by his double-mindedness he brings about a strained relation between the Good and the punishment. He wishes that the punishment did not exist, and thereby he really wishes also that the Good did not exist, for otherwise he must have another relation to the Good than the one that he has through punishment. Now punishment does exist, and so he performs the Good out of fear of punishment. But the one that wills the Good in truth, understands that punishment only exists for the sake of the transgressors. He devoutly understands that punishment is like all other things which fall to the lot of one who loves God. It is a helping hand. The double-minded person shuns punishment as a suffering, a misfortune, an evil, and thereby detaches himself and his understanding from punishment, and wholly detaches punishment from the Good. This obstinacy is like the infantile notion of a child, who in his lack of judgment even sets up a cleft in the father's nature; for the child imagines that the father is the loving one, that punishment on the other hand is something that a bad man has invented. That the loving father himself should have invented the punishment out of love for the child would not become apparent to the child. So also with the relation between the Good and punishment. It is the Good who, out of love for the pupil, has invented punishment. We all go to school, only life's school is for adults. For this reason the punishment is of a more serious kind than in a children's school. It is less obvious, and therefore all the more serious; less immediate, and therefore all the more serious; less external, and therefore all the more serious. It does not follow blow for blow upon the mistake, and therefore [is] all the more serious; one has not been spared because it may seem as if the punishment had been forgotten, hence it is all the more serious. Yet by this seriousness punishment does in truth press one toward the Good, if one really wills it. Doubleness of mind has no desire to do that. It continues to have an effeminate, sensuous conception of punishment, and an impotent will for the Good. It often happens with such a double-minded person, that the older he gets the more impoverished his life becomes: when his youth, in which there was something better than fear, is spent, and when fearfulness and cleverness conspire together in order to make him into a slave, if one wishes to put it so—to the Good. It is so different with the one who wills the Good in truth. He is the only one who is free, made free by the Good. However, a man does not in truth will the Good if he only wills it out of fear of punishment, and hence is only in a state of slavery to the Good.

Yet double-mindedness seldom dwells on eternity's punishment. The punishment it fears is more often understood in an earthly and temporal sense. Of a man who only wills the Good out of fear of punishment, it is necessary to say with special emphasis that he fears what a man should not and ought not to fear: loss of money, loss of reputation, misjudgment by others, neglect, the world's judgment, the ridicule of fools, the laughter of the frivolous, the cowardly whining of consideration, the inflated triviality of the moment, the fluttering mist-forms of vapor. Yes, this double-minded man becomes as unsteady in all his ways as the one who willed the Good for the sake of the reward, because he is continually intent upon what is in flux, upon what is always changing, and he fears continually that which no man should fear. He fears that which has power to wound, maltreat, ruin, or strike dead the body, but which has no power whatever over the soul unless it obtains it through fear. Should a man love neither the earth, nor the pleasures of the eye, nor the pleasures of the flesh, nor a haughty life; should he covet neither what is the world's, the possession of money and prestige among men, then he shall fear neither what is the world's, neither the world nor men, neither poverty nor the expelling hand of persecution. If he fears these things, then he is the prey of double-mindedness, just as in this double-mindedness he is the slave of mankind.

Yes, there is a sense of shame that is favorable to the Good. Woe to the man who casts it off! This sense of shame is a saving companion through life. Woe to the man that breaks with it! It is in the service of sanctification and of true freedom. Woe to the man who is scandalized by it as if it were a compulsion! If a man goes alone through life, according to the word of the Scriptures[13] that is not good, yet if he goes accompanied by that shame, oh, he shall become good and become one thing. And if the solitary one should stumble, if this sense of shame were still his companion, then we should not cry out as the book of Ecclesiastes does, "Woe to him that is alone," nor say of the solitary one, as does Ecclesiastes, "If he falls, who shall help him up."[14] For this sense of shame intends to serve him better than the best friend. It will help him better than all human sympathy which easily leads into double-mindedness —not into willing one thing. There is no question but that a man usually acts more intelligently, shows more strength, and to all appearances more self-control, when under the scrutiny of others than when he believes himself to be unobserved. But the question is whether this intelligence, this strength, this self-control is real, or whether through the devotion of long-continued attention to it, it does not easily slip into the lie of simulation which kindles the unsteady blush of double-mindedness in his soul. Each one who is not more ashamed before himself than before all others, if he is placed in difficulty and much tried in life, will in one way or another end by becoming the slave of men. For to be more ashamed in the presence of others than when alone, what else is this than to be more ashamed of seeming than of being? And turned about, should not a man be more ashamed of what he is than of what he seems? For otherwise he cannot in truth will one thing, since by trying to appear well in the eyes of others he is only striving after a changing shimmer and its reflection in human favor.

The clever one, who fears the judgment of others and is ashamed before others—if he is not ashamed most of all before himself, ah, perhaps his cunning might succeed in becoming undetectable, it might permit him to imagine that it was already unfathomable; and so, what then? This one who does not misuse his power because he fears the judgment of men and of being ashamed before men—if he is not ashamed most of all before himself, ah, perhaps either he himself or some eye-servant might even succeed in imagining that it could be done so craftily that not even God could see through it; and so, what then? Indeed it is unnecessary for the talk to wait for what will happen, that is, to wait for the outcome of his double-mindedness. For the talk is only about the presence of double-mindedness in him, and that is already obvious. Whether it becomes obvious to men or not, double-mindedness is none the less present, and the double-minded person is to be pitied. For let us not forget that truth is right in saying of each one who is in untruth, that he is indeed to be pitied, even when he himself and all men think him fortunate. Because, in the sense of truth, it does not help a man that he does not know that he is to be pitied, for this is only a further misfortune. But the one that is most ashamed of himself when he is alone, is thereby strengthened in willing one thing. However crafty this cunning may have been, the inventor himself can still see through it. Let it, then, be hidden from all men, no matter how its hiddenness might be able to support him, yet he could not hide it from that inner companion, before whom he is most of all ashamed.

We do not mean to imply here, that a man has ever lived, even in the most corrupt age, for whom no person existed whose judgment he might and could well fear with a wholesome shame, a person whose judgment could be a guide to him in order to will the Good in truth. But if this shame before the honored person is in truth to become a source of benefit to the humble man, then there is an indispensable condition: that the person must be ashamed most of all before himself. Therefore one could rightly say that in truth it is most beneficial of all to a man to feel shame before one who is already dead. And if he feels this humiliation before a living person, then to feel it before him as if he were already dead, or (if it seems more to your liking, my listener, I will use another expression, that means the same thing, although it contains the explanation in an aesthetic form): to feel ashamed before him as before a transfigured one. One already dead is just such a transfigured one. One who is living can indeed be mistaken, can be changed, can be stampeded in a moment and by the moment. If, in truth, he is a genuinely honorable person, he himself will, by way of warning, remind you of this in order that by your relationship with him you may not be led into that double-mindedness which lies in being the follower of another. The living person may perhaps favor you too much—perhaps too little. If you see him each day, your shame will perhaps lose something of its intensity or perhaps bring on itself an acute disease, so that you could wish to possess a magic means of deceiving the revered one, so that you wished to be able to ingratiate yourself with him or by any means to raise yourself up in his good graces, because his judgment has become for you the most important thing of all. How much danger and temptation to doublemindedness! It does not disappear until you conduct yourself with him as with one who is dead. Withdraw from him—but never forget him. That only leaves when you are separated from him as though by death, when in earthly or temporal fashion you do not come too near him, but only forever remember what he himself would have termed the best thing in his nature! A man cannot get round a transfigured one. Favor and persuasion and overhastiness belong to the moments of earthly life. The departed one does not notice these appearances, the transfigured one cannot understand them. He does not wish to understand them.

If you will not give them up, then you must give him up; then you must, if you dare, offend the transfigured one, break with him, yes, annihilate him. For when he is not the transfigured one, then he simply does not exist. With the living one, you may speak in another manner, because he also exists in the earthly sense, and if you get him changed a little—alas, to what other end than to your own destruction and to his disparagement! It would be as if you still had him to hold to, you had his words, his audible approval, and in the union between you two perhaps it would escape you both that a change had taken place. But the transfigured one exists only as transfigured, not visibly to the earthly eye, not audibly to the earthly ear, only in the sacredly still silence of shame. He cannot be changed, not in the least particular, without its being instantly noted, and without all being lost, and without his vanishing. The transfigured one exists only as transfigured. He cannot be changed into anything better. He is the transfigured one. He cannot be altered. He is indeed a departed one. He remains true to himself, one and the same—this glorified one! How, then could it be possible for one to become double-minded who by feeling ashamed before such a one is strengthened in willing the Good! However, even the most upright man can nevertheless be surprised by many frailties and oc-

casionally may go astray. But then he has a hope: that there exists a
God, a just government of the universe, that by punishment will
awaken him and lead him back. How different it is! He that wills
the Good in truth even hopes for the punishment; but that man who
in his double-mindedness only wills the Good out of fear of punishment is far from willing the Good in truth.

The double-minded person stands at a parting of the ways,
where two visions appear: the Good and the terrifying figure of
punishment. The two do not belong together in his eyes, for while
punishment, which God in His wisdom has connected with every
transgression, is a Good, there is no denying that it is such a Good
only when it is gratefully received, not when it is simply feared as
an evil. But the double-minded person rarely has this Divine punishment in mind. He thinks rather of the world's punishment. But
the Good and the punishment the world metes out are not identical. Or has the world perhaps really become so perfect and so holy
that it is like God, and that what it rewards is the Good and what it
punishes, the evil? Or would any person who believes that he has
received at God's hand an intimation of the life according to which
he desires to model his own life, could such a man really think of
worshipping the world in this way? To be sure, one may hear—
especially in the places where men festively gather in order to
deceive one another by many speeches—one may hear magnificent
words about how the world progresses, and about our age and
about our century. But, my listener, would you dare, as a father
(and I feel confident that you have a lofty conception of the meaning of this name, a responsible conception of the charge which it
lays upon you) would you dare, as a father, to say to your child as
you sent him out into the world, "Go, with your mind at ease, my
child, pay attention to what the many approve and what the world
rewards, for that is the Good, but what the world punishes, that is
evil. It is no longer true as it used to be, that the judgment of the
masses is like foam on water—nonsense, though loudly proclaimed;
blind, though sharply decisive; impossible to follow because it
changes more swiftly than a woman changes color. Now, there is no
longer any doubt about the outcome, the Good is immediately victorious. Now, the Good exacts no sacrifice, no self-denial, for the
world desires the Good. Now, the judgment of the masses is the
judgment of the wise men, the solitary ones are the fools. Now, the

earth is the kingdom of God, and Heaven is only a reflection of it. Now, the world is the highest certainty, the only one a man can build upon, the only one a man can swear by."

Surely, my listener, the speech need not ask you, for it rests assured in advance what your answer would be. But I would like to ask of the most ardent attender of those festivities: would you dare, if you should speak as a father to your own child, would you dare say any such thing? Or if it were the youth that, with all the earnest devotion of his soul, fixed his trusting gaze on you, assured that if you said it, it must be so, and in gratitude, bound by a solemn vow to follow the guidance of your counsel through life; would you dare give him any such counsel? Or if you were witness to that lovable young man's beautiful enthusiasm when he read and heard of the great men who fought with a heavy destiny and suffered badly in the world, the glorious ones whom earth renounced because it was not worthy of them, would you dare, when no clamor caused your speech to wander but when the stillness of intimacy, of the lovable one's confidence, the inexperience of the young man, all obliged you to tell the truth; at such a time would you dare lay your hand on your heart and say, "Such things no longer happen. Now the world has become enlightened and perfect. Now: to seek first after this world and its customs is identical with what was meant in former times by seeking first God's kingdom and His righteousness."

Alas, gradually as a man gets older, he grows accustomed to a great deal in life. Among other things, he gets in the habit of saying much that he has not properly reflected upon. Among contemporaries he gets into the way of hedging round what he says by so many presuppositions that that which is plain and elevating is almost forgotten. Now and then a word is let drop that expresses a plain and solid exasperation of long standing. "You know well enough what kind of world we live in." And at other times the world is praised to the point of idolatry, without either of these statements making any very deep impression on the one who speaks them. For the first does not arouse him. It does not frighten him into a condition of fear and trembling in which he resolves to save himself since the world is so bad. And the other does not strengthen the speaker into an eager desire for the Good by confidence in the perfection of the world. Alas, along with others in this life, he gets accustomed, amid the dull round of habit, almost to abandon himself as he plays about with mere words.

But when even the most tragic of life's spoiled children seriously admonishes a child, a youth, a maiden, he speaks with shame. There is at this point a beautiful reciprocity, for the youth approaches his elder with shame and the elder in admonishing the youth always speaks with shame. May God grant that all who have an opportunity to admonish youth may themselves derive some benefit from the shame which comes with the admonishment!

In the act of admonishing, and this deserves emphasis, the older person shall by no means set before the youth a horrifying picture of the world. To do so is never earnestness, but is only sickly imagination. But in the act of admonishing, he will shrink before the thought of leading the youth straight into the danger of double-mindedness by deceptively focusing his attention upon the punishment the world metes out. For in this, instead of impressing upon him a holy fear and shame before the Good, he is polluting the pure one by teaching him the fear of loss of money, loss of reputation, misjudgment by others, neglect, the world's judgment, the ridicule of fools, the laughter of the frivolous, the cowardly whining of consideration, the inflated triviality of the moment, the fluttering mist-forms of vapor. Alas, for many men these elevated thoughts are only too often like a gilding, that wears off in life's double-mindedness, which gnaws and gnaws. But even the man whom double-mindedness has eaten most bare, when he speaks admonishingly to a youth, is reminded that, out of shame, he dare say but one thing. In the act of admonishing even he will say (for it is no rare speaker that is here introduced to talk, and just on that account the praise of the Good is so much the more glorious because it does not require the approval of eloquence, for here it is well to note that it is one of life's most tragically spoiled children who speaks admonishingly to a youth) even he will say, "Do not be afraid, be slow to judge others, but attend closely to yourself, hold firmly to willing one thing, to willing the Good in truth, and thus, from now on, let this lead you wherever for now it will lead you—because eternally it will lead you to victory. In this world let it lead you to prosperity or poverty, to honor or insult, to life or death: only do not let go this one thing. By its hand you may walk confidently even in danger. Even in danger of your life itself you may go as confidently as a child who clasps the mother's hand. Yes, even more confidently, for the child does not even know the danger." In the act of admonishing, therefore, a man should warn against fear of the world's punishment, which is double-mindedness.

Now and then someone speaks of "suffering punishment, when one does the Good." How is that possible? From whom shall that punishment come? Certainly not from God! Is it, then, from the world—so that when in its wisdom the world is mistaken, it rewards the bad and punishes the Good? And yet no, it is not as that word "world" implies. The word does not mean what it says. It is improperly expressed. For the word "world" sounds great and terrifying, and yet it must obey the same law as the most insignificant and miserable man. But even if the world gathered all its strength, there is one thing it is not able to do, it can no more punish an innocent one than it can put a dead person to death.

To be sure the world has power. It can lay many a burden upon the innocent one. It can make his life sour and laborious for him. It can rob him of his life. But it cannot punish an innocent one. How wonderful, here is a limit, a limit that is invisible, like a line that is easy to overlook with the senses, but one that has the strength of eternity in resisting any infringement. This may be overlooked by the world whose attention is focused upon that which is big—and the limit is insignificant, is for the present, a quiet-mannered nobody, but yet it is there. Perhaps it is completely hidden from the eyes of the world. For that, too, can be a part of the innocent one's suffering, that the world's injustice takes on the appearance of punishment—in the world's eyes. But the limit is nevertheless there, and is in spite of all the strongest. And even if all the world rose up in tumult and even if everything were thrown into confusion: the limit is nevertheless there. And on the one side of it with the innocent ones is justice; and on the other side toward the world is an eternal impossibility of punishing an innocent one. Even if the world wishes to annihilate an innocent man and put him out of the way, it cannot put the limit out of the way, even though it be invisible. (Perhaps it is just on that account.) Even in the moment of his sacrificial death, the limit is there; then it stretches itself with the strength of eternity, then it cleaves itself with eternity's all-encompassing depth. The limit is there, and on the one side with the innocent ones is justice, and on the other side toward the world is an eternal impossibility of punishing an innocent one.

When the good man truly stands on the other side of the boundary line inside the fortification of eternity, he is strong, stronger than the whole world. He is strongest of all at the time when he seems to be overcome. But the impotent double-minded one has removed the boundary limit, because he only wills the Good out of fear of earth's punishment. If the world is not really the land of perfection, then by his double-mindedness he has surrendered himself to the power of mediocrity or pledged himself to the evil.

6. BARRIERS TO WILLING ONE THING:

EGOCENTRIC SERVICE OF THE GOOD

3. *Furthermore it must be said that the man who wills the Good and wills its victory out of a self-centered willfulness does not will one thing. He is double-minded.*

Suppose a man wills the Good simply in order that *he* may score a victory, then he wills the Good for the sake of the reward, and his double-mindedness is obvious, as the previous section of the talk has sought to point out. Actually he does not care to serve the Good, but to have the advantage of regarding it as a fruit of conquest. When, on the contrary, a man desires that the Good shall be victorious, when he will not call the outcome of the battle "victory" if *he* wins, but only when the Good is victorious: can he then, in any sense, be called and be double-minded? Yes, and yet if he be double-minded (for the decision as to the boundary line between the pure and the double-minded is here of a singular complexity), then his double-mindedness is more subtle and concealed, more presumptuous than that obvious and out and out worldly sort. It is a powerful deception that seems nearest of all to approach the purity of heart that wills the Good in truth, even though it is at the other pole from it, just as the high place is from the deep chasm, just as heaven-storming pride is from humility's dwelling in the low places, just as if a pretentiously plausible approximation had been won by falsifying a line of separation that was eternally real. He does not will the Good for the sake of the reward. He wills that the Good shall triumph through *him*, that he shall be the instrument, he the chosen one. He does not desire to be rewarded by the world—that he despises; nor by men—that he looks down upon. And yet he does not wish to be an unprofitable servant.[15] The reward which he insists upon is a sense of pride and in that very demand is his violent double-mindedness. Yes, violent, for what else does he wish than to take the Good by storm, and by force to press himself and his service upon the Good! And if he will not give up this last presumptuousness, if he, in some way, does not desire what the Good wills, if he does not desire the Good's victory after the fashion that the Good wills it: then he is double-minded. Even if he knows how to hide it from men, even if he hides it from himself, even if the true expression of the language seems for a moment to hide it by calling his condition of mind self-will, willfulness, for that sounds well, especially when it is strong enough to venture the most extreme things: does that seem to be double-mindedness? No, it does not seem to be double-mindedness, but it is.

In the eyes of this double-minded person the Good is one thing, its victory is another, and its victory through him may even be something else. Now it is indeed the case that eternally the Good has always been victorious. But in time it is otherwise, temporally it may take a long time. The victory is slow, its uncertainty is a slow measure of length. Again and again the faithful servant's life ends, and it seemed, at his death, as if he had accomplished nothing for the Good. And yet he was a faithful servant, who willed the Good in truth, and he was also loved by the Good, that prizes obedience more than the "fat of the ram." "Alas, why does time exist; if the Good eternally has always been victorious, why should it then creep slowly forward throughout the length of time or almost perish in time's slowness? Why should it fight laboriously through that which makes time the longest, through uncertainty? Why should the solitary 'individuals,'[16] who sincerely will the Good, be so scattered, so separated, that they can scarcely call out to one another, scarcely catch sight of one another? Why should time hang like a weight upon them? Why should separation involve them in delay, when it is so swiftly accomplished in eternity? Why was an immortal spirit placed in the world and in time, just as the fish is drawn up out of the water and cast upon the beach?" Whoever talks in this questioning vein (and even if he say it amid groans, the utterance is the same), should be on his guard, for he scarcely knows by what spirit he is speaking. Alas, men often enough confuse impatience with humble, obedient enthusiasm; impatience even lends itself to this confusion. When a man is active early and late "for the sake of the Good," storming about noisily and restlessly, hurling himself into time, as a sick man throws himself down upon his bed, throwing off all consideration for himself, as a sick man throws off his clothes, scornful of the world's reward; when such a man makes a place among men, then the masses think what he himself imagines, that he is inspired. And yet he is at the other pole from that, for he is double-minded, and double-mindedness no more resembles inspiration than a whirlwind resembles the steadiness of the standing wind.

So it is with all impatience. It is a kind of ill-temper. Its root is already in the child, because the child will not take time for things. With the double-minded one, it is thus clear that time and eternity cannot rule in the same man. He cannot, he will not, understand the Good's slowness; that out of mercy, the Good is slow; that out of love for free persons, it will not use force; that in its wisdom toward the frail ones, it shrinks from any deception. He cannot, he will not, humbly understand that the Good can get on without him. He is double-minded, he that with his enthusiasm could apparently become an apostle, but can quite as readily become a Judas, who treacherously wishes to hasten the victory of the Good. He is scandalized, he that by his enthusiasm seems to love the Good so highly. He is scandalized by its poverty, when it is clothed in the slowness of time. He is not devoted to the Good in service that may profit nothing. He only effervesces, and he that effervesces loves the moment. And he that loves the moment fears time, he fears that the course of time will reveal his double-mindedness, and he falsifies eternity; for otherwise eternity might still more effectively reveal his double-mindedness. He is a falsifier. For him eternity is the deceptive sensory illusion of the horizon; for him eternity is the bluish haze that limits time; for him eternity is the dazzling sleight-of-hand trick executed by the moment.

Such a double-minded person is perhaps hardly recognizable in this world, because his double-mindedness is not evident inside the world. The world's reward and punishment do not serve as informers against him; for he has overcome the world, even if by a higher deception. Hence his double-mindedness is first recognizable at the boundary where time and eternity touch upon each other. There it is clear and is always recognized by the all-knowing One. He will not be content with the blessed assurance which is a security that passeth all understanding; the blessed assurance that the unprofitable servant may have within himself at each moment, even when the time is the longest and he seems to have accomplished least of all, the blessed assurance which allows the unprofitable servant if he loses honor to speak more proudly than that royal word: All is lost save honor.[17] And when even honor is lost to say: Nothing is lost, but all is gained.

But this double-minded person is not so easily recognizable on earth. He does not will the Good for the sake of reward, for then he would have become obvious in his aspiration or in his despair. He does not will the Good out of fear of punishment, for then he would have become obvious in his cowardice, in his shunning of punishment, or in his despair, when he was not able to avoid it. No, he wishes to sacrifice all, he fears nothing, only he will not sacrifice himself in daily self-forgetfulness. This he fears to do.

The double-minded man stands at a parting of the ways, and sees there two apparitions: the Good, and the Good in its victory, or even in its victory through him. This latter is presumptuousness, but even the first two apparitions are not wholly the same. In eternity they are the same, but not in time. And they must be kept apart. The Good so wills it. The Good puts on the slowness of time as a poor garment, and in keeping with this change of dress one who serves it must be clothed in the insignificant figure of the unprofitable servant. With the eye of his senses he is not permitted to see the Good in victory. Only with the eye of faith can he strive after its eternal victory. Therein lies his double-mindedness. For as there is a double-mindedness which divides up the nature of the Good which the Good has united for all eternity: so is his double-mindedness of that sort that unites what the Good in time has set apart. The one double-minded person forgets the Eternal and on that account misuses time, the other misuses eternity.

7. BARRIERS TO WILLING ONE THING:

COMMITMENT TO A CERTAIN DEGREE

4. Before finally leaving the subject of double-mindedness
for a similar examination of purity, *the talk should at least
touch upon that versatile form of double-mindedness: the double-mindedness of weakness* as it appears
in the common things of real life; *upon the fact that the
person who only wills the Good up to a certain degree
is double-minded.*

At bottom this is the way all double-mindedness expresses itself
in relation to the Good, in that it wills the Good only up to a certain degree. But what has been set forth above, what of double-
mindedness might perhaps be spoken of as its deceptive transactions in the "big," still had a certain semblance of unity, and of
inner consistency, in so far as it was one single thing and that betrayed into one-sidedness, yet this one-sidedness, however strange it
may seem, was precisely the double-mindedness in that one-sided
person.

It is otherwise with the transactions of daily life, for they are not
in the "big." It is rare in daily life, to see anyone who wills some
perverse thing with fixed consistency and effort. The transactions
of daily life are made in the little things so that double-mindedness
presents a much greater diversity within the "individual."

A merchant who deals in only one kind of ware is a rare sight,
and so is that double-mindedness which has a certain unreal unity.
A merchant generally deals in different wares, and double-mindedness, too, is generally a number of different things. On that account the false road is harder to detect than that clear-cut one.
Nay, the false roads cross each other and the right road in the most
different ways and the "individual" shares in this crossing in an
equally varied way. To be sure his life is distinguishable as falling
within double-mindedness. But it is not double-mindedness, he is

not at one with himself in anything definite, but is tossed about in vacillation by every breeze. For he learns and learns and yet never comes to a knowledge of truth.[18] Or if he comes almost to it, then he quickly turns further and further away the more he learns of this confused and confusing instruction. In preference to the earlier double-mindedness, this has the Good on its side, in that it wills the Good, even though weakly; and in that it is without obstinacy that marked the previously mentioned double-mindedness. But upon occasion weakness may be just as incurable.

This double-mindedness is difficult to speak of because it approximates both the one and the other, and because it alters itself continually, changing so swiftly that it may have transformed itself several times before the talk had hardly finished describing a single expression. It plays about gaily not only in all possible colors, but there is not even any law for this play of colors that blends colors and color relations in ever new confusion. Hence there is always something new under the sun—and yet the old double-mindedness persists. Indeed what makes it even more difficult to speak of, is that in daily life, where it is right at home, double-mindedness, within limits, keeps comparatively to itself, so that a double-minded person, by being a little less double-minded than the others, claims distinction even though his degree of difference is quite within an essential sameness. Hence in the end it would seem as if that true eternal claim that demands purity of heart, by willing one thing, were done away with, as if it had been withdrawn from government, set away in retirement at such a distance from daily life that there simply could be no talk about it. For among the many-colored seething populace in the noise of the world from day to day and from year to year, there is no scrupulous check made as to whether a person wholly wills the Good if he has influence and might, runs a great business, is something in his own and in others' eyes. "What frightfully niggardly pettiness," one thinks, "to be so scrupulous!" One does not consider that there is any presumptuousness in what one has spoken. Nay, one drops the clever remark in passing and hurries on, while the remark also hurries on from mouth to mouth amid the many-colored seething populace. And in the rush of life, in trade and commerce from morning to night, there is no such scruple about whether a person wholly wills the Good, just so that in his business he is keen, not to say a "thief," just so that he saves and piles up money, just so that he has a good reputation and by good fortune manages to avoid slander (for whether he actually is guilty or not is here of little importance, for neither he nor the world has time to look into that. Slander is merely a danger as an obstacle to his business). "To what purpose such a delay in the midst of busyness?" And in the world, it is always busy. Yes, it is entirely true that this is the way things look in the world, the way they seem in the world, and the way they must seem within the deceptive horizon of the temporal order. But in eternity it will make a tremendous difference whether a person was scrupulous or not.

And yet eternity is not like a new world, so that one who had lived in time according to the ways of the time world and of the press of busyness, if he were to make a happy landing in eternity itself, could now try his luck in adopting the customs and practices of eternity. Alas, the temporal order and the press of busyness believe that eternity is so far away. And yet not even the foremost professional theatrical producer has ever had all in such readiness for the stage and for the change of scenes as eternity has all in readiness for time: all—even to the least detail, even to the most insignificant word that is spoken; has all in readiness in each instant—although eternity delays.

Oh, that this talk, far from detaining anyone who sincerely wills the Good, or calling anyone away from fruitful activity, might cause a busy man to pause. For this press of busyness is like a charm. And it is sad to observe how its power swells, how it reaches out seeking always to lay hold of ever-younger victims so that childhood or youth are scarcely allowed the quiet and retirement in which the Eternal may unfold a divine growth. And suppose that busyness in its haste should make a concession, believing even in its superficial wisdom that there is something beneficial in having a busy man on hand who now and then hurriedly proclaims that higher reflection on life about willing the Good in truth. Alas, is this, then, the true relationship? Are almost all to be excused from that which every man should do for himself? But then for the sake of completeness is someone in the midst of busyness to be delegated the task of setting forth that higher claim—that higher claim, which, if by some means it could be satisfied, even if in feebleness and in imperfection, would command a man's whole mind, his unrelenting industry, his best strength?

Thus in the midst of busyness, double-mindedness is to be found. Just as the echo dwells in the woods, as stillness dwells in the desert, so double-mindedness dwells in the press of busyness. That the one who wills the Good only to a certain degree, that he is double-minded, that he has a distracted mind, a divided heart, scarcely needs to be pointed out. But the reason may need to be explained and set forth, why, in the press of busyness, there is neither time nor quiet to win the transparency that is indispensable if a man is to come to understand himself in willing one thing or even for a preliminary understanding of himself in his confusion. Nay, the press of busyness into which one steadily enters further and further, and the noise in which the truth continually slips more and more into oblivion, and the mass of connections, stimuli, and hindrances, these make it ever more impossible for one to win any deeper knowledge of himself. It is true that a mirror has the quality of enabling a man to see his image in it, but for this he must stand still. If he rushes hastily by, then he sees nothing. Suppose a man should go about with a mirror in his possession which he does not take out, how should such a man get to see himself? In this fashion the busy man hurries on, with the possibility of understanding himself in his possession. But the busy man keeps on running and it never dawns upon him that this possibility which he has in his possession is rapidly fading from his memory. And yet one hardly dares say this to one of these busy ones, for however rushed he otherwise may be, yet upon occasion he has plenty of time for a multitude of excuses by the use of which he becomes worse than he was before: excuses whose wisdom is about the same as when a sailor believes that it is the sea, not the ship, that is moving.

One hardly dares say this to him, for however rushed he otherwise may be, yet upon occasion when in the company of congenial spirits, he has ample time: "to rob the unripe fruit of ridicule of its wisdom," in order to poke fun at the speaker as one of life's incompetents, as a man whom the busy one in his cleverness ignores—from the exalted viewpoint of his excuses. Then, too, the general approval is everywhere upon the side of the busy one—everywhere, in the ever-increasing sum of the pressure of busyness, and in the swarming mass of excuses. For like a poisonous breath over the fields, like a mass of locusts over Egypt, so the swarm of excuses is a general plague, a ruinous infection among men, that eats off the sprouts of the Eternal. For with each one who is attacked, there is always just one more excuse for the next person. And while a person cannot, as a rule, prevent a sickness becoming more and more dangerous, more and more malignant, the more it attacks those around him, yet with excuses it is just the reverse. There the sickness seems to become milder and milder, the condition become more and more agreeable, the more persons there are attacked by it. And if we all agree that the wretched, stunted state of health of these excuses is the highest of all, then there is no one to say anything to the contrary. Should there be an "individual" who could not feel easy about yielding, and who raised a strong objection to this widespread practice of excusing, alas, we have not yet heard all; for there is always one excuse held in reserve, that lies in wait at his door and demands of him, "What good does it do for a single individual to insist upon opposing this?" Hence once again with excuses it is even worse than with a virulent disease, for no one dies of a disease simply because others have died of it.

So the double-minded person, then, may have a feeling—a living feeling for the Good. If someone should speak of the Good, especially if it were done in a poetical fashion, then he is quickly moved, easily stimulated to melt away in emotion. Suppose the world goes a little against him and then someone should tell him that God is love, that His love surpasses all understanding, encompassing in His Providence even the sparrow that may not fall to the earth without His willing it. If a person speaks in this way, especially in a poetical manner, he is gripped. He reaches after faith as after a desire, and with faith he clutches for the desired help. In the faith of this desire he then has a feeling for the Good. But perhaps the help is delayed. Instead of it a sufferer comes to him whom he can help. But this sufferer finds him impatient, forbidding. This sufferer must be content with the excuse "that he is not at the moment in the spirit or the mood to concern himself about the sufferings of others as he himself has troubles." And yet he imagines that he has faith, faith that there is a loving Providence who helps the sufferer, a Providence who also uses men as his instruments. Possibly now the desired help comes. Again he quickly flares up with gratitude, basking in a soft conception of the loving

Goodness of Providence. Now he thinks he has rightly grasped faith. Now it has been victorious in him over every doubt and every objection. Alas, and that other sufferer has been completely forgotten. What else is this condition if it is not double-mindedness! For suppose, after all, that there should be talk of objections to faith, of incidents and occurrences that seem as it were to cry out against the care of a loving Providence: then that other sufferer who with the excuse that by chance he was not in the mood was turned away sharply by the very one who could have helped him, that sufferer is an even more powerful objection. But the double-minded one is wholly blind to the fact that at the very moment when he believes faith to have conquered in him, he has, precisely by his action, refuted this conviction. Or is this not double-mindedness that thinks to have a conviction while by his own action a man contradicts it? Is this not, in truth, the sole proof that a man has a conviction: that his own life actually expresses it? Is this not the sole certainty: that one's so-called conviction is not altered from moment to moment as a result of the different things that happen to one, things that momentarily alter a person and alter everything for a person so that today he has faith, and tomorrow he has lost it, and he gets it again day after tomorrow until something completely out of the ordinary happens, at which time he almost inevitably loses it, assuming that he has ever had it!

Suppose that there were two men: a double-minded man, who believes he has gained faith in a loving Providence, because he had himself experienced having been helped, even though he had hard-heartedly sent away a sufferer whom he could have helped; and another man whose life, by devoted love, was an instrument in the hand of Providence, so that he helped many suffering ones, although the help he himself had wished continued to be denied him from year to year. Which of these two was in truth convinced that there is a loving Providence that cares for the suffering ones? Is it not a fair and a convincing conclusion: He that planted the ear, shall he not hear?[19] But turn it around, and is the conclusion not equally fair and convincing: He whose life is sacrificing love, shall he not trust that God is love? Yet in the press of busyness there is neither time nor quiet for the calm transparency which teaches equality, which teaches the willingness to pull in the same yoke with other men, that noble simplicity that is in inner understanding with every man. There is neither time nor quiet to win such a conviction. Therefore, in the press of busyness even faith and hope and love and willing the Good become only loose words and doublemindedness. Or is it not double-mindedness to live without any conviction, or more rightly, to live in the constantly and continually changing fantasy that one has and that one has not a conviction!

In this fashion feeling deceives the busy one into double-mindedness. Perhaps after the flaming up of the contrition of repentance, if this turns into emptiness, he had a conviction, at least so he believed, that there is a mercy that forgives sins. But even in the forgiveness he strongly denied any implication that he had been guilty of anything. Hence he had, so he thought, believed in a conviction that such a mercy exists, and yet in practice he denied its existence; in practice his attitude seemed designed to prove that it did not exist. Suppose that there were two men, that double-minded one, and then another man who would gladly forgive his debtor, if he himself might only find mercy. Which of these two was in truth convinced that such a mercy exists? The latter had indeed this proof that it exists, that he himself practices it; the former has no proof at all for himself, and only meets the contrary proof which he himself presents. Or the double-minded one perhaps had a feeling for right and wrong. It blazed strongly in him, especially if someone would describe in a poetical manner the zealous men who, by self-sacrifice in the service of truth, maintained righteousness and justice. Then some wrong happened to this man himself. And then it seemed to him as if there must appear some sign in heaven and upon earth since the world order could no more sleep than he until this wrong was put right again. And this was not self-love that inflamed him, but it was a feeling for justice, so he thought. And when he obtained his rights, no matter how much wrong it had cost those around him, then once again he praised the perfection of the world. Feeling had indeed carried him away, but also it had so enraptured him that he had forgotten the most important of all: to support righteousness and justice with self-sacrifice in the service of the truth. For which of these two is really convinced that justice exists in the world: the one that suffers wrong for doing the right, or the one that does wrong in order to obtain his right?

The immediate feeling is indeed—primary. It is the *élan vital* out of which life flows, just as it is said that the heart is the source of life. But then this feeling must be "kept," understood in the sense that one says, "Keep thy heart with all diligence, for out of it are the issues of life."[20] It must be cleansed of selfishness, kept from selfishness. It must not be delivered up to its own devices. On the other hand, that which will be kept must always put its trust in a higher power who will keep it; hence, even the loving mother begs God to keep her child.

In immediate feeling one man never understands another. As soon as something happens to himself, all things seem different to him. When he himself suffers he does not understand the suffering of another and neither is his own happiness the key to understand the happiness of another. The immediate feeling selfishly understands all in relation to itself, and is therefore in the discord of double-mindedness with all others. For only in the well-understood equality of sincerity can there be unity, and in selfish shortsightedness his conviction is continually being altered. If it is not altered it is an accident, since the cause of its exemption is only that by sheer chance his life was not touched by any change. But the stability of such a conviction is mere fantasy on the part of the one whom fate has pampered. Because a conviction is not firmly fixed when all press upon it equally and hold it firm. Rather, its true stability is revealed when everything is changed. It is rare indeed that a man's life is able to escape all changes, and in the changes the conviction based on immediate feeling is a fantasy, the momentary impression simply inflated into a consideration of the whole life.

Perhaps the double-minded one had a knowledge of the Good. In the moment of contemplation it stood out so distinctly before him, so clearly, that the Good, in truth, has all the advantage on its side, that the Good, in truth, is a gain both for this and for the future life. Yes, it lay on his heart, as though he must be able to convince the whole world of it. Perhaps it was not demanded of him that he should go out with his acquired conviction in order to convince others, but the testing that should try this newly won conviction nevertheless was not left out. Alas, contemplation and the moment of contemplation, in spite of all their clarity, readily conceal a deception; because the moment of contemplation has something in common with the falsified eternity. It is a foreshortening that is necessary in order that the contemplation may take place. It must foreshorten time a good deal. Indeed it must actually call the senses and thoughts away from time in order that they may complete themselves in a spurious eternal well-roundedness. It is here as when an artist sketches a country. The sketch cannot be as big as the country, it must be infinitely smaller; but on that account it also becomes all the easier for the observer to scan the outlines of that country. And yet it may well happen to the observer, if suddenly he were actually set down in that country where the many, many miles really exist and are valid, that he would be unable to recognize the country, or to make any sense of it, or as a traveler, to find his way about in it. So it will be with the double-minded person. His knowledge has indeed been a sense-deception. What was there, in airtight fashion pressed together in the completeness of contemplation, shall now be stretched out at its full length. It is now no longer rounded off but is in motion. For life is like a poet, and on that account is different from the observer who always seeks to bring things to a conclusion. The poet pulls us into the very complex center of life.

Now the double-minded person stands there with contemplation's sketch. Time, that was ignored by contemplation, begins to assert its validity. And it is obvious that in all eternity, time has no right to deny that the Good has all the advantage on its side. But it has permission to stretch time out, and thereby to make somewhat more difficult what in contemplation is apparently so plainly understood. So the understanding does not, in this way, simply become less plain because it has become crooked and awry, but rather it has become less plain—to go by. Now instead of keeping his contemplation to himself and holding himself to the contemplation in order to penetrate time with it in a direct but gradual manner, the double-minded person lets time cut him off from contemplation. Is this not double-mindedness: to be in time without any contemplation, without any distinct thoughts, or to put it more exactly, to be within time deceived over and over again about having or having had an experience of contemplation! The moment of contemplation he had recklessly misunderstood as being earnest, and then as this earnestness really approached, he threw off contemplation, and misunderstood the moment of contemplation as a delusion, until he again becomes earnest in the moment of contemplation. Or perhaps the double-minded one himself admitted that he had done wrong, had acted badly, had gotten upon a false road. But then after reflection it became so evident, so attractive, that punishment really is like a medicine. It seemed to him that no physician had ever made his medicine so agreeable or inviting as this reflection upon punishment had succeeded in rendering it. However, when the punishment came, momentarily, as a physician knows, it made the condition worse, in order that real health might break through. He then became impatient. In reflection he had thought himself healed; thought how good it was, when it was all over—when it was all over. In this fashion the lazy man always has a disproportionate power of imagination. He thinks immediately how he will establish himself, and how fine it will be for him when now this and now that is done: he is less given to thinking—that he should do this and that. And in reflection this looks very inviting, but when he must step out upon the road (for reflection is up above the road) then all is changed. Now instead of keeping the reflection and the estimate to himself, and conforming to them, he throws off reflection. He has lightly taken the reflection in vain, as if it were the healing quality of the medicine, and as the healing is about to begin, he light-mindedly misunderstands the reflection as a delusion. Is this not double-mindedness: to be ill, to put oneself under the physician's treatment, and yet not be willing to trust the physician, but arbitrarily to break off the treatment! Is this not double-mindedness, when the sick person is perhaps getting into the bath, where the heat increases, but now finding it suddenly too warm he springs out, regardless of all danger! Is it not double-mindedness, when he still has a remnant of deliberation left and with it an intimation that actually he is ill and so he begins to go through his cure all over again—in the same fashion!

In the recognition that contemplation and reflection are the distance of eternity away from time and actuality, there is indeed a truth: the knower can understand that truth, but he cannot understand himself. It is certain that without this recognition a man's life is more or less thoughtless. But it is also certain that this recognition, because it is in a spurious eternity before the imagination, develops double-mindedness if it is not slowly and honestly earned by the will's purity.

So the double-minded person may have had a will to the Good, for the one who is betrayed into double-mindedness by feeling, or by that distant recognition, he too has a will; but it received no power, and the germ of double-mindedness lay in the inner psychical disagreement. He also has a will to the Good. He is not without intentions or purposes, and resolutions and plans for himself, and not without plans of participation for others. But he has left something out: namely, he does not believe that the will in itself is, or should be, the most solid of all, that it should be as hard as the sword that could hew stone, and yet be so soft that it could be wrapped around the body. He does not believe that it is the will by which a man should steady himself, yes, that when all fails, that it is the will that a man must hold to. He does not believe that the will is itself the mover, but rather that it should itself be moved, that in itself it is fluctuating and on that account should be supported, held firm, that it should be moved and supported by causes, considerations, advice of others, experiences, rules of life. If we, quite properly, should compare the will in man with the headway impetus of a ship in which he (the man) is carried forward: then he believes, on the contrary, that the will, instead of its propelling all, is itself something that should be tugged forward, that there are grounds, considerations, advice of others, experiences, rules of life, that go alongside of and push or pull the will forward as if the will could be compared to a barge—yes, to a freight barge. But in the same stroke the will is made impotent, "up to a certain degree" discounted in relation to causes, considerations and advice, and in relation to how these react upon one another. He has turned everything around. What for each one, who with the impetus of eternity steers for a better world, would be a hindrance in life, he takes for an advantage in hastening forward, and what should be an advantage in hastening forward, he makes into a delay, or at least into something that is in itself neutral. Such a person must certainly remain in double-mindedness, upon the inland lake of double-mindedness, busy with trivialities, if, instead of charting a course out of all this delaying by means of the will to the Good, he only sails with the speed of the hindrance.

A man enters upon his life, hoping that all will go well for him and with good wishes for others. He steps out into the world's multiplicity, like one that comes from the country into the great noisy city, into the multiplicity where men engrossed in affairs hurry past

one another, where each looks out for what belongs to him in the
vast "back and forth," where everything is in passing, where it is as
though at each instant one saw what he had learned borne out in
practice, and in the same instant saw it refuted, without any cessa-
tion in the unrest of work, in multiplicity—that all too vast a school
of experience. For here one can experience everything possible, or
that everything is possible, even what the inexperienced man would
least believe, that the Good sits highest at the dinner table and
crime next highest, or crime highest and the Good next highest—in
good company with each other. So this man stands there. He has in
himself a susceptibility for the disease of double-mindedness. His
feeling is purely immediate, his knowledge only strengthened
through contemplation, his will not mature. Swiftly, alas, swiftly he
is infected—one more victim. This is nothing new, but an old story.
As it has happened to him, so it has happened with the double-
minded ones who have gone before him—this in passing he now
gives as his own excuse, for he has received the consecration of excuses.

Perhaps at this point a speaker, who was just as double-minded
as that double-minded one, and therefore really only wishes to
deceive, will describe the willing of the Good for us in an alluring
fashion, yet, in an alluring fashion with the prospect of becoming
something in the world. Perhaps he will close his description by
saying that that double-minded person came to nothing in the
world—just to terrify us. But we do not wish to deceive. Still less do
we wish to stir up terror, to frighten by a fraud, which is much like
commending a falsehood. We wish only to say that, eternally understood, the double-minded one came to nothing. On the other
hand, in the time order, in keeping with his ability and his inde-
fatigable industry, he probably became a well-to-do man, a respected man—or to a certain degree, a respected man, or at least
what a man can become within the circumference of "to a certain
degree." And by this it is not denied that he could readily become
the richest man in the world. For that, too, the condition of being
the richest man, is only something "to a certain degree." Only the
determinations of eternity are above "a certain degree." Like its
truths, the time order with all that belongs to it is to a "certain degree"; only eternity and its truth is eternal. Therefore let us not
deceive and say that in an earthly sense a man advances furthest in

the time order by willing the Good in truth. Do not let the talk be as double-minded as the world is. No, in the time order a man advances furthest, in an earthly sense, by means of double-mindedness, and, it must be admitted mainly by that double-mindedness that has about it a spurious gloss of unity and of inner coherence.

Behold! Honesty is the most enduring of all. It endures, too, at the time when the rich man becomes poor by his honesty. It still endures when the once rich but later poor man is dead and gone, and when the world has been destroyed and forgotten, and when there is neither poverty nor wealth nor money; or further still, when the once rich, but later poor man has long since forgotten the suffering of poverty, yet his honesty still endures. And yet suppose a man should believe that honesty is only related to money and to money values, that the same thing happens to it as to dishonesty, that it ends with the end of the order of money values. Yes, to be sure, honesty stands related to wealth, and poverty and money, but it also stands related to the Eternal. And it does not stand related in a double-minded fashion to money and to the Eternal, so as to aim at joining itself in a financial relationship—to the Eternal. Because of this it endures. It does not "to a certain degree" endure the longest of all. It endures. That assertion is, therefore, no mere proverb. It is an eternal truth. It is the invention of eternity.

On the other hand, there is a proverb that says: One needs a little more than honesty to get through this world. But the questions to which these assertions are a reply differ most widely. It is asked, what is it that endures; and it is asked, how may I pass through? He that merely asks, how may I pass through, has no desire for real knowledge. But he that asks what it is that endures has already passed through; he has already gone over from the time order to eternity, although he is still alive. The one inquires of things only in comparatives. The other questions eternally and if in the hour of temptation, when his honesty is tested, he asks properly, he will receive now, and in the next world he will again receive eternity's answer: Yes, it endures! Yes, it is better to go to the house of mourning than to the house of feasting,[21] for there one can learn that after a hundred years, all is forgotten. Yes, to be sure, long ago the feat and the gallant brothers were forgotten, but truly the Eternal is not forgotten, not after a thousand years.

8. THE PRICE OF WILLING ONE THING:

COMMITMENT, LOYALTY.
READINESS TO SUFFER ALL

B. IF A MAN SHALL WILL THE GOOD IN TRUTH, THEN HE MUST
BE WILLING TO DO ALL FOR THE GOOD OR BE WILLING TO
SUFFER ALL FOR THE GOOD.

My listener, before going further, if it seems right to you, we shall look at the course our talk has taken up to this point. For the talk, too, has its laborious development, and it is only when this is completed in the necessary slowness that we may come to an understanding with each other about what the talk presupposes. Only at that point can the talk, being then secure, make use of the agreeable speed that is properly the very life of conversation. Thus, purity of heart is to will one thing, but *to will one thing could not mean to will the world's pleasure and what belongs to it,* even if a person only named one thing as his choice, *since this one thing was only by a deception. Nor could willing one thing mean willing it in the vain sense of mere bigness,* which only to a man in a state of giddiness appears to be one. FOR IN TRUTH TO WILL ONE THING, A MAN MUST WILL THE GOOD. This was the first, *the possibility of being able to will one thing.* But in order GENUINELY TO WILL ONE THING, A MAN MUST IN TRUTH WILL THE GOOD. On the other hand, as for each act of willing the Good which does not will it in truth, it must be declared to be double-mindedness. Then there was a type of double-mindedness that in a more powerful and active sort of inner coherence seemed to will the Good, but deceptively willed something else. It willed the Good *for the sake of reward, out of fear of punishment, or as a form of self-assertion.* But there was another kind of double-mindedness *born of weakness,* that is commonest of all among men, that versatile double-mindedness that wills the Good in a kind of sincerity, but only wills it "to a certain degree."

Now the talk may continue. If, then, a man in truth wills the

Good, then HE MUST BE WILLING TO DO ALL FOR IT OR HE MUST BE
WILLING TO SUFFER ALL FOR IT. Once more we understand that this
classification divides mankind, or rather reminds us of a division
that exists in reality: a division into the active ones and the
sufferers, so that when the talk is about willing to do all, we may
think about the suffering which this act may entail without calling
such a man a sufferer, since he actually is an active person. But by
the sufferers, we think of those to whom life itself seems to have assigned the speechless, and if you will, the useless sufferings, useless
because the sufferings are not benefitting others, are helping nothing at all, but rather are a burden both to others and to the
sufferers themselves.

1. *If a man shall will the Good in truth, then he must be
willing to do all for the Good.*

Let us first consider: the willingness to do all for the Good. All—
yet will not this talk easily exceed all bounds, if all is named? Will
it not become an impossibility to master all the differences included
under the term "all," and as a result will the talk not become
vague, since the Good can demand the most different things of
different people? It can sometimes demand that a man leave his es-
teemed calling and put on lowliness, that he give away all his possessions to the poor, that he shall not even dare to bury his father.[22]
Again it can demand of others that they shall assume the power
and the dignity that are offered them, that they shall take over the
working power of wealth, that they shall bury the father, and that
perhaps a large part of their lives shall be consecrated to faithfulness which is to be faithful over the little to this extent, that their
own life has no claims of its own, but rather is faithful to the memory of a departed one. Now let us not multiply confusion and distraction in a host of individual details. For these also remind us of
the struggle of pettiness for preference, where one person thinks
that by doing one thing he is doing more for the Good than another
who does something else. For if both in relation to the demand do
all, then they do equally much. And if neither of them does all,
then they do equally little. Instead of multiplying details, let us
simplify this all into its essential unity and likeness by saying that
to will to do all is: *in the commitment to will to be and to remain*

loyal to the Good. Because the commitment is just the committing of all, just as it is also that which is essentially one thing. In this way no tempting occasion for the mistaken quarrel of pettiness about preference need arise. Then, too, the talk can be briefer, for it is unnecessary to enumerate variety's many names and yet be in keeping with strict accuracy, since this essential brevity answers to that rich brevity which is present in life, in the act of commitment to will to be and to remain loyal to the Good. No one believes that this is a long-drawn-out affair. On the contrary, from the standpoint of eternity, if I dare say so, it is this abbreviating of all of life's fractions (for eternity's length is the true abbreviation) that frees life of all its difficulties, and it is through deciding to will to be and to remain loyal to the Good that so much time is gained. For that which absorbs men's time when they complain about the lack of time is irresoluteness, distraction, half thoughts, half resolutions, indecisiveness, great moments—great moments. It was because of these that we said: to be and to remain loyal to, so that the commitment should not be confused with the extravagance of an expansive moment. The person who in decisiveness wills to be and to remain loyal to the Good can find time for all possible things. No, he cannot do that. But neither does he need to do that, for he wills only one thing, and just on that account he will not have to do all possible things, and so he finds ample time for the Good.

The commitment of willing to be and to remain loyal to the Good is truth's brief way of expressing: to be willing to do all. And in this expression there is apparent that leveling insight that recognizes no distinction proportionate to that actual difference of life or of human circumstances: to be an active person or to be a sufferer, because the sufferer too, can be committed to the Good. This is of importance to the thought and to the talk, so that discord shall neither exist nor be kindled; so that the talk shall not incite the active person who is able to accomplish much in the outer world to compare himself in a conceited way with the sufferer; nor provoke the heavily laden sufferer who apparently spends his time in useless suffering, despairingly to compare his uselessness, his pain, his not merely superfluous, but for others even burdensome existence, with the great accomplishments of the active ones. Alas, often enough such an unfortunate person, in addition to his heavy, innocent suffering must bear the severe judgment of the arrogant, the busy, and the stupid, who are indeed able to irritate and hurt him, but who can never understand him.

So now let us talk of doing all, and speak of the men who, in this or that way, are assigned to the external world as to a stage. It makes no difference at all, God be praised, how great or how small the task may be. In relation to the highest of all this simply does not matter when it comes to being willing to do all. Oh, how great is the mercy of the Eternal toward us! All the ruinous quarreling and comparison which swells up and injures, which sighs and envies, the eternal does not recognize. Its claim rests equally on each, the greatest who has ever lived, and the most insignificant. Yes, the sun's rays do not shine with more equality on the peasant's hut and the ruler's palace than the equality with which the Eternal looks down upon the highest and the lowest. Yet not equally, for if the most exalted is not willing to do all, then eternity gazes in wrath upon him. And, even though the rich man by human ingenuity should at last succeed in being able to trick the sun into shining more invitingly upon his palace than over the poor man's hut, man will never be able to trick the Good and eternity in this fashion. The demand upon each is exactly the same: to be willing to do all. If this be fulfilled then the Good bestows its blessing equally upon each one who makes and remains loyal to his commitment.

Suppose that we should now in earthly and temporal fashion recommend the commitment. Suppose we should say, "It does not matter whether you leap into it or creep into it. You may as well risk it first as last. For although you may very well succeed for a time in dancing on roses, nevertheless the difficult time of trouble will come, and so it is always well to be prepared." Oh, let us never wish to see what is holy, or more properly, let us never forget that in this sense eternity is not for sale, that it regards itself as too good to be sold where it might be bought by a bargainer—a brazen one. Yes, for the same reason that a temple-robber is the most contemptible of criminals, so it is with this highly painted clever one who cunningly wills the highest thing of all without willing it in truth. The temple-robber may even succeed in plundering the sacred treasures, and may actually get them into his possession since these treasures are something external. But that clever one never succeeds in stealing the commitment or in stealing himself into the commitment. The ever-active righteousness that eternally dispenses justice is so vigilant that every criminal not only does not become dangerous to the Eternal, but in the sense of imperfection does not even actually come into existence, since it becomes a self-accusation. In relation to the Eternal, the criminal's worst act is much as if the temple-robber instead of stealing the sacred vessels went to the high temple officials and said, "I wish to steal the sacred vessels." So with the matter of stealing the commitment, it does not succeed, but instead the guilty one announces himself to the Eternal and says, "I wish to steal the commitment." For in eternity there is no sensory illusion, and so neither is there what in a moral sense is the same thing, any actual possession—of stolen goods. Let us not, then, deceptively and uselessly recommend the coming to a decision. If someone wishes to sneak through life, let him do it. The truth might still take occasion to seize him so that he would will the decision for the sake of the Good. But let us not make him believe that by an artifice he could cunningly carry the commitment with him on his stealthy way through life.

The decision is to be willing to do all for the Good; it is not cleverly to wish to have the advantage of the Good. Alas, there is in every man a power, a dangerous and at the same time a great power. This power is cleverness. Cleverness strives continually against the commitment. It fights for its life and its honor, for if the decision wins, then cleverness is as if put to death—degraded, to become a despised servant whose talk is attentively listened to, but whose advice one does not stoop to follow.

Now in the inner world man uses cleverness in a ruinous way, in order to keep himself from coming to a decision. In countless ways cleverness can be so misused; but in order once again not to multiply that which is not important and thereby to divert attention from the really important, we will again simply designate this misuse by a definite expression: to seek to evade. To forsake one's post, to desert in battle is always disgraceful, but cleverness has invented an ingenious device that apparently prevents flight: it is evasion. By the help of evasion, namely, one does not come into danger, and neither does he lose his honor by running away in danger—on the contrary one does not come into danger—that is one advantage. And one wins great honor as being especially clever—that is a second advantage. Only eternity, the Good, and so also the Holy Scriptures, are of another opinion about this matter of evasions and about the much-honored clever ones. For they are referred to when it speaks of "those that draw back into perdition" (Hebrews x. 39). How strange that a man can, therefore, avoid a danger, and when he believes himself secure and saved (which one indeed should believe after he has escaped danger), just at that point he has sunk into perdition.

A clever one speaks in this way, "Afterwards it is too late. If I have already ventured too far out and been crushed, who will help me then? Then I should be a cripple for all the rest of my life, an object of mockery and a by-word among men. Who will help me then?" Who will help him then? Who other than the power in which he trusted in venturing so far out? Yet surely not as one who is stronger helps a weakling, but rather as when the unprofitable servant[23] does everything in order to do his lord's will. But now with the help of evasions the clever one talks as if the Good itself was no power, or as if its power counted for nothing, so, therefore, that it could be the clever one who (if he chose to risk it), by doing all, would help out the Good. If this is so, then it is true enough that no one exists who can help him—in case he actually should venture out—and that which a clever ingenious imagination invents in order to be able to forget the troublesome background of evasion above the terrifying foreground, actually comes to pass. Evasion thus accomplishes nothing.

And even if the terrible thing now happens: the confident venturer is injured. Even an earthly government is accustomed to care for its faithful servants who risk danger in loyalty to the state, then shall not God and the Good also care for their faithful servants, if only they are sincere!

And even if the terrible thing happens that when the sincere person had risked all, that it was then that the government said to him, "My friend, I cannot use you." Oh, how clear it is that the smallest crumb of grace in the service of the Good is infinitely more blessed than to be the mightiest of all outside that service. Verily, verily, it is indeed true, it is with trembling true, in relation to the ungodly, but it is also by grace happily true for the sincere, that God is not tricked by a man. Even if the sincere one comes to grief, perhaps it was just this that the government needed. Has it not often happened that the well is first covered only after the child has fallen in, while before this the most reasonable arguments and warnings had been of no avail? Now if the sincere one is willing to be the child who falls in, has his venture been wholly in vain?

Another says, "I have not the strength to risk all." Again evasion, an evasion by the aid of the word "all." For the Good is quite capable of reckoning and computing its demand in relation to the strength that this man has. And what is more, if he will venture in all sincerity, then he will certainly receive strength enough in the act of decision. But the clever one desires by the help of evasions to have strength in advance. He wishes to misuse it like the soldier who, in order to be sure of being distinguished in battle, demands his distinction in advance. And yet this picture is untrue, for it is doubtful how far the battle gives strength. But it is certain that the confidence wherewith he has ventured does give superhuman strength. Yet it is also certain (oh, wonderful accuracy!) that the one who does not have trust does not receive this strength. Look, the great battleship first gets its orders when it is far out at sea, the little sloop knows all in advance. And in a spiritual sense, a person is only really out at sea who is willing to do all, irrespective of whether he is the highest or the least. The little sloop is the clever person, no matter whether he be the highest or the least.

One says, "The bit that I can do is not worth while." The clever one is polite, he understates, he says, "Do excuse me." He acts as if the Good were a distinguished man, and as if willing the Good were a distinguished act. But it is a misconception. No, here it is an evasion. The Good is not distinguished. It demands neither more nor less than all; whether that is a mere bit or not is neither here nor there. The widow's mite was all that she owned. Before God it was as great a sum as all of the world's gold in a single heap, and if one who owned all the gold in the world gave it all, he would give no more. Yes, when that public collection of money was made, it was possible that the collectors both kindly and politely might have said to the widow, "No, Mother, you keep your mite." But the Good—how shall we express it? Its goodness is so great, that it recognizes no difference.

One man says, "I am not justified in doing that because of my wife and children." Alas, even the civil government looks after, yes . . . yet this is out of place here. But I wonder if he, as man and father, really could do anything better for wife and children than to impress upon them this trust in Providence. Here, then, it is not as in civil life that the person who risks dares hope that the state will look after his wife and children. No, spiritually understood, he has by his venture cared for them in the best possible way, for by this he has shown them that he at least has faith in Providence. Here, then, it is not as in civil life that the person who undertakes to risk can do it by caring for wife and children. For spiritually understood, the fearful one shows that he has no concern for the true welfare of wife and children.

One may say, "Experience teaches that it is best to divide one's energies in order that one can win by the one when he loses by another. I owe it to myself, and to my future, not to place all upon a single thing." Yes, God grant that he will not restrict his pains to his future, for that is too little; but may this alone be set before his eyes, and ever called to his mind; that his future is—an eternity.

Yet how could one ever finish talking about all the evasions? Who would undertake this fruitless work, this battle with the air! And even if someone should, even if he succeeded in enumerating them all and for an instant succeeded in holding them together so that they could not, like true runaways, slip away and assume another role while remaining in essence the same, still one evasion would always remain behind even if none ought to be there, even if by repeated inspection a commendable cleverness should be unable to discover that a single ground had been overlooked and hence that a single evasion was still possible.

So the double-minded person, seduced by cleverness, yielded to the evasions. "But this brought him nothing." Oh, let us not deceive youth, let us not sit and bargain in the outer court of the holy, nor formulate a profane introduction to the holy, as if one should in truth will the Good in order to prosper in the world. Readily grant that the clever one amounts to something, even to something great in the world. There is, however, a power that is called memory. It should be dear to all the good ones as well as to all lovers. Yes, it may even be so dear to lovers that they almost prefer this whisper of memory to the sight of each other, as when they say, "Do you remember that time, and do you remember that time?"

Now memory also visits the double-minded person. Then it says to him, "Do you remember that time? . . . You as well as I knew well enough what was there required of you, but you shrank back (to your own destruction), do you remember that! It was by this that you won a great deal of your property (to your own destruction). Do you remember that! Do you recall that time? . . . You knew as well as I what you should venture, you knew what danger it involved, do you remember, you shrank back (to your own destruction), do you remember? . . . Yet it served you well, for the badge of honor on your breast calls you back to a memory of how you shrank back to your own destruction!

"Do you remember that time . . . you knew well enough by yourself and by my solitary voice in your heart, what you should choose, but you shrank back (to your own destruction), do you remember that? It was that time when the popular favor and the exultation of the masses hailed you as the righteous one, do you remember that?" Yes, it indeed becomes your concern to remember the popular exultation and favor, for in eternity such things are not recognized. But in eternity it is not forgotten that you shrank back! For what shall it profit a man if he shall gain the whole world and lose his own soul?[24] What shall it profit him if he shall gain the time order and all it possesses, if he breaks with the Eternal? What shall it profit him if he comes through the world under full sail aided by the favorable winds of popular exultation and admiration, if he runs aground upon eternity? What shall it profit the sick man to imagine himself, as all men do, to be well, if the physician says he is sick!

Outwardly, too, cleverness is used in a ruinous way, in the matter of the decision, that is to say, it is outwardly misused. And we are indeed speaking of the active ones, and of being willing to do all for the Good. Here cleverness may be misused in a multitude of ways. But, once more, let us not increase the distracting element. Let us, rather, simplify that which is significant, and call all these different kinds of misuse by a single name: deception. The clever one knows just how the Good must be altered a tiny particle in order to win the world's good will. He knows how much should be added to it and how much should be subtracted. He knows just what ingratiating thing should be whispered in men's ears, what should be entrusted to their hands, and how the hand should be pressed, how it should be swung away from truth's decision, how the turning should be done, and how he himself in suppleness should shift and turn—"in order that he can accomplish all the more for the Good." But the secret of deception, to which in one way or another all the expressions can be traced back, is this: that certainly it is not men that stand in need of the Good, but that it is the Good that stands in need of men. On that account it is men who must be won. For the Good is a poor beggar that is in desperate need, instead of its being men who are in need of the Good, and so much in need of it that it is the one thing necessary to them, that it must be bought at any price, that absolutely all must be given up and sold in order to buy it, but that also, the one who owns it owns all. Yet it happens that all are naturally fooled by the deception. Someone makes an attempt to fool the Good, which in all eternity inevitably fails, for that it seems to succeed for a fortnight or a life-time is only a jest. The clever one, on the other hand, wins great distinction in the world—and he, too, is fooled. The crowd delights itself with the flattering sweets of imagination—and is fooled! This was deception's secret, that it is the Good that stands in need of men. The clever one's secret is that he cannot be wholly content with the Good's poor reward, but must cast about to earn a little extra by eluding the Good a little.

Seduced by cleverness, the double-minded person yielded, "but he accomplished nothing in this world." No, let us not give a false impression; he accomplished much. A large number of friends of the Good, or of good friends rallied admiringly around him. Of course, they believed by this to attach themselves once more to the Good, but that certainly must be a deception, for the clever one himself went outside the Good. Many joined together, for they had the idea that the Good is something extraordinary, and all honor be to them and all honor be to this true idea. But they also had the idea that the Good is something so exceptionally great that many must join together in order to buy it. Yet this conception is not worthy of honor, even if it be deceptively called humility. It is an insult to the Good, which in its infinite goodness does not refuse the most insignificant, but allows him also to bid and to buy—if he is willing to do all and so in truth to honor the Good. On the other hand, the Good rejects all stupid honor and distinction, where its greatness would be compared with an estate which the "individ-ual" has not money enough to buy so that it is necessary to take up a collection. With the help of the masses the clever one now erected an enormous building. True enough, it was only a frame building (there were many others like it), but it looked well as long as it stood. But memory, memory that in the highest and most sober sense purifies even the coarser expressions is what in plain everyday language is called a "dunner." Now and then memory even pays a visit to the popular idol. Upon these occasions, memory murmurs softly to him, "Can you remember the deceptive turn you gave the thing, by which you won the blind masses, and by which you were able to build the tower so high?" But the popular one says, "Only keep quiet, never let anyone get to know it." "Very well," memory answers. "You know that I am no petty bickerer who is in desperation over what is owed him. Let it rest. No one shall get to know it, as long as you live, perhaps not even when you are dead and forgotten. But eternally, eternally it will continue to be remembered." Oh, what did it net the unprofitable servant if his Master went away, if his Master traveled so far away that he should never more see him in this life, what good was this to him, if the Master that traveled away was memory with which he must be together throughout eternity! What help is it indeed to the condemned one, if the day of punishment is put off throughout his whole life; how does this help him, if indeed the judgment that was passed on him is the judgment of eternity and shall be carried out in eternity!

The clever one, therefore, accomplishes much. Let us for once think through this thought: *to accomplish something in this world.* One hears so much of both impatient and misleading talk about this. To be sure, it is well that all should wish to do something. It is indeed earnestness to desire it, but should it not also be earnestness to understand in oneself and in life precisely what is meant by saying that one man accomplishes such an exceptional amount, or that another man seems to accomplish nothing at all. Suppose the temporal order is not understood as it pictures itself, but rather as the recognizable fact that it is in reality. Suppose the temporal order was a homogeneous transparent medium of the Eternal. Then every eternal volition in a man, and every volition of the Eternal would straightway become perceptible in the temporal order, if the same kind of powers of comprehension be assumed in the temporal order: so that when the man who wills does get on in the temporal order, and is accounted to be something in the eyes of the many, the eternal volition in a man would be plainly evident, just as the quantity of a cry is obvious by the quantity of the sound in a room, just as when a stone is cast into the water its size is evident by the size of the circle it makes. If matters stood like this between the temporal order and the Eternal, so that they answer each other as the echo answers to the sound, then that which is accomplished would be a trustworthy rendering of the eternal volition in a man. By what a man had accomplished, one could immediately see how much will toward the Eternal there was in him. But in that case it could never have come to pass in the temporal order (in order to mention the highest and the most horrible, but also what is the key that explains all) that God's son, as He was revealed in human form, was crucified—repudiated by the temporal order. For He truly willed the Eternal in the eternal sense, and yet in the temporal order He became distinguished by being repudiated, and so accomplishing but little. As it had happened to God's son, so it went with the Apostles, just as they themselves had expected, and so it has gone with so many witnesses of the Good and the true in whom this eternal will has burned fiercely.

It is obvious, then, that the temporal order cannot be the transparent medium of the Eternal. In its given reality the temporal order is in conflict with the Eternal. This makes the determination to accomplish something less plain. The more active the Eternal is toward the witness, the stronger is the cleavage. The more the striver, instead of willing the Eternal, is linked with temporal existence, the more he accomplishes in the sense of the temporal existence. So it is in many ways or in all possible ways in the temporal order. When a peculiar thinker, who just by his peculiarity is more tied up with the Eternal and less with time's moment, addresses his speech to men, he is rarely understood or listened to. When, on the other hand, a voluble follower comes to his aid in order that the peculiar one can become—misunderstood: then it succeeds, then there are many who instantly understand it. The thinker becomes a kind of superfluous element in life, the follower an effective man who accomplishes such an extraordinary amount in the temporal order. Only upon a rare occasion does it ever happen that the Eternal and the temporal's accomplishments conform after a fashion to each other—by accident. For let us not insult God and the God-Man by assuming that what happened to Him there was an accident, that His life expressed something accidental, perhaps something that had He lived at another time, among another people, would not have happened to Him. If, then, there is to be significance in the talk about accomplishing, a distinction must be made between the momentary and the eternal view of the thing. These are two opposed views which each man has to choose between in regard to his own striving and in regard to each contemporary striving. For to judge by the outcome (whereby an attempt is made to unite a judgment of temporal existence and of eternity into a judgment that comes after the event is past) is not humanly possible in the instant that a man himself acts, nor is it possible in the instant when others act.

By the help of a sense deception, a living generation often believes itself able to pass judgment on a past generation, because it misunderstood the Good. And it is even guilty of committing the same offense against a contemporary. And yet it is just in regard to his contemporary that a man should know whether he has the view of the moment, or the view of the Eternal. At some later date, it is no art to decorate the graves of the noble and to say, "If they had only lived now," now—just as we are starting in to do the same thing against a contemporary. For the difficulty and the test of what dwells in the one who judges is precisely—the contemporary. The view of the moment is the opinion which in an earthly and busy sense decides whether a man accomplishes anything or not. And in this sense, nothing in the world has ever been so completely lost as was Christianity at the time that Christ was crucified. And in the understanding of the moment, never in the world has anyone accomplished so little by the sacrifice of a consecrated life as did Jesus Christ. And yet in this same instant, eternally understood, He had accomplished all. For He did not foolishly judge by the result that was not yet there, or more rightly (for here is the conflict and battleground of the two interpretations of what is meant by "accomplishing") the result was indeed there. Question His contemporaries, if you ever meet them. Do they not say of the crucified one, "The fool, he would help others and he cannot help himself, but now the outcome also shows, so that everyone may see what he was."[25] Was it not said by His contemporaries, especially where the clever led the conversation, "The fool, he who had it in his power to become king if he cared to make use of his opportunity, if he had only half my cleverness, he would have been king. In the beginning I really believed that it was ingenuity, that he let these people express themselves in this fashion without wishing to give himself up to them. I believed it was a trick in order to inflame them still more. But now the result shows clearly enough what I more recently have myself been quite clear about, that he is a shallow, blind visionary!" Was it not said by many intelligent men and women, "The result shows that he has been hunting after phantasies; he should have married. In this way he would now have been a distinguished teacher in Israel."

And yet, eternally understood, the crucified one had in the same moment accomplished all! But the view of the moment and the view of eternity over the same matter have never stood in such atrocious opposition. It can never be repeated. This could happen only to Him. Yet eternally understood, He had in the same moment accomplished all, and on that account said, with eternity's wisdom, "It is finished."

For it is not after the passage of eighteen hundred years that He will now again appear, and referring to the outcome, say, "It is finished." In contrast to this, He would still not say that. Perhaps it would require many centuries before He would be able to say that in regard to temporal existence. Yet what He is still unable to say after the passage of eighteen triumphant centuries, He said in His own age, eighteen centuries ago, in the very moment when all was lost. Eternally understood, He said, "It is finished." "It is finished." He said that just when the mass of the people, and the priests, and the Roman soldiers, Herod and Pilate, and the idle ones on the street, the crowd in the gateway, and the newspaper reporters (if there were any such at that time), in short, when all the powers of the moment, however different their sentiments might have been, were agreed upon this view of the matter: that all was lost, hopelessly lost. "It is finished," He said, nailed to the cross as He was, at the very time when His Mother stood there—as if nailed to the cross, when His disciples' eyes were as if nailed to the cross by horror at this sight. Hence Motherhood and faithfulness submitted to the moment's view of the matter, that all was lost. Oh, then let us by this most horrible thing, which once took place (and that it has happened only once is not to the world's credit, but rather that the crucified one is eternally and essentially different from every other man), let us learn wisdom in the lesser relationships. Let us never deceive youth by foolish talk about the matter of accomplishing. Let us never make them busy in the service of the moment, instead of in patience willing something eternal. Let us not make them quick to judge what they perhaps do not understand, instead of willing something eternal and being content with little for themselves! Let us rightly consider that a generation is not on that account superior because it understands that a previous generation acted wrongly, if in the present moment they themselves do not understand how to discriminate between the momentary and the eternal aspect of the thing at hand.

9. THE PRICE OF WILLING ONE THING:

THE EXPOSURE OF EVASIONS

But the one who in truth wills the Good puts cleverness to an inward use: in order to prevent all evasions and thereby to help him enter into and persist in the commitment.

Cleverness is indeed a great power, yet it is treated by him as an insignificant servant, as a shrewd contemptible one. He hears the servant, to be sure, but in action he is not guided by him. He uses cleverness against himself as a spy and informer, which informs him instantly of each evasion, yes, even gives warning at any suspicion of an evasion. Now just as the thief knows the hidden way—and goes by it, so the authorities also know it and go by it in order to detect the thief, but the knowledge as knowledge is the same in both cases.

This is the way he makes use of cleverness. I do not know whether it is true that at each man's birth two angels are born, his good and his bad angel. But this I do believe (and I will gladly listen to any objection, although I will not believe it) that at each man's birth there comes into being an eternal vocation for him, expressly for him. To be true to himself in relation to this eternal vocation is the highest thing a man can practice, and, as that most profound poet has said: "Self-love is not so vile a sin as self-neglect-

ing."[26] Then there is but one fault, one offense: disloyalty to his
own self or the denial of his own better self. One who is guilty of
such a fault is not like a thief or a robber. The civil authority will
not lie in wait for him. This fault may begin its course in complete
silence so that none will be aware of it. Is it, therefore, perhaps of
no account? Certainly many believe that a man can search out and
grasp the Truth just as well, creatively express the Beautiful just as
well, vitally perfect the Good just as well, even if, in order to win
some advantage in the world, he was secretly a little unfaithful to
himself, even if he did shift the boundary stones of his inner life a
particle by just a shade less scrupulousness, so that even though he
had won this material advantage by doubtful means, yet he "can
truly work for the Good, the Beautiful, and the True." So low an estimate of the Good and the Beautiful and the True is expressed by
this as to think that it ought to be able to make use of anyone as a
serviceable instrument from whom to elicit a harmonious strain,
anyone—even the one that had polluted himself!

Yes, man can deceive himself and men. But when eternity listens
attentively, listens in order to discover whether the playing of the
strings is pure and in time with itself—alas, it instantly detects false
tones and hesitation. It rejects such a man just as a connoisseur
rejects a stringed instrument when it is damaged. Alas, it is indeed
a sorry cleverness (however much it boasts of the material advantage that it won as a proof—of its folly; however much it points to
the badges of distinction and thereby again to—the hidden dejec-
tion within), a sorry cleverness that deceives itself about what is the
highest of all. The only genuine cleverness is that which helps a
man in all devotedness truly to will the Good.

The one who truly wills the Good, therefore, makes use of cleverness against evasions. But by this does he not achieve something
great in the world? Perhaps so, perhaps not. But one thing definitely he does become: he becomes a friend, a lover of memory. And
so when in a quiet hour, memory visits him (and already at this
point how different it is from that visit when memory threateningly
knocks at the door of the double-minded man!), then it says to him,
"Do you remember that time, that time when the good resolution
conquered within you?" And he answers, "Yes, dear one!" But then
memory continues (and between lovers memory is so dear that
they almost prefer to the sight of each other the whisper of memory

when they say, "Can you remember that time?" and "Can you remember that time?"), memory continues, "Can you remember all the hardships and sufferings you endured for the sake of the resolution?" He answers, "No, dear one, I have forgotten that—let it remain forgotten! But when in the toils of life and struggle, when in my troubled thoughts all is in confusion, it may seem to me as if even that was forgotten which I know I had willed in sincerity. Oh, thou hast thy very name from that act of remembering, thou messenger of the Eternal: Memory. At that hour, visit me, and bring with thee the long-desired, the strengthening meeting with thyself once more." And memory answers in parting, "I promise you that, I swear it to you by all eternity." Then they part one from another, for so it must be here in the world of time. Deeply moved, he takes one more look after memory's vanishing form as one looks after a glorified saint. Now it has gone and so has the quiet hour. It was only a quiet hour, it was not some great moment—on that account he hoped that memory would keep its promise. He preserved in his own soul that stillness in which he met with memory when it was pleased to visit him. To him this is his reward, and to him this reward is above all others. Yes, just as a mother, who carries her beloved child asleep at her breast along a difficult road, is not troubled about what may happen to her, but only fears that the child may be disturbed and upset, so he, too, does not fear the troubles of the world on his own account. He is only troubled lest these should upset and disturb that possibility of a visit that slumbers in his soul.

The one who in truth wills the Good also uses cleverness on the outer world. It is no disgrace to be clever; it is a good thing. It is no disgrace that the authorities are clever, that they shrewdly know how to trace the criminal's hidden trail in order to seize him and make him harmless. In so far as the good man is clever, he, too, knows, how in the very face of truth the world wishes to have the Good made agreeable, how the crowd desires to be won—the much feared crowd, who "desire that the teacher shall tremble before his hearers and flatter them." He knows all about this—in order not to follow it, but rather by the very opposite conduct to keep as free as possible of these deceptions, that he himself may not adopt any illicit way of deriving some advantage from the Good (earning money, distinction, and admiration) and so that he may deceive no one by a figment of the imagination. Whenever possible he will prefer to withdraw the Good from contact with the crowd. He will seek to split the crowd up in order to get hold of the individual or to get each by himself. He will be reminded of what that simple old sage remarked in ancient times, "When they meet together, and the world sits down at an assembly, or in a court of law, or a theater, or a camp, or in any other popular resort, and there is a great uproar and they praise some things which are being said or done, and blame other things, equally exaggerating both, shouting and clapping their hands, and the echo of the rocks and the place in which they are assembled redoubles the sound of the praise or blame—at such a time will not a young man's heart, as they say, leap within him?"[27] And indeed this is exactly what is necessary in order in truth to will the Good—that a man's heart should leap, but leap with the unspoiled quality of youth. And therefore the good man, in case he is also a clever one, will see that if anything is able to be done for the Good, then he must try to get men to be alone. The same persons, who singly, as solitary individuals are able to will the Good, are immediately seduced as soon as they associate themselves and become a crowd. On that account the good man will neither seek to secure the assistance of a crowd in order to split up the crowd, nor will he seek to have a crowd back of him, during the time that he breaks up the crowd in front of him.

But just how the good man will make use of cleverness in the outer world does not permit of being more precisely specified in general terms, for that which is necessary can be totally different with respect to each time and to the circumstances of each time. That stern prophet[28] who went out into the desert and lived on locusts knew how, in relation to his contemporaries, he ought to express this decisively: that it is not the truth that is in need of men, but men who are in need of the truth. Hence they must come to him, come out into the desert. Out there, there was no opportunity for them to be able to decorate the truth, to be able most graciously to do something for it; out there where the ax did not lie in the woods, but at the foot of the solitary tree, and where each tree that did not bear good fruit was bound to be chopped down. Yes, to be sure, there have been self-appointed judges since that time, who have erred and chopped away at the whole forest—and the crowd found it most flattering. Again, there was that simple wise man who worked for the Good under the form of a joke. He knew by his cleverness exactly what his frivolous people needed, in order that they should not simply take the earnestness of the Good in vain, and thereby be led to pay the wise man a good deal of money as a reward for having deceived them. The form of the joke prevented their misusing the Good's earnestness; the opposition of the joke, on the other hand, made their frivolity obvious: it was the judgment.

Without this cleverness, the frivolous ones would in all probability have imitated him in being earnest. Now, on the contrary, he confronted them with the choice, and see, they chose the joke. They never even noticed that there was anything earnest in it—because there was no earnestness in them. This was the judgment, and the judge's conduct. His art was paganism's highest ingenuity, for the Christian type has still another consideration.

Yet this, too, may not be generalized upon. It applies only to that initiated one whose secret it is, so that by paying close attention to such an individual, one can learn to know a whole generation, concluding from him, from the form he found it necessary to clothe himself in, how the entire age must have been. But it is certain and acknowledged by all, that each one who in truth wills the Good, is not in the world in order to conjure up an appearance of the Good, thus winning approval in the eyes of the world and becoming a man who is beloved by all. He has not the task of changing the Good into a thing of the moment, into something that shall be voted upon in a noisy gathering, or something that swiftly gains some disciples who also will the Good up to a certain degree. No, he has always the task, not by word, nor by intention, but by the sincere inner concentration of his own life—the task of making it most obvious of all that his surroundings have been set in opposition to him, not in order that he shall judge in terms of words, but in order that his life may unconditionally serve the Good in action. The task is his own obligation in the service of the Good. Judging is not his real function, not his act, but is an accompaniment whereby the surrounding world relates itself to him. Judging is not his activity, because to will the Good in truth is his activity. Yet his suffering is an act of judging, because the surrounding world becomes manifest by the manner in which it lets him suffer; and at the same time by these sufferings he is helped to test himself as to whether it actually is the Good that he wills or whether he himself is caught up in a deception.

Above all, the one who in truth wills the Good must not be "busy." In quiet patience he must leave it to the Good itself, what reward he shall have, and what he shall accomplish. He dare not allow himself a single word of compromise, not a glance. He dare not ask the slightest relief from the world. He has only to give himself up to the Good and to that thing and to that person that might possibly be helped by him. He is no judge. On the contrary, he is just the opposite, he is the one who is judged. He effects a judgment only in the sense that the surrounding world becomes manifest by how it judges him.

But in this way does he accomplish nothing at all, since he is weighed down with men's opposition, and then gets the worst of the battle? Now in this life indeed no, and in eternity, never. In this life indeed no, for the one who sincerely trusts in God is enthusiastic. He is not like a candle-stub, whose tiny flame goes out before a wind. No, he is like a great fire; a storm cannot quench it! And the flame in his fire is like that one in Greece: water cannot put it out! And even if finally the world does make him suffer, on that account neither the Good nor he has lost—for to be too far up in the world is most often, as in the ordeal that is called "trial by water," a sign of guilt. To be sure, since the world puts more store by the fashionable than by the truly Good, just on that account in the reckoning of the moment, he will accomplish far less by not giving in, not bargaining, not even making himself comfortable and powerful, by not willing to have profit for himself. But the remembering, the remembering! Let us indeed never forget the remembering, although a person might certainly believe that he would at least be able to forget. And shall not memory be able to remind him of that time when he sneaked away by underhanded means, in order to avoid a decision; of that time when he gave the matter another turn, in order to please men; of that time that he deserted his post, in order to let the storm pass over; of that time he knuckled under, in order to secure an easing off of his painful position; of that time he sought refuge and association with others—perhaps, as it is called, in order to work all the more effectively for the Good's victory, that is, in order to make his own position a little less difficult than as though at the midnight hour, somewhat terror-stricken, one stood all alone "with heavily loaded weapons at his dangerous post."[29]

Nay, what he accomplishes, and what he does not accomplish, in the sense of the moment, that is not his concern. He always accomplishes this—that he becomes the friend and lover of memory. He accomplishes this whether he is remembered in the world or not. For this world's memory is like the moment: a series of moments. Eternity's memory, that he is certain of. When he leaves this world, he leaves nothing behind him, he takes all with him, he loses nothing, he gains all—for "God is all to him."

10. THE PRICE OF WILLING ONE THING:

AN EXAMINATION OF THE EXTREME CARE OF AN INCURABLE SUFFERER

2. *If a man in truth wills the Good then he must be willing to suffer all for the Good.*

This applies to the active ones. But from the sufferer, if he shall in truth will the Good, it is demanded that he must be willing to suffer all for the Good, or, as was previously explained, for the expression is essentially the same (and therein lies precisely the equal participation of the Eternal in the differentiations of earthly life), *he must be willing in his decision to be and to remain with the Good.* For he may also suffer and suffer and continue to suffer without ever arriving at any decision, in the true sense, of assenting to the suffering. A man may have suffered throughout his whole life without it ever, in any true sense, being able to be said of him that he has been willing to suffer all for the Good. But in that respect the sufferer's suffering is different from the active person's suffering, for when the active one suffers, then his suffering has significance for the victory of the Good in the world. When the sufferer, on the other hand, willingly takes up his appointed sufferings, he is willing to suffer all for the Good, that is, in order that the Good may be victorious in him.

Therefore, the sufferer must be willing to suffer all. All; but now how at this point shall the talk be conducted: For alas, even now the sight and the knowledge of suffering can easily rob anyone of composure. How shall the talk be briefly formulated? For the sufferings are able to be so different, and of such long duration. Here, once again, let us not multiply distractions but rather let us simplify that which is really important. Let us center all the talk about suffering upon *the wish*. For the wish is the sufferer's connection with a happier temporal existence (faith and hope are related to the Eternal through the will); and at the same time the wish is the sore spot where the suffering pains, the sore spot which the suffering continually touches. Even if suffering could still be spoken of where there is no longer any wish, it is an animal-like suffering, not suffering that befits a man. It is a kind of spiritual suicide to will to put the wish to death. For we are not talking about wishes, but rather about *the wish* with the real emphasis of distinction, just as we also are not talking about passing sufferings, but of the real sufferer. The wish is not the cure. This happens only by the action of the Eternal. The wish is, on the contrary, the life in suffering, the health in suffering. It is the perseverance in suffering, for it is as one thinker has said, "The comfort of temporal existence is a precarious affair. It lets the wound grow together, although it is not yet healed, and yet the physician knows that the cure depends upon keeping the wound open." In the wish, the wound is kept open, in order that the Eternal may heal it. If the wound grows together, the wish is wiped out and then eternity cannot heal, then temporal existence has in truth bungled the illness.

And so let us speak of the wish and thereby of the sufferings; *let us properly linger over this, convinced that one may learn more profoundly and more reliably what the highest is by considering suffering than by observing achievements, where so much that is distracting is present.* There are wishes that die in being born; there are wishes that are forgotten like our yesterdays; there are wishes that one outgrows, and later can scarcely recall; there are wishes that one learns to give up, and how good it was to have given them up; there are wishes from which one dies away, which one hides away, just as a departed one is hidden away in glorified memory. Those are the wishes to which an active person is exposed. They may be more or less dangerous diseases. Their cure may be accomplished by the extinction of the individual wish.

Yet there is also a wish that dies slowly, a wish that remains with the real sufferer even in the pain of his loss, and that only dies when he dies. For wishes concern particular objects, and a great number of objects, but the wish applies essentially to the whole life.

Yet sad as it is with the wish, how joyful it is with hope! For there is a hope that is born and dies; a short-lived hope, that tomorrow is forgotten; a childish hope, that old age does not recognize; a hope that one dies away from. But then—in death, in death's decision, a hope is born that does not die in being born because it is born in death. By this hope the sufferer, under the pain of the wish, is committed to the Good. So it is with the hope in which the sufferer, as though from afar off, reaches out toward the Eternal.

With faith it is still more joyful. For there is a faith that disappoints and vanishes; a faith that is lost and is repented of; there is a faith, which, when it droops is like death. But then—in death, in death's decision a faith is won that does not disappoint, that is not repented of, that does not die; it seizes the Eternal and holds fast to it. By this faith, under the pain of the wish, the sufferer is committed to the Good. So it is with faith in which the sufferer draws the Eternal nearer to himself.

But with love it is most joyous of all. For there is a love that blazes up and is forgotten; there is a love that unites and divides—a love *until* death. But then—in death, in death's decision, there is born a love that does not flame up, that is not equivocal, that is not —*until* death, but beyond death, a love that endures. In this love under the pain of the wish, the sufferer is committed to the Good. Oh, you sufferer, whoever you may be, will you then with doubleness of mind seek the relief that temporal existence can give, the relief that permits you to forget your suffering (yes, so you think) but rather that allows you to forget the Eternal! Will you in doubleness of mind despair, because all is lost (yes, so you think) yet with the Eternal all is to be won! Will you in doubleness of mind despair? Have you considered what it is to despair? Alas, it is to deny that God is love! Think that over properly, one who despairs abandons himself (yes, so you think); nay, he abandons God! Oh, weary not your soul with that which is passing and with momentary relief. Grieve not your spirit with forms of comfort which this world affords. Do not in suicidal fashion murder the wish; but rather win the highest by hope, by faith, by love—as the mightiest of all are able to do: commit yourself to the Good!

Once again let us speak of the wish, and hence of sufferings. A discussion of sufferings may always be profitable if it does not confine itself to the stubbornness of the affliction but is concerned whenever possible with the edification of the sufferer. It is both permissible and an act of sympathy to dwell upon suffering in order that the sufferer may not become impatient with our superficial discussion in which he does not recognize his own suffering and in order that in such impatience he may not thrust aside all consolation and be strengthened in double-mindedness. It is indeed one thing to move out into life with the wish when that which is wished for, continued to be work and a task. It is another thing to move out into life away from that wish. Look at Abraham.[30] He had to leave the home of his fathers and journey out among a strange people, where there was no reminder of that which he loved—yes, it is true that sometimes it may be a consolation that nothing reminds one of what he wishes to forget, but it is a bitter consolation for one who is filled with longing. Hence a man can also have a wish that for him contains all, so that in the hour of separation, when the journeying is begun, it is as if he wandered out into a strange land where nothing but the contrast with what he has lost reminds him of that which he wished for. It can be to him as if he journeyed into a stange land, even if he remains in his home, perhaps on the same spot—through the loss of the wish; indeed, it may be as if he were among strangers, so that to suffer the loss of the wish seems to him heavier and more critical than the loss of his mind. Even if he does not leave the spot, his life moves along a laborious path away from that wish, perhaps into useless sufferings, for we are talking of the real sufferer, hence not of the ones who have the consolation that their sufferings are serving some good cause, are of benefit to others. It must have been like this: The journey to the strange country was not long; in a moment he was there, there in that strange country, where the sufferers were gathered, only not those that had stopped grieving; not those whose tears eternity cannot wipe away, for the reason that, as an old religious writing so simply and so touchingly says, "how shall God be able in heaven to dry up your tears when you have not wept?"[31]

Another comes perhaps by another way but to the same place. Silently, the guiding necessity leads him onward. Austere and earnest, not cruel, for it is never cruel, duty comes behind and brings up the rear of the company. But the path is not the path of the wish. Now he halts for a moment, even the two austere guides are touched by his suffering: look, there a side path branches off; "good-by, thou wish of my youth, thou friendly place, where I had hoped to be able to build and to dwell with my wish!" So they move on; the guiding necessity silently in advance, duty austere and silent comes behind, not cruel, for duty is never cruel. Alas, look, there a road runs off to the side that leads to the wish; "good-by, my place of work where by the full joy of work I had hoped to be able to forget the wishes I was denied in youth." So the company moved on. Yet the manner in which it happens does not matter, whether it be the spot that is altered and the sufferer remains at that same spot, or whether the sufferer changes his whereabouts and journeys away; this does not matter, if the place is the same, if they are gathered at this one place, which human language may well be tempted to call: the useless suffering that is beyond the reach of any comfort. The sufferings themselves could have different names, but let us not multiply names. Let us consider what is essential; that the real sufferer does not benefit others by his suffering, but rather is a burden upon them. If this latter is not the case, the former must then be so if the suffering is to be regarded as useless, that is, if the sufferer is in the strictest sense to be called a sufferer. In the strictest sense, and let us really be strict with ourselves in order that we may not venture to call ourselves sufferers the first time anything goes against us; but let us be all the more tender with those who are in the strictest sense sufferers. Oh, such a sufferer, whoever you may be; if a man is come to the point in the land of his birth where every way of making a living is closed to him, then he thinks seriously of emigrating to a foreign country and there seeking his fortune. But perhaps you answer, "What does that mean; how shall I be able to emigrate, and what good would it do me to change my location? My lot is cast, everywhere on earth it would be just the same." Of course, but let us understand one another; the journey of which we speak is not long, neither is the lot cast, unless you have already found the way out of your suffering: it is only a single step, a decisive step, and you, too, have emigrated, for the Eternal lies much nearer to you than any foreign country to the emigrant, and yet when you are there the change is infinitely greater. So then, go with God to God, continually take that one step more, that single step that even you, who cannot move a limb, are still able to take; that single step, that even the prisoner, who has lost his freedom, even the one in chains, whose feet are not free, is still able to take: and you are committed to the Good. Nobody, not even the greatest that has ever lived, can do more than you.

But bear in mind: [that] your sufferings might well be called useless, and that we men can certainly be tempted to speak of useless suffering as beyond the reach of comfort. But this is only human speech. In the language of eternity, the suffering that helped you to reach the highest is far from useless. Alas, it is only useless and unused when you will not let yourself be helped by it up to the highest—for perhaps you killed the wish and became spiritually like dead flesh that feels no pain, otherwise it is just at the point of the wish that the sufferer winces and that the Eternal comforts.

Let us once again speak of the wish, and hence of sufferings. It is well not to turn away from the sight of suffering too soon. *Let us properly dwell upon it, being convinced that for the deadly disease of "busyness" there is no medicine so specific as the pondering of the hard path of the true sufferer* and as a fellow human being sharing with him in the common lot of suffering. But alas, how often man's sympathetic sharing in the suffering of others stands in inverse ratio to the length of the suffering! For if the suffering is drawn out in length, sympathy tends to pall: as the suffering increases, the sympathy decreases. At the first appearance of suffering, men's sympathy rushes out to the victim. But when the suffering lingers on, then sympathy subsides, and, on the part of the busy individual when the first active stage of his sympathy has waned, this sympathy at times changes into a certain bitterness against the sufferer. Yes: wishes could be healed after a time, they could become a part of the past: but not *the wish*. There is a real distinction here, for there is a pain of the wish which sympathy can fix upon, but there is also a pain of the wish that eludes all scrutiny, that conceals itself and secretly follows through an entire life. Yes, it follows, but in the sense of privation. Yes, like a faithful companion this pain follows the sufferer throughout his whole life and keeps him company, but there is no sympathy in attendance. Now in what way ought we to speak of this wish that may possibly exist but that withdraws into concealment, and yet speak so that the sufferer will acknowledge the description, so that he will not take offense and impatiently turn away from our officious account of sufferings which we are either not capable or have not had the time to think ourselves into? Let us then, wherever possible in the description, speak with the sufferer's own tongue and leave it to God to communicate to his heart any light that he may have for him.

Let us assume that dumb animals could have thoughts and could make themselves understood to one another even though we could not make out what they said, let us take that for granted. It seems almost as if this were so. For when in summer the peasant's horse stands in the meadow and throws up his head or shakes it, surely no one can know with certainty what that means; or when two of them who throughout their lives have walked side by side pulling in the same yoke are turned out at night, when they approach one another as if in intimacy, when they almost caress each other by movements of the head; or when the free horses neigh to one another so that the woods echo, when they are gathered on the plains in a big herd as if at a public meeting—assume then that they really could make themselves understood to one another.

But then there was one horse that was all alone. Now when this horse heard the call, when he saw that the herd was gathering in the evening, and he understood that they were about to hold a meeting, then he came running in the hope that he might learn something about life in its ways. He listened carefully to all that the elders had to say about how no horse should think himself fortunate until he is dead, how the horse of all creatures is most subject to the tragic changes of fate. And now the elder went over the many agonies: to suffer hunger and cold, to all but kill oneself through overwork, to be kicked by a cruel driver, to be abused by unskilled persons whom not a single step you take will satisfy, yet who blame and punish the horse for their own blunders, and then at last some winter, when old age has come on, to be driven out into the bare woods.

At this point the meeting broke up and that horse who had come

with such eagerness went away dejected: "by sorrow of the heart
the spirit is broken" (Proverbs xv. 13). He had understood perfectly
all that had been said, but no one there had even as much as mentioned his sufferings. Yet each time he noticed the other horses hur-
rying off to a gathering he came running eagerly, hoping always
that now it would be spoken of. And each time he listened he went
away with a heavy heart. He came to understand better and better
what the others were concerned about, but he came to understand
himself less and less, just because it seemed as though the others
excluded him, although he, too, was present.

Oh, you sufferer, whoever you may be, if your suffering was not
hidden because you wished to hide it (for then you can manage;
your action calls for a different comment) but if it is because of
misunderstandings then you, too, have gone among men, listened
carefully to their explanations, sought out their instruction, taken
part in their meeting. But each time you finished the book, and
each time the conversation was over, and each time the "Amen"
was pronounced: then was your spirit broken because your heart
grew troubled as you sighed: "Oh, that such a thing was all that I
suffered from!" Oh, but you are not wholly wanting in being understood, for even if you yourself may have done nothing to deserve it,
you shall be bidden to the highest thing of all, and to the Most
High Himself. Nor are you wholly without human sympathy. There
is a common human concern that is called edification. It is not so
common as those undertakings about which the crowd shouts and
clamors, for each participant is in reality alone with himself, but yet
in the highest and most inclusive sense, edification is a common
human concern. The edifying contemplation finds no rest until it
has come to understand you. Is not one sinner who repents more
important to Heaven than ninety-nine righteous men[32] who have no
need of repentance? So it is with you if you are one who truly
suffers, your edifying contemplation is more important than the ac-
tions of ninety-nine busy ones who have no need of edification. Yes,
even if you did not exist, the edifying contemplation finds no rest
before it has also plumbed this sorrow. For woe to the edifying talk
that wishes only to chat between man and man about all the
different inconveniences in life but does not dare risk touching
upon the more terrible sufferings: such a talk is without frankness
and can but have a bad conscience if it poses under the name of

"edifying." The busy ones that neither toil nor are oppressed[33] but are just busy think that they have escaped when they have contrived to avoid sufferings in this life; hence they do not wish to be disturbed either by hearing or thinking of that which is terrible. Yes, it is true that they have escaped. They have also escaped having any insight into life and have escaped into meaninglessness.

Oh, you sufferer, alone and abandoned as you are by the generation to which you belong, know that you are not abandoned by God, your creator. Everywhere you are surrounded by His understanding which offers itself to you at each moment. In it you unite your will with the Good. And the edifying contemplation is always ready to remind you of that presence; and its very existence is a source of security to the living.

As it is a comfort to seafarers to know that no matter on what strange water they may venture there are always pilots within call, so the edifying contemplation stands near the breakers and reefs of this life prepared by daily sight of terrible sufferings swiftly to render what little aid it can. Yet it cannot help in the way that a pilot helps the ship. The sufferer must help himself. But then neither shall we owe to this or to any other man what the seafarer owes to the pilot. Indeed if this sufferer like anyone else sincerely wills the Good, then he must be ready to suffer all. Then he is committed, not in that commitment by which he is exempted from suffering, but in that by which he remains intimately bound to God, in which he wills only one thing: namely, to suffer all, to be and to remain loyally committed to the Good—under the pain of the wish.

My listener! Perhaps you are tired of so much talk about suffering—but an edifying talk never tires of it, no, a mother may sooner tire of nursing her sick child than the edifying talk of speaking of suffering. You are perhaps what is called a "happy one" whom talk of this kind tires. Yet surely you are not so happy as to wish to remain coldly ignorant of sufferings; on the contrary you aspire to this knowledge of suffering for your own sake in order that your education may be improved by its somber spectacle! Or perhaps you are a sufferer, who is wearied by talking of so many different kinds of suffering when yours is not even mentioned. Oh, to edify oneself in a living way with the sufferings of others is a comfort, and to dwell too exclusively on one's own suffering may easily become that doubleness of mind which thinks that there is comfort for all others but none for itself. But this is not so. For with suffering each has his own, be it great or small. But with comfort it is certainly true that there is comfort for all, and in fact the same comfort for all.

Now let us once again speak of the wish, and hence of sufferings, for the duration of the suffering makes it heavier and heavier. But its duration depends as a matter of fact upon when the suffering began. A shrewd pagan has wisely observed that a man can accustom himself to protracted sufferings.[34] But the question here is whether such comfort is the right thing. For what is being considered here is not how to find the readiest and best source of comfort, but rather how to will the Good in truth, how to will to suffer all in order to be and to remain committed to the Good.

Let us speak of a whole life of sufferings or of some person whom nature, from the very outset, as we humans are tempted to say, wronged, someone who from birth was singled out by useless suffering: a burden to others; almost a burden to himself; and yes, what is worse, to be almost a born objection to the goodness of Providence. Alas, the career of many a busy man is described by and gives rise to fresh *busyness*. The contemplation of such an unfortunate one is an excellent antidote for busyness. *For just by observing such a sufferer, one comes to know unmistakably what the highest is.* But we will not speak carelessly or in passing, hastening away from the sight of this suffering, absorbed in rejoicing over our having been spared it. Neither shall we speak despondently.

To be sure it is wonderful to be a child, to fall asleep upon the mother's breast only to awaken to see the mother again; to be a child and to know only the mother and the toy! We laud the happiness of childhood. The very sight of it soothes us by its smile, so that even the one to whom fortune is granted does not forget this down through the years. But, God be praised, it is not so ordered that this should be the highest thing of all. It may be dispensed with without losing the highest thing of all. It may be absent without having lost the highest thing of all.

And to be sure it is fine to be young, to lie sleepless with the ferment of joyful thoughts, and to fall asleep only to wake up early with the song of the birds to continue the gaiety! We laud the happiness of youth. We rejoice with the joyful ones. We wish that youth might feel grateful for its happiness, and in the future we wish that it might be thankful for that which has vanished. But, God be praised, it is not so ordered that this should be the highest thing of all. It may be dispensed with without losing the highest thing of all. It may be absent without having lost the highest thing of all.

And to be sure it is blessed to love, to be reduced to a single desire. What does it matter if all other desires are fulfilled or denied? There is but one desire, the loved one; one longing, the loved one; one possession, the loved one! We laud the happiness of love. Oh, that the fortunate one may be steadfast in the daily thankfulness of domestic life; that he may be faithful in the continuing thankfulness of remembrance. But, God be praised, it is not so ordered that this should be the highest thing of all. It may be dispensed with without losing the highest thing of all. It may be absent without having lost the highest thing of all.

But now the sufferer! Alas, there was no happy childhood for him. Of course a mother's love is faithful and tender, especially toward an ailing child. But a mother is also a human being. When he lay at his mother's breast, she did not gaze joyfully upon him. He saw that she was troubled. Sometimes when he awakened he noticed her weeping.

Even among grown-ups when they sit about depressed, let a man appear at the door, a happy, gifted one with light heart and gay spirit, and let him say, "Here am I!" and at once the merriment begins, and the clouds of care are routed. Such a gifted one is uncommon. But even the rarest genius of all, when can he bring in comparison to a child, when it makes its entrance amid the agonizing pain of the birth hour, opens the door and says, "Here am I!" Oh, the good fortune of childhood, to be so welcome!

Then he grew into a youth, but he never played with the others, and if someone asked him, "Why do you not play with the others?" he might well have replied, "How have you the heart to ask me such a question?" So he withdrew from life, yet not with the object of dying, for he was still only a youth.

Then came the season of love, but no one loved him. Of course there were a few that were friendly toward him, but it was out of compassion and sympathy. Then he became a man, but he stood apart from life. Then he died, but even here he was not spared. For the little band that made up the mourner's train all said it was a blessing that God took him away, and the priest said the same thing. Then he was dead, and then he was forgotten—together with all of his useless sufferings. When he was born there was no gladness or rejoicing, only fearful dismay; when he died there was no grief or affliction, only a melancholy joy. In this fashion his life was passed, or, to speak more accurately, is passed, for this is not an ancient fairy tale that I am telling, of what has happened to an "individual" in bygone days. The same thing happens frequently. It lies close enough to us even though frivolity and sensuousness, worldly cleverness and godlessness wish to remain ignorant of it. It lies close enough to us even though they wish to keep away from any such unfortunate ones and to avoid all sober reminders not alone from the careless judgment of the storyteller's art, but also from the church and from the edifying insight that must certainly know that the Holy Scriptures have almost a predilection for the halt and the lame, the blind and the lepers. When the disciples began to seem "busy," Christ set a little child in their midst.[35] The crowd that storms and blusters in the bewildered name of the century might well tempt a serious man to set just such an unfortunate sufferer in their midst. The sight of him certainly would not detain anyone that willed anything eternal; but busyness has nothing whatever to do with the Eternal.

He, the sufferer, took part in life—by living. But to his life one thing was unknown, a thing which in all relations of life, as in the passion of love, makes for happiness: to be able to give and to receive "like for like." This "like for like" he never received, and he himself could never give; for as a sufferer he was always an object of sympathy and compassion. No, he never got like for like, not as a child, so that if others saddened his mother he might make her happy merely by smiling as he wakened. No, he never got like for like, for he loved his playmates in a different way than they loved him. No, he never got like for like, and therefore he got no mate. All through his life he could never do anything to repay others. And even in death he did not get like for like, for he was not mourned, as he had mourned those dear to him. He died, but what did the mourners and the priest say there except, "God be praised." Do not all these things cut him off from the highest?

Oh, you sufferer, wherever you may be, wherever you hide from the sight of men in order to spare them from being reminded of the pitiable, oh, do not forget that you, too, can accomplish something. Do not let your life consume itself in a futile counting up of the worthless sufferings of the days and years. Do not forget that you can accomplish something. If some feigned sufferer wishes to throw himself upon others because of a slight adversity, this does not mean that he should be told, as is sometimes done, that he can accomplish something for others. For one who is capable of accomplishing something for others is not regarded by the edifying contemplation as in the strictest sense a sufferer. Instead he would be harsh with him. Oh, you true sufferer, even though your very suffering cuts you off from any such service to others, you can still do—the highest thing of all. You can will to suffer all and thereby be committed to the Good. Oh, blessed justice, that the true sufferer can unconditionally do the highest quite as well as fortune's favorite child! Honor and praise be to the Eternal, in whom is no shadow of turning, in whom is neither malice nor favoritism but perfect justice. By willing to suffer all, you are committed to the Good, having changed your garments—yes, as when the dead rise up and cast off their grave clothes, so you have cast off the mantle of your misery. Now you are indistinguishable from those whom you wish to be like—those that are committed to the Good. All are clothed alike, girded about the loins with truth, arrayed in the armor of righteousness and wearing the helmet of salvation![36] If it be so, and it is the hope of every good man that there is a resurrection where there shall be no difference, where the deaf man shall hear, the blind man see, where he that bore a form of misery shall be fair like all the others, then there is indeed on this side of the grave some such resurrection each time a man, by willing to do all or to suffer all, rises up by entering into the commitment, and remains bound to the Good in the commitment. The sole difference is the pain of the wish in the sufferer. But at the same time this may be a help to bring him into the decision.

The sufferer must therefore be willing to suffer all. This means equally to be willing to do all: to bring it to a commitment, to be and to remain loyal to the Good in the commitment. While it is true that the pain of the wish is the sign that the suffering in a way continues; yet the healing also continues, as long as the sufferer remains firm in the commitment. But there is a force that is momentarily powerful. It is cleverness. From cleverness and from the moment, or through it and from the moment, a man's destruction is born—if it is a fact that a man's salvation comes in the Eternal and by the Eternal. Now cleverness may be inwardly misused; for outwardly a true sufferer has little chance of misusing it. Cleverness in this inner realm is rich in evasions by which the time is put off and the decision is postponed. It will come to understand the decision only in an earthly and temporal sense. From its momentary standpoint, it has in view only a decision by which the suffering shall be brought to an end. But be assured, the Eternal does not heal in this fashion. The palsied man does not become whole, because he has been healed by the Eternal, nor the leper clean, nor the deformed made physically perfect. "But then it is a useless device, this help of the Eternal," cleverness suggests, "and what is still worse, is this decision, where the sufferer dedicates himself to his suffering, which indeed makes his condition hopeless"—because the decision renounces the juggling hope of temporal existence. Where the Eternal does not come to heal such a sufferer, what happens, with the aid of cleverness, is about as follows: first, the sufferer lives for some years by an earthly hope; but when this is exhausted and the suffering still continues, then he becomes superstitious, his state of health alternates between drowsiness and burning excitement. As the suffering continues, there settles over him finally a dull despair, broken only rarely by an unnatural and terribly enfeebling intensity, as when the gambler hopes on and on that some day he will meet with luck. Alas, at length a man sees what cleverness and this earthly hope amount to! For to cleverness it seems so clever "that one should not foolishly give up an earthly hope for a possible mythical healing"—in order to win the Eternal. To cleverness it seems so cunning "that one would not decide to say farewell to the earth; indeed, one can never know what possibly could happen . . . and then one would regret"—that one had let himself be healed by the Eternal. The earthly hope and the heavenly hope grew up well together and played together in childhood like born equals, but the difference reveals itself in the decision. Yet, this hinders cleverness which steadily hinders the decision. Those who cling to life put off the time, have countless inventions whose genius is this: that one must not take life and his own sorrows too much to heart, that it was just possible, who can know that—etc.

When the sufferer actually takes his suffering to heart, then he receives help from the Eternal toward his decision. Because to take one's suffering to heart is to be weaned from the temporal order, and from cleverness and from excuses, and from clever men and women and from anecdotes about this and that, in order to find rest in the blessed trustworthiness of the Eternal. For the sufferer, it is as if one should liken him to a sick man who turns himself from side to side, and now at last discovers the position in which there is relief—even if the wish still pains. Even if it was only a trifle, one can never have taken something too much to heart, when in taking it so to heart he thereby wins the Eternal.

But the sufferer who does not wish to be healed by the Eternal is double-minded. The double-mindedness in him is a disease that gnaws and gnaws and eats away the noblest powers; the injury is internal and infinitely more dangerous than being deformed and palsied. This double-minded one wishes to be healed and yet does not wish to be healed: eternally, he does not wish to be healed. But the temporal cure is uncertain, and the different stages in the scale of uncertainty are marked by increasing restlessness, in his double-mindedness. When the double-minded man comes to the final moment of his life, cleverness will still be sitting at his deathbed and explaining that one cannot know what might suddenly and unexpectedly happen. Under no circumstances should a messenger be sent after the clergyman, for cleverness is so afraid of the decision that it even regards the clergyman's coming as a tacit decision, and indeed one can never know what suddenly and unexpectedly might happen. So the double-minded one dies, and now the survivors know for certain that the deceased was not cured of his long-standing suffering by any sudden and unexpected means. Alas, the Eternal is a riddle for the one who, in the clever sense of the moment, loves the world. Over and over again he thinks, what if some temporal help should suddenly appear, then I would be trapped, I, who by commitment to the Eternal had died to the temporal. He prefers to say, one still regards the temporal as the highest, one looks upon the Eternal as a kind of desperate "last resort." Therefore, one objects to giving it the decision for as long as possible. And even if temporal help is the most absurd and unreasonable of all expectations, yet one would sooner whip up his superstitious imagination to hope for it than to lay hold on the Eternal. One is constantly afraid that he might live to regret it, and yet the Eternal, if one honestly lays hold on it, is the only thing, absolutely the only thing of which it may be said without reservation, it will never be regretted. But because of this fear that he should one day regret committing himself to the Eternal, a man deserves some day to be compelled to regret bitterly that he allowed the time to pass by.

Oh, it is indeed a shallow cleverness (no matter how much it brags or how loquacious it may be) that stupidly cheats itself out of the highest consolation, getting along with a mediocre and even less than mediocre consolation and ending in inevitable remorse. Even if the sufferer is able to use his cleverness in such a way as to give his double-mindedness a little better public appearance than is depicted here, that in no way affects the real situation. If he uses cleverness to hinder commitment to the Eternal, he is double-minded. He is, and he remains double-minded, even if temporal help did come and he did revel in the cleverness by which he had managed his shrewd escape; yes, one should still believe that it was a calamity that he cleverly managed to evade commitment to the Eternal. Commitment to the Eternal is the only true salvation. Therefore it is also double-mindedness when the sufferer uses his strength to conceal the pain instead of letting himself be healed by the Eternal. Such a sufferer is not seeking release from the suffering but only from a sympathy, in so far as this also can be an affliction. Therein lies the contradictory character of double-mindedness. For only by commitment to the Eternal may he become really free from the painfulness of sympathy, since by the commitment he really overcomes the suffering. Hence only the wish pains, while the Eternal cures.

In relation to the sufferer, all double-mindedness has its ground in and is marked by the double-minded one's unwillingness to let go of the things of this world. In the same way the double-minded talk that is from time to time addressed to the sufferer may be recognized by the fact that it puts its trust in the things of this world. It is only too often the case that the sufferer shrinks from receiving the highest comfort, and the speaker is ashamed to offer the highest consolation. Contrary to the truth, the consoling talk seeks to offer comfort by saying that the illness will soon be better—perhaps; and begs for some little patience. It coddles the sufferer a little, and says that by Sunday all will surely be going well. Yet why give a pauper, if we may for a moment compare the sufferer with a pau-

per, silver or even counterfeit coin when one has a rich supply of
gold to offer him? For the Eternal's comfort is pure gold. Let us
remember the active one even though his suffering is always
different from that of a real sufferer. We read of the Apostles,[37] that
when they were scourged they went on their way rejoicing and
gave thanks to God. Here there is no talk of having a little patience,
and of things going well by Sunday; but here is found the Eternal's
victorious comfort, and these scourged Apostles have more than
conquered. So, too, shall it be with the true sufferer. For when the
Eternal heals, the wish continues to pain (for the Eternal does not
remove the sufferer from time), but there is no whining, no tempo-
rary distraction, no deceitful evasion. One knows well enough that
when the true sufferer has whined himself through time and by all
kinds of imaginings has managed to pass away the time or to kill
time: still eternity stands open to him. Alas, no, the true sufferer
must also answer for the manner in which he has used his time, answer for whether or not he has used the earthly misery to allow
himself eternally to be healed. But cleverness asserts, "still, one
should never give up hope." "You hypocrite," answers the Eternal,
"why do you speak so equivocally? You know well enough that
there is a hope that should be put to death; that there is a lust and
a desire and a longing that should be slain. Earthly hope should be
put to death, for in just this way did man first come to be saved by
the true hope." Therefore the sufferer should never be willing to
"accept deliverance" (Hebrews xi. 15) on this world's terms.

11. THE PRICE OF WILLING ONE THING:

THE SUFFERER'S USE OF CLEVERNESS
TO EXPOSE EVASION

*But the sufferer who sincerely wills the Good, uses this very
cleverness to cut off evasions and hence to launch himself into the
commitment* and to escape the disillusionments of choosing the
temporal way. He does not fear the mark of the commitment that,

as it were, draws the suffering over him; for he knows that this mark is the breaking through of the Eternal. He knows that in the commitment the nerve of the temporal order is being cut, even though pain continues in the wish. There is no doubt that what often makes a sufferer impatient is that he takes upon himself in advance the suffering of a whole lifetime and now quails before what would be lighter to bear if he were to take each day's burden as it comes.

The commitment should not concentrate sufferings in this way. For the error is just this, that in spite of all his advance acceptance of suffering, the sufferer wins nothing that is eternal but only becomes terrified in a temporal sense. Because of the uncertainty of the temporal order, it is also true that over a period of many years a sufferer may talk himself out of the original impression of the commitment. And this is a calamity. On that account the sufferer who sincerely wills the Good knows that cleverness is a treacherous friend, and that only the commitment is fully trustworthy.

The active one will do all for the Good, the sufferer will suffer all for the Good. The similarity is that they both may be and remain committed to the Good. Only the direction in which they work is different, and this difference must not be understood as making them mutually exclusive. The active one works from without in order that the Good may conquer; even his suffering has significance from its bearing upon this goal. The true sufferer does everything inwardly (by being willing to suffer all) for the Good in order that it may conquer in him. Yet the Good must have conquered and must continue to conquer in the active one's own heart, if he sincerely works for the Good outwardly. The true sufferer can always work for the Good outwardly by the power of example, and work effectually. For his life, just because so much is denied him, contains a great challenge to the many to whom much is given. His life, when he is and remains committed to the Good, contains a severe judgment upon the many, who use in an inexcusable way the much that has been given them. Yes, even if the sufferer were denied this working by the power of example, even if he were cut off from all other men, he would still be sharing in mankind's great common concern. On his lonely outpost he, too, would be defending a difficult pass by saving his own soul from all of the ensnaring difficulties of suffering. Although not a single man should see him, mankind feels with him, suffers with him, and conquers with him! For everywhere that the Good truly conquers, the victory is really as great whether the Good conquers in a solitary forsaken one by his own efforts; in reality the victory is equally great. Oh, praised be the blessed justice of the Eternal!

Yet one thing still remains to be discussed before leaving the matter of sufferings: Can one be said to will suffering? Is not suffering something that one must be forced into against his will? If a man can be free of it, can he then will it, and if he is bound to it, can he be said to will it? If we would answer this question, let us first of all distinguish between what it is to will in the sense of inclination, and what it is to will in the noble sense of freedom. Yes, for many men it is almost an impossibility for them to unite freedom and suffering in the same thought. Hence, when they see a man of means who could spend his time easily and comfortably, when they see him straining himself as much as a scrupulous workman, exposing himself to many sufferings, choosing the burdensome way of a higher calling: they look upon him as either a fanatic or a lunatic. They all but complain that Providence has given all of these fortunate circumstances to someone that simply does not know how to make use of them. They think in their hearts even when they do not say it aloud, even when they do not consider how tragically they are betraying their own inner life: "We should have been there in his place, we should have really known how to enjoy that life." According to this if one can be free of suffering it is either fanaticism or insanity to will it.

But what then is courage? Is it courage to go where pleasure beckons in order to see where pleasure is? Or, in order for courage to be revealed, is it not required that there be opposition (which even language seems to indicate)[38] as though the courageous person looks the danger in the eye, even though the danger is not what the eye wants to see? To illustrate, is it not as when the courageous knight spurs his horse forward against some terrifying object? There is no tremor of fear in his eye because courage controls even the expression of the eye. Yet the knight and the horse illustrate the structure of courage. The knight is the courageous one, the horse is skittish. The horse and its skittishness answer to that which is low in a man and its skittishness is that which courage checks. In this way, courage voluntarily wills suffering. The courageous one has a treacherous opposition within himself that is in league with the opposition without. But just on that account, he is the courageous one, because in spite of it he voluntarily wills the suffering.

On the other hand (and this is what we must primarily consider, for we are speaking of the true sufferer), the sufferer can voluntarily accept that suffering which in one sense is forced upon him, in so far as he does not have it in his power to get rid of it. Can anyone but one who is free of suffering, say, "Put me in chains, I am not afraid"? Can even a prisoner say, "Of my own free will I accept my imprisonment"—the very imprisonment which is already his condition? Here again the opinion of most men is that such a thing is impossible, and that therefore the condition of the sufferer is one of sighing despondency. But what then is patience?[39] Is patience not precisely that courage which voluntarily accepts unavoidable suffering? The unavoidable is just the thing which will shatter courage. There is a treacherous opposition in the sufferer himself that is in league with the dread of inevitability, and together they wish to crush him. But in spite of this, patience submits to suffering and by just this submission finds itself free in the midst of unavoidable suffering. Thus patience, if one may put it in this way, performs an even greater miracle than courage. Courage voluntarily chooses suffering that may be avoided; but patience achieves freedom in unavoidable suffering. By his courage, the free one voluntarily lets himself be caught, but by his patience the prisoner effects his freedom—although not in the sense that need make the jailer anxious or fearful.

The outward impossibility of ridding oneself of suffering does not hinder the inward possibility of being able really to emancipate oneself within suffering—of one's own free will accepting suffering, as the patient one gives his consent by willing to accept suffering. For one can be forced into the narrow prison, one can be forced into lifelong sufferings, and necessity is the tyrant; but one cannot be forced into patience. If the tyrant necessity presses upon a soul which neither possesses nor wills to possess the elasticity of freedom, then the soul becomes depressed, but it does not become patient. Patience is the counterpressure of resiliency, whereby the coerced ones are set free from restraint. Or can only the rich man be economical because he may, if he likes, be extravagant? Cannot the poor man also be economical even though he is powerless to be extravagant, even though he is forced to be—economical? No, he cannot be forced to be economical even though he is forced to be poor. Alas, the wisdom of many men seems calculated to abolish the Good. When a person of means voluntarily chooses the hard way, then he is called strange, "he who could be so well off without working and who could indulge his every desire for comfort." And when the victim of unavoidable suffering bears it patiently, one says of him, "to his shame, he is coerced, and he is making a virtue out of a necessity." Undeniably he is making a virtue out of a necessity, that is just the secret, that is certainly a most accurate designation for what he does. He makes a virtue out of necessity. He brings a determination of freedom out of that which is determined as necessity. And it is just there that the healing power of the decision for the Eternal resides: that the sufferer may voluntarily accept the compulsory suffering. Just as it is a relief to the sufferer to open himself in confidence to a friend, so it is deliverance to the sufferer to commit himself to the Eternal even though the compulsion of necessity should press against his heart, it is deliverance to open himself to the Eternal and to consent eternally to be willing to suffer all.

For that man is captive indeed for whom a door stands open: the trapdoor of eternity! And he is indeed in bonds who is eternally free! When Paul said, "I am a Roman citizen,"[40] the prefect did not dare to put him into prison, and he was placed in a voluntary confinement. In like fashion when a man dares declare, "I am eternity's free citizen," necessity cannot imprison him, except in voluntary confinement.

My listeners! If you are willing, let us recall the direction that our talk has taken. If a man should will one thing, then he must will the Good, for in this way alone was it possible for him to will a single thing. If, however, it is to be genuine, he must will the Good in truth. According to whether he is *an active one or a sufferer he must be willing either to do all for the Good, or he must be willing to suffer all for the Good.* He must be willing either to do all for the Good, or to be and to remain committed to the Good. But cleverness may be misused internally, to seek evasions; and misused externally in deception. The good man, on the contrary, uses cleverness to cut off all evasions and thereby to launch out and to remain constant—in the commitment. He also uses cleverness to prevent such external deception. He must be willing to suffer all for the Good, or to be and to remain committed to the Good. And the talk went on to describe the true sufferer's condition, because by looking at sufferings one may really learn what the highest is. Once again in regard to suffering, cleverness may be misused internally to seek ways of escape, but the good man makes use of just this very cleverness against ways of escape, in order that he may be and remain committed to the Good, by being willing to suffer all, by accepting the enforced necessity of suffering.

But purity of heart is to will one thing. It is this thesis that has been the object of the talk which we have linked to the apostolic words: "Draw nigh to God, and he will draw nigh to you. Cleanse your hands, ye sinners, and purify your hearts, ye double-minded!" For commitment to the Good is a whole-souled decision, and a man cannot by the craft and the flattery of his tongue lay hold of God while his heart is far away. No, for since God is spirit and truth, a man can only draw near to Him by sincerity, by willing to be holy, as He is holy:[41] by purity of heart. *Purity of heart:* it is a figure of speech that compares the heart to the sea, and why just to this? Simply for the reason that the depth of the sea determines its purity, and its purity determines its transparency. Since the sea is pure only when it is deep, and is transparent only when it is pure, as soon as it is impure it is no longer deep but only surface water, and as soon as it is only surface water it is not transparent. When, on the contrary, it is deeply and transparently pure, then it is all of one consistency, no matter how long one looks at it; then its purity is this constancy in depth and transparency. On this account we compare the heart with the sea, because the purity of the sea lies in its constancy of depth and transparency. No storm may perturb it; no sudden gust of wind may stir its surface, no drowsy fog may sprawl out over it; no doubtful movement may stir within it; no swift-moving cloud may darken it: rather it must lie calm, transparent to its depths. And today if you should see it so, you would be drawn upwards by contemplating the purity of the sea. If you saw it every day, then you would declare that it is forever pure—like the heart of that man who wills but one thing. As the sea, when it lies calm and deeply transparent, yearns for heaven, so may the pure heart, when it is calm and deeply transparent, yearn for the Good. As the sea is made pure by yearning for heaven alone; so may the heart become pure by yearning only for the Good. As the sea mirrors the elevation of heaven in its pure depths, so may the heart when it is calm and deeply transparent mirror the divine elevation of the Good in its pure depths. If the least thing comes in between, between the heavens and the sea, between the heart and the Good, then it would be sheer impatience to covet the reflection. For if the sea is impure it cannot give a pure reflection of the heavens.

12. WHAT THEN MUST I DO?

THE LISTENER'S ROLE IN A
DEVOTIONAL ADDRESS

My listener! This talk was brought forth upon the occasion of the office of Confession. If after the opening references to this occasion no more has been said of it, yet it has never been forgotten in the talk. For what has been given is most intimately connected with what is appropriate to an address of invitation to such an occasion. From its single point of departure—*to will one thing*—the talk has moved out in different directions, ever returning, however, to this point of departure. It has at the same time scanned the earth, making note of human differences. From time to time it has depicted the individual error and the state of soul of one who has lost his way. This has been done on a magnified scale, so that man may the better become aware of, and look out for, what in the trivial circumstances of daily life so rarely appears unmixed that it is much harder to detect than are these instances that are "writ large." As it has proceeded, the talk, holding tenaciously to the demand—*to will one thing*—has taught how to recognize many errors, disappointments, deceptions, and self-deceptions. It has striven to track down double-mindedness into its hidden ways, and to ferret out its secret. By striving at every possible point to make itself intelligible, the talk has sought to bring these things within the reach of each listener. But the intelligibility of the talk, and the listener's understanding of it, are still not the talk's true aim. This by no means gives the meditation its proper emphasis. For in order to achieve its proper emphasis the talk must unequivocally demand something of the listener. It must demand not merely what has previously been requested, that the reader should share in the work with the speaker—now the talk must unconditionally demand the reader's own decisive activity, and all depends upon this.

So, my listener, turn your attention now to the occasion, while consciousness of sin sharpens the need until it becomes the one thing necessary; while the earnestness of this holy place strengthens the will in holy determination, while the all-knowing One's presence makes self-deception impossible, consider your own life! The talk, which is without authority, will not have the presumption to pass judgment upon you. By vigorously pondering the occasion you will stand before a higher judge, where no man dares judge another since he himself is one of the accused. The talk does not address itself to you as if to a particularly designated person, for it does not know who you are. But if you weigh the occasion vigorously, then it will be to you, whoever you may be, it will be as if it spoke precisely to you. This is not due to any merit in the talk. It is the product of your own activity that for your own sake the talk is helpful to you; and it will be because of your own activity that you will be the one to whom the intimate "thou" is spoken. This is your own activity, it really is. Alas, above all let us not be drawn away from the decision by any attention to the speaker and the artistry of the talk. If this happens, then busyness and double-mindedness are again to blame that the emphasis in the composition is wrongly placed. In this case the devotional speaker is admired for his art, his eloquence, while that decision of which each man is capable, and that which, it may be well to note, is the highest thing of all, is completely ignored. In a devotional sense, to be eloquent is a mere frill in the same way that to be beautiful is a happy privilege, but is still a non-essential frill. In a devotional sense, earnestness: to listen in order to act, this is the highest thing of all, and, God be praised, every man is capable of it if he so wills. Yet busyness places its most weighty emphasis upon the frills, the capacity to please, and looks upon earnestness as nothing at all. In a contemptuous and frivolous fashion, busyness thinks that to be eloquent is the highest thing of all and that the task of the listener is to pass judgment on whether the speaker has this gift.

In order that no irregularity may be admitted or no double-mindedness left unmentioned, let me then at this point, where the demand is being made for a person's own activity, briefly illustrate the relation between the speaker and the listener in a devotional address. Let me, in order once again to take up arms against double-mindedness, make this illustration by borrowing a picture from worldly art. And do not let the two senses in which this may be taken disturb you or give you grounds for accusing the address of impropriety. For if you have dared to attend an exhibition of worldly art, then by doing this, you yourself must have come to understand what is meant by spiritual. Therefore you must have considered the spiritual with the worldly art even though it was the means of your first distinct recognition of the difference between the two. If you did not, discord and double-mindedness are in your own heart, so that you live for periods of time on the worldly plane with only an occasional thought of the spiritual. It is so on the stage, as you know well enough, that someone sits and prompts by whispers; he is the inconspicuous one, he is, and wishes to be overlooked. But then there is another, he strides out prominently, he draws every eye to himself. For that reason he has been given his name, that is: actor.[42] He impersonates a distinct individual. In the skillful sense of this illusory art, each word becomes true when embodied in him, true through him—and yet he is told what he shall say by the hidden one that sits and whispers. No one is so foolish as to regard the prompter as more important than the actor.

Now forget this light talk about art. Alas, in regard to things spiritual, the foolishness of many is this, that they in the secular sense look upon the speaker as an actor, and the listeners as theatergoers who are to pass judgment upon the artist. But the speaker is not the actor—not in the remotest sense. No, the speaker is the prompter. There are no mere theatergoers present, for each listener will be looking into his own heart. The stage is eternity, and the listener, if he is the true listener (and if he is not, he is at fault) stands before God during the talk. The prompter whispers to the actor what he is to say, but the actor's repetition of it is the main concern—is the solemn charm of the art. The speaker whispers the word to the listeners. But the main concern is earnestness: that the listeners by themselves, with themselves, and to themselves, in the silence before God, may speak with the help of this address.

The address is not given for the speaker's sake, in order that men may praise or blame him. The listener's repetition of it is what is aimed at. If the speaker has the responsibility for what he whispers, then the listener has an equally great responsibility not to fall short in his task. In the theater, the play is staged before an audience who are called theatergoers; but at the devotional address, God himself is present. In the most earnest sense, God is the critical theatergoer, who looks on to see how the lines are spoken and how they are listened to: hence here the customary audience is wanting. The speaker is then the prompter, and the listener stands openly before God. The listener, if I may say so, is the actor, who in all truth acts before God.

Oh, let us never forget this, let us not reduce the spiritual to the worldly. Even though we may earnestly think of the spiritual and the worldly together, let us forever distinguish between them. As soon as the spiritual is looked upon in worldly fashion (an observation for which one has the same foolishness to thank as that which would look upon the prompter in a play as more important than the actor) then the speaker becomes an actor and the listeners become critical theatergoers. In the same way, from the secular point of view, the devotional address is simply held for a group of attenders and God is no more present than he is in the theater. God's presence is the decisive thing that changes all. As soon as God is present, each man in the presence of God has the task of paying attention to himself. The speaker must see that during the address he pays attention to himself, to what he says; the listener, that during the address he pays attention to himself, to how he listens, and whether during the address he, in his inner self, secretly talks with God. If this were not done, then the listeners would be presuming to share God's task with him, God and the listeners together would watch the speaker and pass judgment upon him. So it is with the true relationship of speaker and listener in a devotional address.

Or to put it in another way, it is as if a subordinate functionary of the church, who is without authority, should read aloud the prescribed prayer. Properly speaking, it is not the church functionary who prays. The one who prays is the listener who sits in the church and opens himself to God while he listens to the reading of the prayer. Yet the listener does not speak, his voice is not heard, nor does he pray softly to himself; but silently and with his heart he is praying in the presence of God by means of the audible voice of the one who reads out the prayer, and whispers to him what he shall say. Yet this is not earnestness: that one man shall tell another or dictate to another what he shall say. But this *is* earnestness: that the other man now should tell it to God speaking for himself. Now we have come to a clear understanding about this, and the demand will only be repeated in order that the speaker may focus his mind actively upon the occasion of the address.

The talk asks you, then, or you ask yourself by means of the talk, *what kind of life do you live, do you will only one thing, and what is this one thing?* The talk does not expect that you will name off any goal that only pretends to be one thing. For it does not intend to address itself to anyone with whom it would not be able to deal seriously, for the reason that such a man has cut himself off from any earnest consideration of the occasion of the address. There is still another reason: a man can, to be sure, have an extremely different, yes, have a precisely opposite opinion from ours, and one can nevertheless deal earnestly with him if one assumes that finally there may be a point of agreement, a unity in some universal sense, call it what you will. But if he is mad, then one cannot deal with him, for he shies away from just that final point in which one at last may hope to find agreement with him. One can dispute with a man, dispute to the furthest limit, as long as one assumes that in the end there is a point in common, an agreement in some universal human sense: in self-respect. But when in his worldly strivings he sets out like a madman in a desperate attempt to despise himself, and in the face of this is brazen about it and lauds himself for his infamy, then one can undertake no disputing with him. For like a madman, and even more terribly, he shies away from this final thing (self-respect) in which one might at last hope to find agreement with him.

The talk assumes, then, that you will the Good and asks you now *what kind of life you live, whether or not you truthfully will only one thing.* It does not ask inquisitively about your calling in life, about the number of workers you employ, or about how many you have under you in your office, or if you happen to be in the service of the state. No, the talk is not inquisitive. It asks you above all else, it asks you first and foremost, whether you really live in such a way that you are capable of answering that question, in such a way that the question truthfully exists for you. Because in order to be able earnestly to answer that serious question, a man must already have made a choice in life, he must have chosen the invisible, chosen that which is within. He must have lived so that he has hours and times in which he collects his mind, so that his life can win the transparency that is a condition for being able to put the question to himself and for being able to answer it—if, of course, it is legitimate to demand that a man shall know whereof he speaks. To put such a question to the man that is so busy in his earthly work, and outside of this in joining the crowd in its noisemaking, would be folly that would lead only to fresh folly—through the answer.

13. WHAT THEN MUST I DO?

LIVE AS AN "INDIVIDUAL"

The talk asks you, then, *whether you live in such a way that you are conscious of being an "individual."* The question is not of the inquisitive sort, as if one asks about that "individual" in some special sense, about the one whom admiration and envy unite in pointing out. No, it is the serious question of what each man really is according to his eternal vocation, so that he himself shall be conscious that he is following it; and what is even more serious, to ask it as if he were considering his life before God. This consciousness is the fundamental condition for truthfully willing only one thing. For he who is not himself a unity is never really anything wholly and decisively; he only exists in an external sense—as long as he lives as a numeral within the crowd, a fraction within the earthly conglomeration. Alas, how indeed should such a one decide to busy himself with the thought: truthfully to will only one thing!

Indeed it is precisely this consciousness that must be asked for. Just as if the talk could not ask in generalities, but rather asks you as an individual. Or, better still, my listener, if you would ask yourself whether you have this consciousness, whether you are actively contemplating the occasion of this talk. For in the outside world, the crowd is busy making a noise. The one makes a noise because he heads the crowd, the many because they are members of the crowd. But the all-knowing One, who in spite of anyone is able to observe it all, does not desire the crowd. He desires the individual; He will deal only with the individual, quite unconcerned as to whether the individual be of high or low station, whether he be distinguished or wretched.

Each man himself, as an individual, should render his account to God. No third person dares venture to intrude upon this accounting between God and the individual. Yet the talk, by putting its question, dares and ought to dare to remind man, in a way never to be forgotten, that the most ruinous evasion of all is to be hidden in the crowd in an attempt to escape God's supervision of him as an individual, in an attempt to get away from hearing God's voice as an individual. Long ago, Adam attempted this same thing when his evil conscience led him to imagine that he could hide himself among the trees. It may even be easier and more convenient, and more cowardly, to hide oneself among the crowd in the hope that God should not be able to recognize one from the other. But in eternity each shall render account as an individual. That is, eternity will demand of him that he shall have lived as an individual. Eternity will draw out before his consciousness all that he has done as an individual, he who had forgotten himself in noisy self-conceit. In eternity, he shall be brought to account strictly as an individual, he who intended to be in the crowd where there should be no such strict reckoning. Each one shall render account to God as an individual. The King shall render account as an individual; and the most wretched beggar, as an individual. No one may pride himself at being more than an individual, and no one despondently think that he is not an individual, perhaps because here in earth's busyness he had not as much as a name, but was named after a number.

For, after all, what is eternity's accounting other than that the voice of conscience is forever installed with its eternal right to be the exclusive voice? What is it other than that throughout eternity an infinite stillness reigns wherein the conscience may talk with the individual about what he, as an individual, of what he has done of Good or of evil, and about the fact that during his life he did not wish to be an individual? What is it other than that within eternity there is infinite space so that each person, as an individual, is apart with his conscience? For in eternity there is no mob pressure, no crowd, no hiding place in the crowd, as little as there are riots or street fights! Here in the temporal order conscience is prepared to make each person into an individual. But here in the temporal order, in the unrest, in the noise, in the pressure of the mob, in the crowd, in the primeval forest of evasion, alas, it is true, the calamity still happens, that someone completely stifles the voice of his conscience—his conscience, for he can never rid himself of it. It continues to belong to him, or more accurately, he continues to belong to it. Yet we are not now talking about this calamity, for even among the better persons, it happens all too readily that the voice of conscience becomes merely one voice among many. Then it follows so easily that the isolated voice of conscience (as generally happens to a solitary one) becomes overruled—by the majority. But in eternity, conscience is the only voice that is heard. It must be heard by the individual, for the individual has become the eternal echo of this voice. It must be heard. There is no place to flee from it. For in the infinite there is no place, the individual is himself the place. It must be heard. In vain the individual looks about for the crowd. Alas, it is as if there were a world between him and the nearest individual, whose conscience is also speaking to him about what *he* as an individual has spoken, and done, and thought of good and of evil.

Do you now live so that you are conscious of yourself as an individual; that in each of your relations in which you come into touch with the outside world, you are conscious of yourself, and that at the same time you are related to yourself as an individual? Even in these relations which we men so beautifully style the most intimate of all, do you remember that you have a still more intimate relation, namely, that in which you as an individual are related to yourself before God? If you are bound to another human being by the holy bond of matrimony, do you consider in this intimate relation that still more intimate relation in which you as an individual are related to yourself before God? The talk does not ask you whether you now love your wife: it hopes so; nor whether she is the apple of your eye and the desire of your heart: it wishes you this. It does not ask what you have done to make your wife happy, about how you both have arranged your household life, about what good advice you have been able to get from others, or what harmful influence others have had upon you. It does not ask whether your marital life is more commendable than that of many others, or whether it perhaps might be looked upon by some as a worthy example. No, the talk asks about none of these things. It asks you neither in congratulation, nor inquisitively, nor watchfully, nor apologetically, nor comparatively. It asks you only about the ultimate thing: whether you yourself are conscious of that most intimate relation to yourself as an individual. You do not carry the responsibility for your wife, nor for other men, nor by any comparative standard with other men, but only as an individual, before God, where it is not asked whether your marriage was in accordance with others, with the common practice, or better than others, but where you as an individual will be asked only whether it was in accordance with your responsibility as an individual. For common practice changes, and all comparison goes lame, or is only half truth. But eternity's practice, which never goes out of fashion, is that you are the individual, that you yourself in the intimate relation of marriage should have been conscious of this.

In truth, it is not divorce that eternity is aiming at, neither is it divorce, that eternity does away with the difference between man and woman. Your wife will have no occasion to grieve because you are pondering this, your most intimate relation to God. And should she be so foolish as to desire for herself only that which is earthly or even foolish enough to desire as well to draw you down to the earthly: yet a woman's folly shall certainly not be able to change the law of eternity. In eternity it will not be asked whether your wife seduced you (eternity will talk with her about that), but simply as an individual you will be asked whether you allowed yourself to be seduced. If your marriage is so blessed that you see a family growing up around you, may you be conscious that while you have an intimate relation to your children you have a still more intimate relation to yourself as an individual. You share the responsibility with your wife, and hence eternity will also ask her as an individual about her share of the responsibility. For in eternity there is not a single complication that is able to make the accounting difficult and evasion easy. Eternity does not ask concerning how far you brought up your children in the way that you saw others do it. It simply asks you, as an individual, how you brought up your children. It does not talk with you in the manner that you would talk with a friend in confidence. For alas, even this confidence can all too easily accustom you to evasions. For even the most trustworthy friend still speaks as a third person. And by much of such confidence, one easily gets used to speaking of himself as if he were a third person. But in eternity, you are the individual, and conscience when it talks with you is no third person, any more than you are a third person when you talk with conscience. For you and conscience are one. It knows all that you know, and it knows that you know it. With respect to your children's upbringing you can weigh various matters with your wife, or your friends. But how you act and the responsibility for it is finally wholly and solely yours as an individual. And if you fail to act, hiding from yourself and from others behind a screen of deliberation, you bring down the responsibility solely upon yourself as an individual.

Yes, in the temporal order where in all directions both this and that are asked about in the manifold complex complications of their reciprocal action, there one may rightly enough believe that it was a fantasy of the imagination, a chimera, that each one among these countless millions of people should be convinced accurately down to the least trifle of what his life consisted. But in eternity this is possible, because each becomes an individual. And this applies to every relation of your life.

If you do not live in some out-of-the-way place in the world, if you live in a populous city, and you direct your attention outwards, sympathetically engrossing yourself in the people and in what is going on, do you remember each time you throw yourself in this way into the world around you, that in this relation, you relate yourself to yourself as an individual with eternal responsibility? Or do you press yourself into the crowd, where the one excuses himself with the others, where at one moment there are, so to speak, many, and where in the next moment, each time that the talk touches upon responsibility, there is no one? Do you judge like the crowd, in its capacity as a crowd? You are not obliged to have an opinion about what you do not understand. No, on the contrary, you are eternally excused from that. But you are eternally responsible as an individual to render an account for your opinion, and for your judgment. And in eternity, you will not be asked inquisitively and professionally, as though by a newspaper reporter, whether there were many that had the same—wrong opinion. You will be asked only whether you have held it, whether you have spoiled your soul by joining in this frivolous and thoughtless judging, because the others, because the many judged thoughtlessly. You will be asked only whether you may not have ruined the best within you by joining the crowd in its defiance, thinking that you were many and therefore you had the prerogative, because you were many, that is, because you were many who were wrong. In eternity it will be asked whether you may not have damaged a good thing, in order that you also might judge with them that did not know how to judge, but who possessed the crowd's strength, which in the temporal sense is significant but to which eternity is wholly indifferent.

You see, in the temporal order, a man counts and says: "One more or less, it makes no difference"—and he applies this even to himself! In the temporal order a man counts and says: "One over against a hundred, after all what can come of that?" So he grows cowardly in the face of—number. And numbers are usually false. Truth is content to be a unity. But a man wins something by this cowardly indulgence. He does not win a bed in a hospital. No, but he wins the amazing thing of becoming the strongest of all, because the crowd is always the strongest. Eternity, on the other hand, never counts. The individual is always only one and conscience in its meticulous way concerns itself with the individual. In eternity you will look in vain for the crowd. You will listen in vain to find whether you cannot hear where the noise and the gathering is, so that you may run to it. In eternity you, too, will be forsaken by the crowd. And this is terrifying. Yet in the temporal order to be forsaken by the crowd, provided that the Eternal comforts, may be something blessed, and the pain of it, a mere jest. What then in eternity will conscience demand of you by the consciousness that you are an individual? It will teach you that if you judge (for in very many cases it will restrain you from judging), you must bear the responsibility for your judgment. It will teach you that you should examine what you understand and what you do not understand as if you stood trembling in the presence of a departed one; it wishes to frighten you from resorting to the brilliant flights into wretchedness to which you are often subject. For many fools do not make a wise man, and the crowd is doubtful recommendation for a cause. Yes, the larger the crowd, the more probable that that which it praises is folly, and the more improbable that it is truth, and the most improbable of all that it is any eternal truth. For in eternity crowds simply do not exist. The truth is not such that it at once pleases the frivolous crowd—and at bottom it never does; to such a multitude the truth must appear as simply absurd. But the man who, conscious of himself as an individual, judges with eternal responsibility, he is slow to pass judgment upon the unusual. For it is possible that it is falsehood and deceit and illusion and vanity. But it is also possible that it is true. He remembers the word of the simple sage of ancient times: "This, that a man's eye cannot see by the light by which the majority see could be because he is used to darkness; but it could also be because he is used to a still clearer light, and when this is so, it is no laughing matter."[43]

No, it is no laughing matter, but it is laughable, or it is pitiable, that the frivolous ones laugh at a man because he is wiser or better than they. For even laughter calls for a reasonable ground, and when this is absent, the laughter becomes the very thing that is laughable. But here in the temporal order, in the midst of earth's appalling prodigality with human beings, here number tempts. It tempts a man to count, to count himself in with the crowd. Here, by the use of round numbers, everything can be manipulated with ease. Yes, here in the temporal order it is possible that no individual can ever succeed, even if it were true that he sincerely willed the Good, in dispersing the crowd. But eternity can do it. Eternity seizes each one by the strong arm of conscience, holding him as an individual. Eternity sets him apart with his conscience. Woe to him, if he is left to this judge alone! For in that case eternity will set him apart with his conscience in that place where there is pressure, to be sure, but not as in the temporal order where the pressure is the excuse, yes, the victory. No, eternity places him where to be under pressure is to be alone, stripped of every excuse; to be alone and to be lost. The royal psalm singer says that while the heathen clamor, God sits in his heaven and laughs at them.[44] I dare not believe this. It would seem to be preferable to say that while the crowd clamors and shouts and triumphs and celebrates; while one individual after another hastens to the place of tumult, where it is good to be if one is in search of oblivion and indulgence from that which is eternal; while at the same time the crowd shouts mockingly at God, "Yes, now see whether you can get hold of us"; yet since it is difficult in

the rush of the crowd to distinguish the individual, difficult to see
the single tree when one is looking at the wood, the sober countenance of eternity quietly waits. And if all the generations that have
lived on earth rose up and gathered themselves in a single crowd in
order to loose a storm against eternity, in order to coerce eternity
by their colossal majority: eternity would scatter them as easily as
the firmness of an immovable rock would scatter frothy scum; as
easily as the wind when it rushes forward scatters chaff. Just as easily, but not in the same way. For the wind scatters the chaff, but
then turns around and drifts it together again. Eternity scatters the
crowd by giving each an infinite weight, by making him heavy—as
an individual. For what in eternity is the highest blessing is also the
deepest seriousness. What, there, is the most blessed comfort, is
also the most appalling responsibility.

In eternity there are chambers enough so that each may be
placed alone in one. For wherever conscience is present, and it is
and shall be present in each person, there exists in eternity a lonely
prison, or the blessed chamber of salvation. On that account this
consciousness of being an individual is the primary consciousness in
a man, which is his eternal consciousness. But that man is slow to
pass judgment who bears in mind that he is an individual, and that
the final and highest responsibility for the judgment rests solely
upon him. For even the most trusted friend in passing judgment as
an impartial observer must necessarily leave out what is crucial. To
be the party directly concerned, the one to whom conscience in this
affair speaks the intimate "thou," is another matter, for conscience
only speaks this intimate "thou" to your friend in regard to the
manner in which he is to give counsel. Such a thoughtful one does
not willingly pass judgment on many things, and just this helps
him to will only one thing. He thinks it is not altogether an advantage to live in a populous city where because of the swiftness of the
means of communication almost everyone can easily have a hasty
and superficial judgment about everything possible. On the contrary, he looks upon this easiness as a temptation and a snare and
he learns earnestness in order as an individual to be concerned
about his eternal responsibility.

"Even a fool might be a wise man if he could keep silent," says
the proverb.[45] And this is so, not merely because then he would not
betray his foolishness, but also because this self-control would help

him to become conscious of himself as an individual, and would prevent him from adopting the crowd's opinion. Or if he had an opinion of his own, it would prevent him from hastening to get the crowd to adopt it. The one who is conscious of himself as an individual has his vision trained to look upon everything as inverted. His sense becomes familiar with eternity's true thought: that everything in this life appears in inverted form. The purely momentary, in the next moment, to say nothing of eternity, becomes nonsense and vanity: the fiery moment of lust (and what is so strong for the moment as lust!) is loathsome in memory; the fiery moment of anger, revenge, and passion whose gratification seems an irresistible impulse is horrible to remember. For the angry one, the vengeful one, the passionate one, thinks in the moment of passion that he revenges himself. But in the moment of remembrance, when the act of revenge comes back to him, he loathes himself, for he sees that precisely in that moment of revenge he lost himself. The purely momentary seems to be profitable. Yet in the next moment its deception becomes apparent and, eternally understood, calls for repentance. So it is with all things of the moment, and hence with the crowd's opinion or with membership in the crowd in so far as this opinion and this membership is a thing of the moment.

My listeners, do you at present live in such a way that you are yourself clearly and eternally conscious of being an individual? This was the question the address was to ask, or rather that you are to ask yourself, if you actively consider this occasion. The talk should not tell you only that which will disturb you, even though many are of the conviction that a man ought ever to live in such an aroused state of consciousness. Nor is it concerned how many or how few hold that conviction. The speaker will not attempt to win you to this conviction, even if he does as a rule hold it himself. He does not wish to force it upon you any more than you would desire to force it upon him if you were of this conviction. For the exalted earnestness of the Eternal wishes neither the commendation of the majority nor the commendation of eloquence. One thing alone the talk does not dare to promise you—nor does it wish to insult you. It does not dare to promise you earthly gain if you enter upon and in dedication persevere in this conviction. On the contrary, if persevered in, it will make your life more taxing, and frequently perhaps wearisome. If persevered in, it may make you the target of others' ridicule, not to mention even greater sacrifices that perseverance might choose to require of you. Of course, the ridicule does not distract you if you continue to persist in your conviction. Ridicule will even be a help to you, in the sense that it is a further proof to you that you are on the right path. For the judgment of the crowd has its significance. One should not remain proudly ignorant of it, no, one should be attentive to it. If after this he sees to it that he does the opposite from the judgment of the crowd, then he, for the most part, does the right thing. Or if at the outset a man does the opposite, and he is then so fortunate as to have the judgment of the crowd express itself to the contrary, then he can be fairly certain that he has laid hold of the right thing. Then he has not only himself inwardly weighed and tested the conviction properly, but he has also the advantage of having it tested a second time by the help of ridicule. Ridicule may wound his feelings but just by that wound it shows that he is on the right path—the path of honor and of victory, like a warrior's wound, when it is on the breast where both the wound and the badge of honor are to be borne.

You have surely noticed among schoolboys, that the one that is regarded by all as the boldest is the one who has no fear of his father, who dares to say to the others, "Do you think I am afraid of him?" On the other hand, if they sense that one of their number is actually and literally afraid of his father, they will readily ridicule him a little. Alas, in men's fear-ridden rushing together into a crowd (for why indeed does a man rush into a crowd except because he is afraid!) there, too, it is a mark of boldness not to be afraid, not even of God. And if someone notes that there is an individual outside the crowd who is really and truly afraid—not of the crowd, but of God, he is sure to be the target of some ridicule. The ridicule is usually glossed over somewhat and it is said: a man should *love* God.

Yes, to be sure, God knows that man's highest consolation is that God is love and that man is permitted to love Him. But let us not become too forward, and foolishly, yes, blasphemously, dismiss the tradition of our fathers, established by God Himself: that really and truly a man should fear God. This fear is known to the man who is himself conscious of being an individual, and thereby is conscious of his eternal responsibility before God. For he knows that even if he could, with the help of evasions and excuses, get on well in this life, and even if he could by this shady path have gained the whole world, yet there is still a place in the next world where there is no more evasion than there is shade in the scorching desert.

The talk will not go into this further. It will only ask you again and again, do you now live so that you are conscious of being an individual and thereby that you are conscious of your eternal responsibility before God? Do you live in such a way that this consciousness is able to secure the time and quiet and liberty of action to penetrate every relation of your life? This does not demand that you withdraw from life, from an honorable calling, from a happy domestic life. On the contrary, it is precisely that consciousness which will sustain and clarify and illuminate what you are to do in the relations of life. You should not withdraw and sit brooding over your eternal accounting. To do this is to deserve something further to account for. You will more and more readily find time to perform your duty and your task, while concern over your eternal responsibility will hinder you from being "busy" and busily having a hand in everything possible—an activity that can best be called: time-wasting.

14. WHAT THEN MUST I DO?

OCCUPATION AND VOCATION; MEANS AND END

This was the principal question. For as only one thing is necessary, and as the theme of the talk is the willing of only one thing: hence the consciousness before God of one's eternal responsibility to be an individual is that one thing necessary. The talk now asks further, "*What is your occupation in life?*" The talk does not ask inquisitively about whether it is great or mean, whether you are a king or only a laborer. It does not ask, after the fashion of business, whether you earn a great deal of money or are building up great prestige for yourself. The crowd inquires and talks of these things.

But whether your occupation is great or mean, is it of such a kind that you dare think of it together with the responsibility of eternity? Is it of such a kind that you dare to acknowledge it at this moment or at any time? Suppose that something terrible happened; suppose that the city in which you live suddenly perished like those cities in the far south, and everything came to rest, each one standing in his once-chosen occupation. But suppose this happened without the excuse of "being in practical harmony with the commonly accepted customs of his age," the excuse pronounced by a later generation, in order to shield you from disgrace! Or what is still more serious, suppose one of the most eminent dead, one whose memory the masses keep green, as is their custom, by noisy festivities and by shouting; suppose such a one should come to you. Suppose he visited you and that you there before him, before his piercing gaze, dared continue in your present occupation! Are you not used to thoughts of this kind? It is in just such a way that the transfigured one might well wish to serve after death: by visiting the individual. For it must certainly fill them with disgust if, in their blessed dwelling place, they should become aware that a frivolous crowd treats the transfigured dead as only a living fool could wish to be treated: paying them honor by noisemaking and handclapping. Do not think that the transfigured one has become an aristocrat. On the contrary, he has become even more humble, more humanly sympathetic with each man. Hence, when, like a superior official, he travels on his visits to individuals, he will not reject the meanest occupation, if it is truly honorable. Oh, in eternity where he dwells, all trivial differences are forgotten. But the transfigured one, like eternity, does not desire the crowd. He desires the individual. On that account, if you should ever be almost ashamed of your mean occupation, because, among the world's distinctions, it is so mean, the transfigured one's visit to you as an individual will give you the courage of frankness. The transfigured one's visit to you as an individual will give you that courage of frankness—but what am I speaking of—and if you actively consider the occasion of this talk, then you will stand as an individual before a still more exalted one who, none the less, thinks still more humanly—about the meanness of the occupation, but also infinitely more purely about which occupation is truly honorable.

In your occupation, what is your attitude of mind? And how do you carry out your occupation? Have you made up your own mind that your occupation is your real calling so that you do not have to make explanation hinge on the result, maintaining that it was not your real calling if the results are not favorable, if your efforts do not succeed? Alas, such fickleness weakens a man immeasurably. Therefore persevere. By God's help and by your own faithfulness something good will come from the unpromising beginning. For there are beginnings everywhere, and there are good beginnings, where you begin with God; and no day is the wrong one to begin upon—not even an unpromising one, if you begin with God.

Or have you let yourself be deceived into regarding something as your calling because it turned out well, because it brought immediate success, perhaps even remarkable success? Alas, it is actually said in the world, often enough even by those who think they speak piously: "The proof that a man's occupation is the right one is that he is able to practice it." As if, because a man *could* so harden his heart that he could placidly practice all manner of cruelty, then this was what he ought to do. As if, because this brazen one could find the most hideous atrocity in his heart, and was able to carry it out, then this was the thing he ought to do! No, an unfavorable result can no more disprove the faithful man's conviction of what his calling should be than a favorable result can of itself prove that he is in his proper calling.

Are you of one mind about the manner in which you will carry out your occupation, or is your mind continually divided because you wish to be in harmony with the crowd? Do you stand firmly behind your offer, not obstinately, not sullenly, but eternally concerned; do you continue unchanged to bid for the same thing and continue in your wish to buy the same thing even though the terms have been altered in a number of respects? Do you think that the Good is no different from gold, that it can be bought too dearly? Is there any profit you could not do without for the sake of the Good, any distinction you could not give up, any relation you could not renounce? Is there any stamp of approval from above that is any more important than this to you or perhaps some approbation from below? If you think that the Good must be bought at any price, then will you become envious when you see others buying for a lower price that which you had to buy so dearly—but which, and do not forget this, is worth any price? If your endeavor succeeds, are you then conscious that you are an unprofitable servant; so that the reward does not affect you, as though you became more useful because you got a reward; and adversity does not affect you, since it merely expresses what you shamefacedly will admit—that you have no right to claim anything? Hide nothing away suspiciously in your soul as though you still wished that it had happened differently, so that you might be able to pounce upon the reward as if it were prey, might be able to assume credit for it, might be able to point to it; as though you wished that adversity did not exist because it constrains the selfish thing in you that, even though repressed, foolishly makes you imagine that if you had luck with you, then you might do something for the Good, something that was worth talking about. Never forget that the devout wise man wishes no stroke of adversity to be taken away when it comes his way, because he cannot know whether or not it may be good for him. Never forget that the devout wise man wins his most beautiful of all victories, when the powerful one who had persecuted him wishes, so to speak, to release him, and the wise man replies: "I cannot unconditionally wish to be released, for I cannot know for certain that the persecution might not be good for me." Do you do good only out of fear of punishment, so that you scowl, even when you will the Good, so that in your dreams at night you wish away the punishment and to that extent also the Good, and in your dreams by day imagine that one can with a slavish mind serve the Good? Oh, the Good is no difficult master, that wills one thing today, and another tomorrow. The Good always wishes one and the same thing. But it reckons with exactness and can be that which demands sincerity and can see whether it is present!

And now the means that you use. What means do you use in order to carry out your occupation? Are the means as important to you as the end, wholly as important? Otherwise it is impossible for you to will only one thing, for in that case the irresponsible, the frivolous, the self-seeking, and the heterogeneous means would flow in between in confusing and corrupting fashion. Eternally speaking, there is only one means and there is only one end: the means and the end are one and the same thing. There is only one end: the genuine Good; and only one means: this, to be willing only to use those means which genuinely are good—but the genuine Good is precisely the end. In time and on earth one distinguishes between the two and considers that the end is more important than the means. One thinks that the end is the main thing and demands of one who is striving that he reach the end. He need not be so particular about the means. Yet this is not so, and to gain an end in this fashion is an unholy act of impatience. In the judgment of eternity the relation between the end and the means is rather the reverse of this.

If a man sets himself a goal for his endeavor here in this life, and he fails to reach it, then, in the judgment of eternity, it is quite possible that he may be blameless. Yes, he may even be worthy of praise. He might have been prevented by death, or by an adversity that is beyond his control: in which case he is entirely without blame. He might even have been prevented from reaching the goal just by being unwilling to use any other means than those which the judgment of eternity permits. In which case by his very renunciation of the impatience of passion and the inventions of cleverness, he is even worthy of praise. He is not, therefore, eternally responsible for whether he reaches his goal within this world of time. But without exception, he is eternally responsible for the kind of means he uses. And when he will only use or only uses those means which are genuinely good, then, in the judgment of eternity, he is at the goal. If reaching the goal should be the excuse and the defense for the use of illicit or questionable means—alas, suppose he should die tomorrow. Then the clever one would be caught in his own folly. He had used illicit means, and he died before reaching the goal. For reaching the goal comes at the conclusion; but using the means comes at the beginning. Reaching the goal is like hitting the mark with his shot; but using the means is like taking aim. And certainly the aim is a more reliable indication of the marksman's goal than the spot the shot strikes. For it is possible for a shot to hit the mark by accident. The marksman may also be blameless if the shell does not go off. But no irregularities of the aim are permissible. To the temporal and earthly passion the end is unconditionally more important than the means. On that very account, it is the passionate one's torment, which if carried to its height must indeed make him sleepless and then insane, namely, that he has no control over time, and that he continually arrives too late, even if it was by merely half an hour. And what is still worse, since earthly passion is the rule, it can truthfully be said that it is not wisdom which saves the worst ones from going insane, but indolence. On the other hand, the blessed comfort of the Eternal is like a refreshing sleep, is like "the cold of snow in the time of harvest"[46] to the one who wills the Eternal. He whose means are invariably just as important as the end never comes too late. Eternity is not curious and impatient as to what the outcome in this world of time will be. It is just because of this that the means are without exception as important as the end. To earthly and worldly passion, this observation must seem shocking and paralyzing. To it conscience must seem the most paralyzing thing of all. For conscience is indeed "a blushing innocent spirit that sets up a tumult in a man's breast and fills him with difficulties" just because to conscience the means are without exception as important as the end.

Therefore, my listeners, in the carrying out of your occupation, which we have assumed to be something good and honorable, are the means without exception as important to you as the end? Or have your thoughts become giddy until the greatness of the goal made you look upon illicit means as of negligible importance? Alas, this state of giddiness is to be found least of all in eternity, for eternity is clear and transparent! Do you think that the greatness of an achievement makes it unnecessary for it to ask about a trivial wrong, that is, do you think that a wrong might exist which would be something of no significance, although as an obligation it is infinitely more important than the greatest achievement! Do you think that it is immaterial the way in which a masterpiece is produced? Well, perhaps that might hold for a masterpiece. But do you think that the master dares to be unconcerned about whether he piously consecrates his powers in holy service, or whether by despair in the midst of glittering sins he simply produces—a masterpiece?

And if the thought does not make you giddy, if you are sober and alert, are you particular in every respect in your use of the means? If a youth (and he is also a blushing and innocent spirit) should turn to you, do you dare without exception to let him know all? In your whole conduct is there not something, yes, how shall I express it, I could describe it at length but I would rather put it briefly in this fashion: is there not something of which you could be fairly certain that the older people and those of your own age would almost admire for its cleverness and ingenuity if you told them of it, but which, strangely enough, a youth would blush over (not over your being so clever, but over your not being big enough to despise acting so cleverly)? Perhaps it is by flattery that you had won over this person and that, by concealing something, won this or that advantage, by a little untruth made a glittering trade, by a false union promoted your cause. Perhaps you had won the victory by allying yourself with admiration based upon a misunderstanding, had won riches and power by clever scheming to enter into the smartest combination. In your whole conduct, open and secret, is there not something that you would not for any price consent to let a youth discover (and it is beautiful that you love the youth so much and wish to guard his purity!)? Is there not something—against yourself —that you can still be willing to admit yourself to be guilty of? Something that you would not for any price confide to a youth? Yet, as I have told you, if you actively consider the occasion of this talk, then you stand before a higher judge, who judges infinitely more purely than the purest innocence of youth; a judge, that you will not out of indulgence let into the secret of your guilt, for He already knows you.

And what is your attitude toward others? Are you at one with all —by willing only one thing? Or do you contentiously belong to a party, or is your hand raised against every man and every man's hand raised against you? Do you wish for all others what you wish for yourself, or do you desire the highest thing of all for you and yours, or do you desire that that which you and yours desire shall be the highest thing of all? Do you do unto others what you will that they should do unto you—by willing only one thing? For this will is the eternal order that governs all things, that brings you into union with the dead, and with the men whom you never see, with foreign people whose language and customs you do not know, with all men upon the whole earth, who are related to each other by blood and eternally related to the Divine by eternity's task of willing only one thing. Do you wish that there should be another law for you and yours than for the others? Do you wish to find your consolation in something other than that in which each man without exception may and shall find consolation?

Suppose that sometime a king and a beggar and a man like yourself should come to you. In their presence would you dare frankly to confess that which you desire in the world, in which you sought your consolation, certain that the king in his majesty would not despise you even though you were a man of inferior rank; certain that the beggar would not go away envious that he could not have the same consolation; certain that the man like yourself would be pleased by your frankness? Alas, there is something in the world called clannishness. It is a dangerous thing because all clannishness is divisive. It is divisive when clannishness shuts out the common citizen, and when it shuts out the nobleborn, and when it shuts out the civil servant. It is divisive when it shuts out the king, when it shuts out the beggar, and when it shuts out the wise man, and when it shuts out the simple soul. For all clannishness is the enemy of universal humanity. But to will only one thing, genuinely to will the Good, as an individual, to will to hold fast to God, which things each person without exception is capable of doing, this is what unites. And if you sat in a lonely prison far from all men, or if you were placed out upon a desert island with only animals for company, if you genuinely will the Good, if you hold fast to God, then you are in unity with all men. And if the terrible thing happened (for religious edification should not, like a woman's finery be intended for a splendid moment) that you were buried alive, if, as you awakened in the coffin you seized upon your accustomed consolation, then even in this lonely torment, you would be in unity with all men. Is this your present attitude? Have you no special privilege, no special talent, none of life's special favors that, either separately or in company with some others, vanity has led you to take, so that you could console yourself by means of it, and that makes you dare not tell the uninitiated the source of your consolation? Thus you give alms to the poor man so that he can console himself, but treacherously you have a further consolation for yourself. To be sure, you give a consolation for poverty, but you console yourself by the fact that your wealth assures you against ever becoming poor. You help to set the simple ones right, but treacherously you have a further consolation for yourself; your talent is so outstanding that it could never happen that when you awakened tomorrow you were the stupidest person in all the land. You wish to instruct the youth, but you do not have the heart to take him into your confidence, because you have a secret of your own, because you are a traitor who deceived youth as to what was the highest thing of all by your secret, and deceived yourself as to what was the highest thing of all—by your secret!

And now a question concerning the sufferer. It is not a question of the state of his health. No, the talk is not sympathetic in this respect. Oh, but if you actively consider the occasion of this talk, then by being in the presence of God you would raise yourself above human sympathy. Then you would no longer pine wretchedly for sympathy. For although it happens all too seldom, if this could properly be proved to you, as you may well wish that it might, then with cheerful frankness you could give thanks for it. You would not give thanks bent over like a beggar—God would prevent that. And if sympathy is denied you, if a man is afraid, and in a selfish and cowardly manner avoids, yes, almost loathes you because he does not dare to think of your suffering, then you should be able to do without sympathy. You should not feel bitter over this lack of sympathy—God will take care of that. The talk asks you then, or you ask yourselves by means of the talk, whether you now live in such a way that you truthfully will only one thing. It is not the intention of the talk to presume to judge of this, far from it. The talk judges no one. Even the Holy Scriptures have an especially tender love for the unfortunate ones. Indeed it is particularly appropriate for a devotional meditation to concern itself principally with the sufferer, just as one in the world addresses the powerful man, the distinguished man. The talk does not ask inquisitively and busily about the name of your particular suffering, about how many years it has continued, about what the doctor or the pastor thinks, how much earthly hope they give you. Alas, out of vanity, sufferings, too, can in this fashion be taken as a mark of distinction that draws the attention of others to oneself.

So on that account, see that you question yourself by means of the talk. If the sufferer talks to himself in private, asks himself which kind of life he leads, whether he truthfully wills only one thing: then he is not tempted to relate in detail what he himself knows best of all, he is not tempted to compare. For all comparison injures. Yes, it is evil. Do you at present genuinely will only one thing? You know that if the only reason you will but one thing is that by this, and by this alone, you will be set free from suffering, then you do not genuinely will but one thing. But even if you could so dull yourself that the wish would die out, so that you could sever the wish's painful tie with that happier sense of being a man, of loving to live, of loving to be a happy one, still you would fail to will only one thing. What at present is your condition in suffering? The doctor and the pastor ask about your health, but eternity makes *you* responsible for your condition. Is it so that it does not frivolously or superstitiously fluctuate in a fever of impatience? Is it so that it is not a dismally sluggish painlessness? Or is it so that you are willing to suffer all and let the Eternal comfort you? As time goes by, how does your condition change? Did you begin well perhaps but become more and more impatient? Or perhaps you were impatient at the beginning, but learned patience from what you suffered? Alas, perhaps year after year your suffering remained unchanged, and if it did change, then its description would be a matter for the doctor or the pastor. Alas, perhaps the unaltered monotony of the suffering seems to you like a creeping death. But while the doctor and the pastor and your friend know of no change to speak of, yet the talk asks you whether under the pressure of the unchanged monotony an infinite change is taking place. Not a change in the suffering (for even if it is changed, it can only be a finite change), but in you, an infinite change in you from good to better. If the talk were to characterize your altered condition through the years, would it dare use the words of the Apostle and say of your life of unaltered suffering: "Suffering taught him patience, patience taught him experience, experience taught him hope?"[47] Would the talk dare say at your grave: "He won the hope that shall never be put to shame"? At your grave, instead of mumbling a prayer of thanks that the sufferer is dead as was described earlier, would the talk dare freely and wholeheartedly to say, as though at a hero's grave, "The content of his life was suffering, yet his life has put many to shame"? For in eternity there will be as little asked about your suffering as about the king's purple, precisely as little. In eternity you as an individual will only be asked about your faith and about your faithfulness. There will be absolutely no asking about whether you were entrusted with much or little, whether you were given many talents of silver to work with or whether you were given a hundred-pound weight to carry. But you will be asked only about your faith and about your faithfulness. In the world of time one asks in other terms. Here one inquires especially about how high a command a man has, and when it is a very high one, then one forgets in one's worldly astonishment to ask after his faithfulness. But if it is very little, then one prefers to hear nothing at all about him, neither about his burden nor his faithfulness. Eternity asks solely about faithfulness, and with equal earnestness it asks this of the king and of the most wretched of all sufferers. It is no excuse to be entrusted with little, nor is it any answer to the question that asks exclusively about faithfulness, the question, which in the eternal mercy knows that sufferings can tempt a man, but knows, too, that they can be a guide. For "sorrow is better than laughter; for by the sadness of the countenance, the heart is made better" (Ecclesiastes vii. 3). This is the change that eternity asks about, not about the unchangeableness of the suffering. This is what eternity asks; and if you yourself actively consider the occasion of this talk, then you will ask yourself about this matter. If the change has not taken place, then this question of whether it has truthfully been done will indeed be helpful to you in bringing about the change. For human sympathy, no matter how painstakingly it inquires about you, cannot by all its questioning alter the fixed character of the suffering. Eternity's question, if you put it truthfully to yourself before God, contains the possibility of change. But I am talking almost as if I meant to edify you, the talk would be embarrassed to press this question upon you. You yourself know best of all that if you put this question, then you must render an account of whether you are living in this way at present.

15. CONCLUSION:

MAN AND THE ETERNAL

This was the issue of the talk. But now if the individual, yes, if you, my listener, and I must admit to ourselves that we were far from living in this way, far from that purity of heart which truthfully wills but one thing; must admit to ourselves that the questions demanded an answer, and yet in another sense, in order to avoid any deception, did not require an answer, in that they were, if anything, charges against ourselves which in spite of the form of the question changed themselves into an accusation: then should the individual, and you, my listener, and I join together in saying, "Indeed your life is like that of most others"? How, then, shall we begin over again, at this time, and once more speak of the evasion which consists of being among the many? For where there are many, there is externality, and comparison, and indulgence, and excuse and evasion. Shall we, even after we have come to understand the calamity of this evasion, in the end take refuge in it? Shall we console ourselves with a common plight? Alas, even in the world of time, a common plight is a doubtful consolation; and in eternity there is no common plight. In eternity, the individual, yes, you, my listener, and I as individuals will each be asked solely about himself as an individual, and about the individual details in his life. If in this talk I have spoken poorly, then you will not be asked about that, my listener; nor will any man from whom I may have learned. For if he has stated it falsely, then he will be questioned about that and I will be made to answer for having learned from another what was false. Nor will any with whom I have had an acquaintance be made to answer. For if his acquaintance was corrupting, then he will be questioned about that, but I shall be made to answer for having sought out or not having avoided his acquaintance, and for letting myself become corrupted. No, if I have spoken poorly and just in so far as I have spoken poorly, then without any excuse whatsoever I, as an individual, will be questioned about that. For in eternity there is not the remotest thought of any common plight. In eternity, the individual, yes, you, my listener, and I as individuals will each be asked solely about himself as an individual and about the individual details in his life.

If it should so happen that in this talk I have spoken the truth, then I shall be questioned no further about this matter. There will be no questioning as to whether I have won men (quite on the contrary, it might well be asked whether I had any notion of having by my own efforts done the least thing toward winning them); no questioning as to whether, by the talk I have gained some earthly advantage (quite on the contrary, it might well be asked whether I had any notion of having myself done the least thing toward gaining it); no questioning about what results I have produced, or whether I may have produced no results at all, or whether loss and the sport that others made of me were the only results I have produced. No, eternity will release me from one and all of such foolish questions. In the world of time a man can be confused, for he does not know which is which: which question is the serious one and which the silly one, especially since the silly one is heard a thousand times to the serious question's once. Eternity, on the other hand, can admirably distinguish between them; yet it is obvious that the thing does not become easier on that account. The seriousness of the plight is only intensified. For in eternity there is not the remotest thought of any common plight. In eternity, the individual, yes, you, my listener, and I as individuals will each be asked solely about himself as an individual, and about the individual details in his life. If it should happen that a true reflection of life is contained in this talk, if it is so that the ability and the occasion is vouchsafed me which enabled me to set it forth; yet it may also have happened, we can suppose such a case, that the circumstances under which it had to be spoken did not seem favorable. If this were so, then eternity would not inquisitively enter into any long-drawn-out discourse about circumstances. Had I remained silent, eternity would hold me as an individual to account. For in the world of time, when the task is to be clever for one's own advantage, when worldly cleverness judges and criticizes, then unfavorable circumstances are not only a ground for silence, but silence becomes admired as cleverness; while favorable circumstances are an invitation for all to join in the conversation. On the other hand, in the eternal order, if the circumstances are difficult the obligation to speak is doubled. The difficulty is precisely an invitation. Eternally, the individual will only be asked whether he knew that they were unfavorable, and whether in this event he dared remain silent and therefore by his silence, yes, to use the proverb, by his consent, he had as an individual contributed to a condition where the circumstances became still more unfavorable for the truth. Eternally, circumstances will provide neither hiding place nor evasion for him, for he will be asked as an individual, and the difficulty of the circumstances will stand against him as a double accusation. As for remaining silent, it is not as with sleeping that he who sleeps does not sin. For in the world the individual has brought the most atrocious guilt upon himself—through remaining silent. The fault was not that he did not manage to get the circumstances changed. The fault was that he was silent not out of discretion, which is silent when it is proper to be silent, but out of cleverness, which is silent because it is the most prudent to be so.

But what, then, shall we do, if the questions sound like accusations? Above all else, each one will himself become an individual with his responsibility to God. Each one will himself be subject to the stern judgment of this individuality. Is this not the purpose of the office of Confession? For just as little as in that silent churchyard "the multitude of dead make up a society," so little does the multitude of those coming to confess make up a society—for not even the king goes to confession alone in order to escape the common company of others. Those who are coming to confess do not belong together in a society. Each one is an individual before God. Man and wife may go to confession in beautiful fellowship with each other, but they may not confess together. The one who confesses is not in company, he is as an individual, alone before God. And if, as an individual, he admits to himself that the questions, which by the help of an insignificant one's whisper he puts to himself, are accusations, then he confesses. For one does not confess merits and achievements, he confesses sins. When one confesses, he sees at once that he has no merits. He sees that merits and achievements are fantasies and sense deceptions that are at home where one moves about in the crowd and engages others in conversation. He sees that it is just on this account that the one who never himself becomes an individual is easily tempted to consider himself a most meritorious man. But the purpose of the office of Confession is certainly not to make a man conscious of himself as an individual at the moment of its celebration, and then for the rest of the time to allow him to live outside this consciousness. On the contrary, in the moment of confession itself he should give account as to how he has lived as an individual. If the same consciousness were not demanded of him for daily use, then the demand of the office of Confession is a self-contradiction. It is as if one now and then demanded of a humble man that he should render account to himself and to God of how he had lived as a king—he that had never been a king. And so it is to ask of a man that he shall render account of his life as an individual when one allows him to lead his life outside this consciousness.

My listener! Do you remember now, how this talk began? Let me call it back to your remembrance. It is true that the temporal order has its time; but the Eternal shall always have time. If this should not happen within a man's life, then the Eternal comes again under another name, and once again shall always have time. This is repentance. And since at present no man's life is lived in perfection, but each one in frailty, so Providence has given man two companions for his journey, the one calls him forward, the other calls him back. But the call of repentance is always at the eleventh hour. Therefore confession is always at the eleventh hour, but not in the sense of being precipitate. For confession is a holy act, which calls for a collected mind. A collected mind is a mind that has collected itself from every distraction, from every relation, in order to center itself upon this relation to itself as an individual who is responsible to God. It is a mind that has collected itself from every distraction, and therefore also from all comparison. For comparison may either tempt a man to an earthly and fortuitous despondency because the one who compares must admit to himself that he is behind many others, or it may tempt him to pride because, humanly speaking, he seems to be ahead of many others.

A new expression of the true extremity of the eleventh hour comes when the penitent has withdrawn himself from every relation in order to center himself upon his relation to himself as an individual. By this he becomes responsible for every relation in which he ordinarily stands, and he is outside of any comparison. The more use one makes of comparison, the more it seems that there is still plenty of time. The more a man makes use of comparison, the more indolent and the more wretched his life becomes. But when all comparison is relinquished forever then a man confesses as an individual before God—and he is outside any comparison, just as the demand which purity of heart lays upon him is outside of comparison. Purity of heart is what God requires of him and the penitent demands it of himself before God. Yes, it is just on this account that he confesses his sins. And heavy as the way and the hour of the confession may be, yet the penitent wins the Eternal. He is strengthened in the consciousness that he is an individual, and in the task of truthfully willing only one thing. This consciousness is the strait gate and the narrow way. For it is not this narrow way that the many take, following one after another. No, this straitness means rather that each must himself become an individual, that through this needle's eye he must press forward to the narrow way where no comparison cools, but yet where no comparison kills with its insidious cooling. The broad way, on the other hand, is broad because so many travel upon it. The crowd's way is always broad. There the poisonous ornamental flower of excuses is found in bloom. The inviting hiding places of evasion are there. There comparison wafts its cooling breath of air. This way leadeth not unto life.

Only the individual can truthfully will the Good, and even though the penitent toils heavily not merely in the eleventh hour of confession, with all the questions standing as accusations of himself, but also in their daily use in repentance, yet the way is the right one. For he is in touch with the demand that calls for purity of heart by willing only one thing.

If you, my listener, unquestionably know much more concerning the office of Confession than has been set forth here; if you know the next thing that follows upon the confession of sins, still this extended talk has not been in vain if it has made you pause, made you pause before something that you already know well, you, who know so much more. But do not forget that the most terrible thing of all is to "live on, deceived, not by what one might expect to be deceived [by] (alas, and on that account horribly deceived) but deceived by too much knowledge." Consider that in these times it is a particularly great temptation for speakers to leave the individual as quickly as possible in order to get as much as possible said, so that nobody might suspect that the speaker did not know what every man in a Christian country knows. Alas, only God knows how the individual knows it. But what does it profit a man if he goes further and further and it must be said of him: he never stops going further; when it also must be said of him: there was nothing that made him pause? For pausing is not a sluggish repose. Pausing is also movement. It is the inward movement of the heart. To pause is to deepen oneself in inwardness. But merely going further is to go straight in the direction of superficiality. By that way one does not come to will only one thing. Only if at some time he decisively stopped going further and then again came to a pause, as he went further, only then could he will only one thing. For purity of heart was to will one thing.

Father in Heaven! What is a man without Thee! What is all that he knows, vast accumulation though it be, but a chipped fragment if he does not know Thee! What is all his striving, could it even encompass the world, but a half-finished work if he does not know Thee: Thee the One, who art one thing and who art all! So may Thou give to the intellect, wisdom to comprehend that one thing; to the heart, sincerity to receive this understanding; to the will, purity that wills only one thing. In prosperity may Thou grant perseverance to will one thing; amid distractions, collectedness to will one thing; in suffering, patience to will one thing. Oh, Thou that givest both the beginning and the completion, may Thou early, at the dawn of day, give to the young man the resolution to will one thing. As the day wanes, may Thou give to the old man a renewed remembrance of his first resolution, that the first may be like the last, the last like the first, in possession of a life that has willed only one thing. Alas, but this has indeed not come to pass. Something has come in between. The separation of sin lies in between. Each day, and day after day, something is being placed in between: delay, blockage, interruption, delusion, corruption. So in this time of repentance may Thou give the courage once again to will one thing. True, it is an interruption of our daily tasks; we do lay down our work as though it were a day of rest, when the penitent (and it is only in a time of repentance that the heavy-laden worker may be quiet in the confession of sin) is alone before Thee in self-accusation. This is indeed an interruption. But it is an interruption that searches back into its very beginnings that it might bind up anew that which sin has separated, that in its grief it might atone for lost time, that in its anxiety it might bring to completion that which lies before it. Oh, Thou that givest both the beginning and the completion, give Thou victory in the day of need so that what neither a man's burning wish nor his determined resolution may attain to, may be granted unto him in the sorrowing of repentance: to will only one thing.

NOTES

1. Ecclesiastes iii. 1.
2. Kierkegaard often takes some liberty with his quotations, paraphrasing what he takes them essentially to mean. "He hath made everything beautiful in his time: also he hath set the world in their heart, so that no man can find out the work that God maketh from the beginning to the end."
3. For example: 2 Thessalonians i. 3.
4. Matthew xxiii. 23. See note 2. The precise text is: "These ought ye to have done, and not to leave the other undone."
5. James iii. 5.
6. Matthew xii. 43, 45.
7. Compare Karl Börne, *Collected Works*, Vol. II, p. 126: "All are not free who scoff at their chains."
8. Compare Thrasymachus in Plato's *Republic* I. 16, 20.
9. Compare Romans viii. 38, 39.
10. 1 John v. 19.
11. Compare Themistocles in Cicero's *De Oratore* II. 74, 299.
12. Plato's *Republic* IX. 572.
13. Genesis ii. 18.
14. Ecclesiastes iv. 10.
15. Compare Luke xvii. 10.
16. See editor's introduction.
17. These words are attributed to Francis I as having been spoken after the battle of Pavia, where he was taken prisoner.
18. Compare 2 Timothy iii. 7.
19. Psalms xciv. 9.
20. Proverbs iv. 23.
21. Ecclesiastes vii. 2.
22. Compare Luke ix. 59.
23. Compare Luke xvii. 10.
24. Compare Mark viii. 36.
25. Matthew xxvii. 41–44.
26. Shakespeare in *Henry V*, Act 2, Scene 4.
27. Socrates, Plato's *Republic* VI. 492 B.
28. John the Baptist.
29. Compare Rosenkranz, *Erinnerungen an Karl Daub*, p. 24: "So as on sentry duty, at night on a lonely post, perhaps before a powder magazine a man has thoughts that under any other circumstances would be quite impossible."

Kierkegaard refers to this same passage again in *Fear and Trembling*, *Collected Works*, Vol. III, p. 100.

30. Genesis xii. 1.

31. Johann Arndt, *True Christianity*.

32. Luke xv. 7.

33. Compare Matthew xi. 28.

34. Epicurus in Diogenes Laetius, 140.

35. Mark ix. 36.

36. Ephesians vi. 14, 17.

37. Acts v. 40–41.

38. The Danish word for "courage" is *Mod* and for "opposition" is *Modstand*. (Tr.)

39. The Danish word for "patience," *Taalmod*, contains the Danish word for "courage," *Mod*, and invites the discourse which follows. (Tr.)

40. Compare Acts xxii. 27–30, and xxiv. 23.

41. Compare 1 Peter i. 16.

42. The Danish word for "actor," *Shuespiller*, means literally *show-* or *display-player*. (Tr.)

43. Socrates in Plato's *Republic* VII. 518 A.

44. Psalm ii. 1–4.

45. The Latin proverb "Tu si tacuisses, philosophus mansisses." See Boethius *Consolatio philos*. II. 17.

46. Proverbs xxv. 13.

47. Romans v. 3–4.

A TESTAMENT
OF DEVOTION

by Thomas R. Kelly

EDITOR'S INTRODUCTION TO
A TESTAMENT OF DEVOTION

Thomas Kelly's *A Testament of Devotion,* the heart of which is included in this volume, is a contemporary classic. Though Kelly incorporated into it many of the rich insights of Quaker spirituality, centered in the Light Within, he enriched them by adding bits from the cornucopia of the whole Christian spiritual heritage and his own personal experience. The result is a wonderfully edifying collection of essays which, not surprisingly, my students in courses on devotional classics have repeatedly selected as their favorite.

Selections from A Testament of Devotion

The essays contained in *A Testament of Devotion* were originally lectures or addresses delivered to Quaker audiences. Shortly before Kelly died, he selected three for a small book on the practice of devotion. These provided a core for the book assembled posthumously by Kelly's long-time friend and colleague Douglas Steere, Professor of Philosophy at Haverford College, Haverford, Pennsylvania, where Kelly once studied and where he taught for three years prior to his death. Collected essays of this type inevitably involve a certain amount of repetition, for most of us feel compelled to repeat basic insights in dealing with various facets of spirituality.

The original edition of *A Testament of Devotion* contains five essays: "The Light Within," "Holy Obedience," "The Blessed Community," "The Simplification of Life," and "The Eternal Now and Social Concern." Due to copyright limitations, this volume will contain only two of these, "Holy Obedience" and "The Blessed Community." These two, however, were a part of Kelly's choice and present insights which are most distinctively his own and, in some way, embrace the best insights found in the others. "Holy Obedience," for instance, includes a splendid discussion of simplification. It was the annual William Penn Lecture delivered to the Yearly Meeting of Quakers in Philadelphia in late March 1939. "The

Blessed Community" resulted from Kelly's association with Friends in Bad Pyrmont, Germany, after delivering the Richard Cary Lecture in the fall of 1938. In letters to his wife, Lael, he exulted over the communion he enjoyed with these ordinary saints, "*giant* souls," he called them.[1] Furthermore, they are especially relevant to the life of faith in the present age.

The forcefulness of these essays lies in simplicity, in style as well as content. The style is unembellished, direct, and, very much like John Woolman's or the Bible's, compelling because born out of experience of Truth. Kelly does not try to convince us that "Holy Obedience" is right; he assumes we will know that, that we will want to obey. He is interested, therefore, in opening for us the "doors" which lead to such obedience.

Similarly, if you know the Christian heritage in spirituality, you will not find any startlingly novel or unique insights in these essays. Obedience, sacrifice, simplicity, and community are words you will have read thousands of times. Thomas Kelly's contribution to you, therefore, is to grasp the exact crucial point of such ideas and to explain in words both plain and compelling how you may make them your own. Kelly is the gentle teacher encouraging the fainthearted and faltering student. He employs always a positive psychology, founded upon the Quaker high estimate of human nature and potential. Guiding us along the path of holy obedience, for instance, he reminds us that the first step is a vision. For those who have had a vision, he offers simple and practical advice. First, "Begin where you are. Obey *now*." Second, "If you slip and stumble and forget God for an hour, and assert your old proud self, and rely upon your own clever wisdom, don't spend too much time in anguished regrets and self-accusations but begin again, just where you are." Third, "Don't grit your teeth and clench your fists and say, 'I will! I will!' Relax. Take hands off. Submit yourself to God." Those are the secrets of holy obedience.

We read in Thomas Kelly some amazingly beautiful and yet profound expressions. Speaking of simplification, for instance, he writes,

I have in mind something deeper than the simplification of our external programs, our absurdly crowded calendars of appointments through which so many pantingly and frantically gasp. These do become simplified in holy obedience, and the poise and peace we have been missing can really be found. But there is a deeper, an internal simplification of the whole of one's personality, stilled, tranquil, in childlike trust listening ever to Eternity's whisper, walking with a smile into the dark.

The words live. Thomas Kelly shared his deepest secret, his most significant discovery, and we discern in them the secret of his attraction for persons living in a hectic, hurried, jostled, overburdened, anxiety-ridden world such as we know.

Thomas Raymond Kelly

The remarkable insights of "Holy Obedience" and "The Blessed Community" were shaped ultimately by experience, in the case of Thomas Kelly, painful experience. He "learned by what he suffered" to live life in another key than he had previously lived it. Douglas Steere has said, "The story of Thomas Kelly's life is the story of a passionate and determined quest for adequacy."[2] But he did not reach his goal until about three years before his death on January 17, 1941. He reached it suddenly, by way of a crushing failure which opened the way for him to be "much shaken by the experience of Presence—something that I did not seek, but that *sought* me."[3]

Thomas Kelly learned early the importance of responsibility and perhaps, like many others in similar circumstances, developed the drive which compelled him always to perform at the very highest level. He was born into a Quaker farm family near Chillicothe, Ohio, on June 4, 1893. His father, Carlton Weden Kelly, died suddenly at the age of thirty-three in September 1897, hemorrhaging internally. His mother, Madora Elizabeth Kersey Kelly; his paternal grandmother, Mahala Kelly; his seven-year-old sister, Mary; and Tom carried on with the farm operation.

In December 1903 the Kelly family moved to Wilmington, Ohio, where Madora Kelly, after taking a business course for a year, secured a job at the Irwin Auger Bit Company. The move allowed the children to attend high school in Wilmington. After completing public and high schools, Tom attended Wilmington College, a small Quaker school, majoring in chemistry. Meantime, he assisted in supporting the family by working part time for the Farquhar

Furnace Company, becoming an excellent sheet-metal worker. He graduated with honors in 1913, receiving the annual scholarship to study at Haverford College in Pennsylvania, one of the elite educational institutions in the East.

Kelly's one-year stint at Haverford proved to be one of the milestones of his life. Although a chemistry major, he came under the spell of Rufus Jones, the brilliant mystical philosopher and interpreter of Quaker thought. One important consequence of this meeting was that Kelly's interest was diverted from chemistry to philosophy and religion. He arranged to read for the M.A. in philosophy. But this result is overshadowed by another, the fact that Kelly was introduced to a quite different brand of Quakerism. The Quakerism he had known up to this time was typical of the Midwest, best characterized by the word "evangelical," not far removed from other evangelical Protestant denominations. The Eastern Quakerism, of which Rufus Jones was a most eminent exponent, was "mystical," closer to the original version of George Fox. Earlier, Kelly had sensed deep feelings of inadequacy in his religious experience, despite being disciplined and active in many areas. When bad weather forbade attendance at meetings, for instance, he had insisted on conducting meetings in the home. At Wilmington he had participated actively in Y.M.C.A., Christian Endeavor, and the Young Friends Movement. Now, more seeds of discontent were being sown.

Kelly never completed his M.A. at Haverford. In the fall of 1914 he began teaching English and science at Pickering College, New Market, Ontario, a small coed Quaker preparatory school. During his two years there, he developed a keen interest in a mission to Japan supported by Canadian Quakers and signed up for missionary service. Two summer vacations spent as a Young Friends Secretary, however, generated a strong countervailing interest in home mission service. Needing theological training whichever direction he decided to go, he enrolled in Hartford Theological Seminary in the fall of 1916. After discussing his dilemma with Rufus Jones during the Thanksgiving holidays, he decided to become a Quaker minister rather than enter missionary service. His interest in the Orient, however, remained with him and figured prominently in his later decisions.

Soon after the United States declared war on Germany, April 6,

1917, Kelly volunteered for Y.M.C.A. canteen work. In this context he became increasingly sensitive to his religious commitments. Assigned first to a British army camp bear Blackpool to serve tea and refreshments and to sell sundries, he was transferred a month later to a new camp and placed in charge. There he worried about the need of soldiers for religious awakening. His pacifist views, moreover, aroused anxiety and made him feel less and less comfortable in the situation. By late summer he had resolved to leave his job and work among German prisoners under auspices of the American Y.M.C.A. In November he was installed in the London office of German POW work. He returned to the United States in December.

Meantime, Kelly's vocational sights had shifted to teaching. His first opportunity opened in March 1918, when the president of Wilmington College wrote to ask if he were interested in teaching Bible and philosophy. He decided to accept when he finished his B.D. at Hartford.

Soon after coming to Hartford, Kelly had met and become attached to the family of the Reverend Herbert Macy, a graduate of Hartford and a minister in the Congregational Church. Lael Macy, one of the daughters, became his bride on May 29, 1919, shortly after he graduated from Hartford.

The Kellys were not happy in Wilmington. Their eagerness to return East was occasioned in part by the serious illness of Lael's mother, who died in December 1921. Having lived and studied in the East, moreover, Kelly was disappointed with the academic level of his alma mater. After one year he resigned, but he stayed a second year at the insistence both of his mother and the college. The second year reinforced his teaching vocation.

In 1921, a fellowship already in hand since graduation, he returned to Hartford Theological Seminary to study philosophy under Arthur Lincoln Gillett. To supplement his stipend, he served as pastor of a nondenominational church in Wilson, Connecticut, several times refusing attractive offers from Quaker parishes. With his usual perseverence he completed his Ph.D. thesis, "The Place of Value Judgments in the Philosophy of Hermann Lotze," in the spring of 1924. The thesis was approved, but on his oral examination his relentless pursuit of perfection, which had shown up earlier in headaches and other symptoms of stress, exacted its toll. He blacked out, unable even to recall his name. Fortunately his examiners granted him a second chance and he performed brilliantly, as had been expected. Just before his graduation, the Hartford chapter of Phi Beta Kappa tapped him for membership.

A semester before he completed his Ph.D., Kelly received an invitation to teach at Earlham College in Richmond, Indiana, and another to work in Germany for the American Friends Service Committee. Having retained an interest in Germany from his service there during World War I, he decided first to follow up on the latter. This mission occupied him for fifteen months, during which he assisted in the establishment of a permanent Quaker center in Berlin. Just before returning to the United States, he visited Eisenach, where an independent German Yearly Meeting of Friends was decided on.

He took up his teaching responsibilities at Earlham College in the fall of 1925. From the first he shouldered a load of responsibilities in Quaker circles in Richmond and frequently preached at the West Richmond Meeting to supplement his income. His sermons during the period reflected the deepening of his spirituality and, by the judgment of his son Richard, "a strong break with his own evangelical background."[4] His last visit to Germany had probably *initiated* the shift in his thinking. In a 1928 letter addressed to Harold H. Peterson, American Y.M.C.A. secretary in Lahore, India, Kelly himself traced the change to "a *new* Quaker movement" in Germany, through which he "had a great 'opening' on the meaning of missionary work" and discovered "a brotherhood relationship in a joint search for truth."[5] But his pilgrimage continued after he left Germany. He was learning "that Quakerism is essentially a mystical fellowship, which transcends the ordinary religious organizations." Evidently he hit upon this truth in an intuitive fashion, for he went on to say, "The meaning of the universal presence of the Inner Light, the Logos, in every man, the essential Christ in all people, glowed out suddenly."[6] To him this amounted to a revelation, reminiscent perhaps of George Fox's in the seventeenth century. "I don't know whence it came," he confessed, "except as one says that all immediate vision of truth is revelation."[7]

This dramatic shift in his perception of Quakerism, coupled with the provincial character of Richmond and his compulsion for perfection, generated dissatisfaction. Midwestern Quakers had shifted too radically from the source. They were, he observed in his letter to Peterson, "caught up in the general stampede toward service—a splendid thing—but that service does not always grow out of a more profound experience of the presence of God."[8] His new perception caused isolation and loneliness for both him and Lael. They felt "strained" and not "at home" in Quaker meetings, hoping for an outburst of "fresh springs of religious experience."[9]

Thomas Kelly's metamorphosis entailed more than a shift to the Quakerism of the East represented by Rufus Jones, however. Actually he seems to have had only limited experience of a mystical presence up to this time. Richard Kelly has noted that he had recorded "a flash of revelation" at Hartford while he was working on a problem in mathematics.[10] But he later discredited his earlier intellectual awakenings. This new discontented phase coincided with his philosophical training and love of scholarship. He was developing also an increasing interest in oriental thought. He needed an environmental change to fulfill his dream.

In the fall of 1930 Kelly obtained a year's leave of absence to study at Harvard. In his mind Harvard offered everything Earlham did not—intellectual stimulation, the most influential group of philosophers in the western world, a chance to acquire the ultimate certification of a scholar. While Hartford was a respected school, it was not especially distinguished in the field of philosophy of religion, and recent developments in logic and the philosophy of science made Kelly feel a need to improve his qualifications.

He paid a great price for his decision. In the early years of the Depression financing was a problem. The Kellys, now with one daughter, Lois, born in 1928, got by on a small fellowship, borrowed money, Kelly's preaching in Fall River, Massachusetts, and teaching part time at Wellesley.

Kelly undertook his studies under Alfred North Whitehead and Clarence I. Lewis with his usual energy and enthusiasm. The excellence of both professors excited him. In the spring of 1932 he took and passed his prelims and prepared to write his thesis on "Explanation and Reality in the Philosophy of Emile Meyerson"; he had been introduced to Meyerson by Whitehead. The study gave him an opportunity to reconcile the world of mind and the world of spirit. During the summer of 1934, while he served on the staff of Pendle Hill, a Quaker conference center, he gave lectures entitled "The Quest for Reality." In these he mentioned Lotze, Whitehead, and Meyerson frequently; each one was a scientist turned philosopher, as was Kelly himself.

The years 1932–37 turned out to be the bleakest of Kelly's life. He wanted desperately to teach in the East, whose cultural stimulus pleased him so much more than the Midwest's. On account of the Depression, however, no position opened. With the encouragement of Rufus Jones, but terribly disappointed, he decided to return to Earlham. Meanwhile, his health began to deteriorate. Never robust, he had pushed too hard and now he complained of frequent headaches, fatigue, hay fever, "woozy spells," and near exhaustion following the spells. The blackouts were not new. According to Richard Kelly, he had experienced one of these in 1919 while driving his stepfather's car, resulting in a serious accident. In 1924 he blacked out during his orals at Hartford. After he returned to Earlham, the spells occurred often. Lael Kelly theorized later that these may have been symptoms of early, small heart attacks. In early 1934 he was hospitalized with a serious attack of kidney stones, from which he recovered slowly and with considerable pain.

In 1934 Kelly was invited to teach at the University of Hawaii in Honolulu. Rufus Jones and Clarence I. Lewis, his most trusted advisers in academic matters, urged him to be cautious, lest he take himself out of the mainstream of American scholarship. But his unhappiness in Richmond and his abiding interest in the Orient prevailed. He agreed to take the post in the fall of 1935.

This decision made urgent the completion of his Ph.D. thesis. Working without letup, he suffered a nervous breakdown in December 1934. He continued to teach anyway. In March 1935 he returned to work on his manuscript and, by pushing himself, finished in May. In a letter to Lewis written from Hawaii shortly after posting two copies he outlined his academic plans in three steps. First, he had gone to Harvard in order to be exposed to the philosophical thought of the whole world. Second, he decided to come to Hawaii in order to get better acquainted with oriental thought. Third, he hoped to return to the United States as a mature scholar. To this he added a word about his distaste for the Midwest. "For the good of our souls it has seemed best to get into a different region."[11]

The geographical solution, however, failed to satisfy his desires and needs. Although it put him in close touch with oriental philosophy, his health worsened. In a letter to his former mentor at Hartford, A. L. Gillett, in November after arrival he complained, "I have not been up to scratch since landing here, but I have been logy, headachey, and unable to drive ahead. I have been fearfully discouraged on account of this, knowing that now is when I must make things move."[12] Susbsequently he underwent surgery to correct a sinus condition, but this proved only a partial solution. He again began to sink into the state of depression and melancholy he had experienced at Earlham the previous winter. In a subsequent letter to Professor Gillett he wrote that Hawaii "certainly is the most unfortunate move ever made. . . ."[13]

Happily, something intruded to lift his spirits. In March 1936 Haverford College offered him a position. This time, he decided immediately to accept the offer, and in July he and his family—now four in number, with the arrival of Richard in February—sailed for the continental United States. At Haverford he had a busy schedule. He was appointed to various Philadelphia Yearly Meeting committees and was often called on to assist the American Friends Service Committee. He was also a frequent speaker at conferences and training sessions for Young Service Committee work-camp volunteers. He loved teaching at Haverford, where he was able to renew old contacts with Rufus Jones and to establish new ones with his colleague Douglas Steere, with whom he felt genuine kinship.

Kelly still sustained his intense drive for academic recognition. He had fought a long battle already. After he took his preliminary examinations in 1932 the Graduate School at Harvard at first had informed him that he could not take the Ph.D. because he had one already from Hartford. He wrote a long explanatory letter mentioning assurances he had received that he could. The decision was reversed. This intensified his desire to obtain the degree. Subsequently he had labored under great physical stress to write his thesis. He borrowed money to publish the latter in the summer of 1937. It was well received by his peers. In the fall he took his orals. But again, as at Haverford, he blacked out. This time, his committee informed him that he could not be considered for the degree again. It was a crushing blow. Years spent in obtaining that one last stamp of approval wiped out at a stroke! Lael Kelly feared a recurrence of Tom's 1935 breakdown. Douglas Steere spent hours talking with him, trying to reassure him that this would not jeopardize his standing at Haverford. President Comfort assured him that the matter need not be made public. In the end, however, Thomas Kelly had to stand alone in the face of failure. But he was not alone. None of us can handle failure alone. Kelly learned here the meaning of God's word to the Apostle Paul, "My grace is sufficient for you, for my power is made perfect in weakness" (2 Cor. xii. 9, RSV). Out of the agony of this experience a *new* Thomas Kelly was born. He echoed his mature perception of the entire experience in a letter to ten-year-old Lois Kelly, dated August 11, 1938: "For sadness, and sorrow, and suffering are not things to run away from, but to live through, and understand."[14]

Richard Kelly has described aptly the transformation which occurred:

> There is no exact record of what happened in the following weeks, but it is certain that sometime during the months of November or December, 1937, a change was wrought within the very foundation of his soul. He described it as being "shaken by the experience of Presence—something that I did not seek, but that *sought* me." The inner awakening of an "Awful Power" surged within him. . . . In the depth of his misery and apparent failure he had found the secret of the pliant spirit as it listens to the interior voice of God. Stripped of his defenses and human self-justification, he found, for the first time, a readiness to accept the outright gift of God's Love, and he responded with unlimited commitment to that leading.[15]

The first public evidence of the *new* Kelly appeared in January 1938, when he delivered a series of lectures to a Young Friends' group in Germantown, Pennsylvania. Two of the lectures, "The Eternal Now and Social Concern" and "Quakers and Symbolism," grew directly out of Kelly's experience that fall and winter. His messages contained a note of authority and authenticity they had not had before, and they had a radically different style.

The experience affected him in many ways. For one, the true center of his interest finally came to focus. While he was working on his thesis, Whitehead had observed that religion was Kelly's true interest. Now he was free to act on earlier intuitions. Whereas before he had "still clung to the basic Quaker notion that God, or Reality, could be known directly, . . . he could not fully accept its apparent nonrational implications."[16] Now he could. He read voraciously in mystical writings—George Fox, the German and Dutch mystics, and others—and checked his own experience.

Similarly, the horizons of his encounter with Reality expanded. He no longer looked only to the philosophers and scholars. His interest in oriental thought, of course, went on growing. But during a journey to Germany in the spring of 1938 he discovered truth in the lives of *ordinary* saints. From Nuremberg in August he wrote Lael:

> I have never had such a sense of *being led* as in the past few days. I have stayed with a family, the man of which is like a little child, simple-minded (perhaps from war injuries), but of amazing simple trust and devotion. The sophisticated modernism and superior attitudes we meet are all gone, here, in these groups, and one seems to feel the bare knuckles of reality, or the enveloping power of love, the Love of God.[17]

He alluded in the same letter to a simple Frenchman as "one of the most profound mystics I have met."

Thomas Kelly laid hold on Quakerism, indeed, on Christianity, in a new way. He perceived the true meaning of incarnation. "The Life of God must be actualized *in men, in life, in lives*," he explained in a letter to his family. "And in such lives there is born the way of *Redemption*."[18] His discovery intensified his concern to share what he had laid hold of, or what had laid hold of him. He pleaded with Lael to "come with" him in embracing a life of childlike trust and simplicity. His visit to Germany as war clouds hovered ominously on the horizon heightened his eagerness to see the formation of "The Blessed Community."

But religious commitment is not all euphoria, discovery of new truth, or exaltation to the sublime. If genuine, it has to mean something in the life of everyday. And that is where Thomas Kelly concentrated his attention after returning from Germany in September. He, like other saints, experienced periods of "dryness." His intense interest in mystical experience notwithstanding, he explained to a friend in September 1939 that "the significant factor in religion is a permanent attitude of the will, rather than a less permanent, more variable state of exaltation."[19]

At Haverford, Kelly continued to develop Eastern studies and sustained a desire to go to the Orient, especially China. He studied Sanskrit at the University of Pennsylvania and Chinese on his own. But the effects of experience were to be seen in all his activities and writings. He cultivated his family life more diligently. He assembled a small "gang" of students on a weekly basis in his home to study the classics of Christian devotion: Augustine's *Confessions, The Imitation of Christ,* and many others. In December 1940 Eugene Exman, editor for Harper's, wrote to ask him for a book on devotional practice. The very day Kelly replied, January 17, 1941, he suffered a massive heart attack and died. The proposed book was put together by his friend and colleague Douglas Steere.

Death came too soon for Thomas Kelly, but not too soon for him to leave his profound testimony. He described his magnificent discovery beautifully in "Holy Obedience":

> It is an overwhelming experience to fall into the hands of the living God, to be invaded to the depths of one's being by His presence, to be, without warning, wholly uprooted from all earth-born securities and assurances, and to be blown by a tempest of unbelievable power which leaves one's old proud self utterly, utterly defenseless, until one cries, "All Thy waves and thy billows are gone over me" (Ps. xlii. 7). Then is the soul swept into a Loving Centre of ineffable sweetness, where calm and unspeakable peace and ravishing joy steal over one. . . .

> One emerges from such soul-shaking, Love-invaded times into more normal states of consciousness. But one knows ever after that the Eternal Lover of the world, the Hound of Heaven, is utterly, utterly real, and that life must henceforth be forever determined by that Real. Like Saint Augustine one asks not for greater certainty of God but only for more steadfastness in Him. There, beyond, in Him is the true Centre, and we are reduced, as it were, to nothing, for He is all.

Need we say more?

—E. GLENN HINSON

NOTES

1. In Richard M. Kelly, *Thomas Kelly: A Biography* (New York: Harper & Row, Publishers, 1966), p. 105.

2. "A Biographical Memoir," in *A Testament of Devotion* (New York: Harper & Row, Publishers, 1941), p. 1.

3. Letter to Lael, Lois, and Richard Kelly, from France, August 16, 1938; in Richard Kelly, op. cit., p. 102.

4. Richard Kelly, op. cit., p. 53.

5. In ibid., p. 54.

6. In ibid., p. 54.

7. In ibid., p. 56.

8. In ibid., p. 58.

9. In ibid., p. 59.

10. Ibid., p. 60.

11. In ibid., p. 82.

12. In ibid., p. 85.

13. In ibid., p. 88.

14. In ibid., p. 96.

15. Ibid., pp. 91–92.

16. Ibid., p. 75.

17. In ibid., pp. 105–6.

18. In ibid., p. 101.

19. In ibid., p. 111.

HOLY OBEDIENCE

Out in front of us is the drama of men and of nations, seething, struggling, labouring, dying. Upon this tragic drama in these days our eyes are all set in anxious watchfulness and in prayer. But within the silences of the souls of men an eternal drama is ever being enacted, in these days as well as in others. And on the outcome of this inner drama rests, ultimately, the outer pageant of history. It is the drama of the Hound of Heaven baying relentlessly upon the track of man. It is the drama of the lost sheep wandering in the wilderness, restless and lonely, feebly searching, while over the hills comes the wiser Shepherd. For His is a shepherd's heart, and He is restless until He holds His sheep in His arms. It is the drama of the Eternal Father drawing the prodigal home unto Himself, where there is bread enough and to spare. It is the drama of the Double Search, as Rufus Jones calls it. And always its chief actor is—the Eternal God of Love.

It is to one strand in this inner drama, one scene, where the Shepherd has found His sheep, that I would direct you. It is the life of absolute and complete and holy obedience to the voice of the Shepherd. But ever throughout the account the accent will be laid upon God, God the initiator, God the aggressor, God the seeker, God the stirrer into life, God the ground of our obedience, God the giver of the power to become children of God.

I. The Nature of Holy Obedience

Meister Eckhart wrote: "There are plenty to follow our Lord halfway, but not the other half. They will give up possessions, friends and honours, but it touches them too closely to disown themselves." It is just this astonishing life which is willing to follow Him the other half, sincerely to disown itself, this life which intends complete obedience, without any reservations, that I would propose to you in all humility, in all boldness, in all seriousness. I mean this literally, utterly, completely, and I mean it for you and for me—commit your lives in unreserved obedience to Him.

If you don't realize the revolutionary explosiveness of this proposal you don't understand what I mean. Only now and then comes a man or a woman who, like John Woolman or Francis of Assisi, is willing to be utterly obedient, to go the other half, to follow God's faintest whisper. But when such a commitment comes in a human life, God breaks through, miracles are wrought, world-renewing divine forces are released, history changes. There is nothing more important now than to have the human race endowed with just such committed lives. Now is not time to say, "Lo, here. Lo, there." Now is the time to say, "Thou art the man." To this extraordinary life I call you—or He calls you through me—not as a lovely ideal, a charming pattern to aim at hopefully, but as a serious, concrete programme of life, to be lived here and now, in industrial America, by you and by me.

This is something wholly different from mild, conventional religion which, with respectable skirts held back by dainty fingers, anxiously tries to fish the world out of the mudhole of its own selfishness. Our churches, our meeting houses are full of such respectable and amiable people. We have plenty of Quakers to follow God the first half of the way. Many of us have become as mildly and as conventionally religious as were the church folk of three centuries ago, against whose mildness and mediocrity and passionlessness George Fox and his followers flung themselves with all the passion of a glorious and a new discovery and with all the energy of dedicated lives. In some, says William James, religion exists as a dull habit, in others as an acute fever. Religion as a dull habit is not that for which Christ lived and died.

There is a degree of holy and complete obedience and of joyful self-renunciation and of sensitive listening that is breath-taking. Difference of degree passes over into utter difference of kind, when one tries to follow Him the second half. Jesus put this pointedly when He said, "Ye must be born again" (John iii. 3), and Paul knew it: "If any man is in Christ, he is a new creature" (2 Cor. v. 17).

George Fox as a youth was religious enough to meet all earthly standards and was even proposed as a student for the ministry. But the insatiable God-hunger in him drove him from such mediocrity into a passionate quest for the real whole-wheat Bread of Life. Sensible relatives told him to settle down and get married. Thinking him crazy, they took him to a doctor to have his blood let—the equivalent of being taken to a psychiatrist in these days, as are modern conscientious objectors to war in Belgium and France. Parents, if some of your children are seized with this imperative God-hunger, don't tell them to snap out of it and get a job, but carry them patiently in your love, or at least keep hands off and let the holy work of God proceed in their souls. Young people, you who have in you the stirrings of perfection, the sweet, sweet rapture of God Himself within you, be faithful to Him until the last lingering bit of self is surrendered and you are wholly God-possessed.

The life that intends to be wholly obedient, wholly submissive, wholly listening, is astonishing in its completeness. Its joys are ravishing, its peace profound, its humility the deepest, its power world-shaking, its love enveloping, its simplicity that of a trusting child. It is the life and power in which the prophets and apostles lived. It is the life and power of Jesus of Nazareth, who knew that "when thine eye is single thy whole body is full of light" (Luke xi. 34). It is the life and power of the apostle Paul, who resolved not to know anything among men save Jesus Christ and Him crucified. It is the life and power of Saint Francis, that little poor man of God who came nearer to re-living the life of Jesus than has any other man on earth. It is the life and power of George Fox and of Isaac and Mary Penington. It is the life and power and utter obedience of John Woolman who decided, he says, "to place my whole trust in God," to "act on an inner Principle of Virtue, and pursue worldly business no farther than as Truth opened my way therein." It is the life and power of myriads of unknown saints through the ages. It is the life and power of some people now in this room who smile knowingly as I speak. And it is a life and power that can break forth in this tottering Western culture and return the Church to its rightful life as a fellowship of creative, heaven-led souls.

II. Gateways into Holy Obedience

In considering one gateway into this life of holy obedience, let us dare to venture together into the inner sanctuary of the soul, where

God meets man in awful immediacy. There is an indelicacy in too-ready speech. Paul felt it unlawful to speak of the things of the third heaven. But there is also a false reticence, as if these things were one's own work and one's own possession, about which we should modestly keep quiet, whereas they are wholly God's amazing work and we are nothing, mere passive receivers. "The lion hath roared, who can but tremble? The voice of Jehovah hath spoken, who can but prophesy?" (Amos iii. 8).

Some men come into holy obedience through the gateway of profound mystical experience.

It is an overwhelming experience to fall into the hands of the living God, to be invaded to the depths of one's being by His presence, to be, without warning, wholly uprooted from all earth-born securities and assurances, and to be blown by a tempest of unbelievable power which leaves one's old proud self utterly, utterly defenseless, until one cries, "All Thy waves and thy billows are gone over me" (Ps. xlii. 7). Then is the soul swept into a Loving Center of ineffable sweetness, where calm and unspeakable peace and ravishing joy steal over one. And one knows now why Pascal wrote, in the center of his greatest moment, the single word, "Fire." There stands the world of struggling, sinful, earth-blinded men and nations, of plants and animals and wheeling stars of heaven, all new, all lapped in the tender, persuading Love at the Center. There stand the saints of the ages, their hearts open to view, and lo, their hearts are our heart and their hearts are the heart of the Eternal One. In awful solemnity the Holy One is over all and in all, exquisitely loving, infinitely patient, tenderly smiling. Marks of glory are upon all things, and the marks are cruciform and blood-stained. And one sighs, like the convinced Thomas of old, "My Lord and my God" (John xx. 28). Dare one lift one's eyes and look? Nay, whither can one look and not see Him? For field and stream and teeming streets are full of Him. Yet as Moses knew, no man can look on God and live—live as his old self. Death comes, blessed death, death of one's alienating will. And one knows what Paul meant when he wrote, "The life which I now live in the flesh I live by the faith of the Son of God" (Gal. ii. 20).

One emerges from such soul-shaking, Love-invaded times into more normal states of consciousness. But one knows ever after that the Eternal Lover of the world, the Hound of Heaven, is utterly, utterly real, and that life must henceforth be forever determined by that Real. Like Saint Augustine one asks not for greater certainty of God but only for more steadfastness in Him. There, beyond, in Him is the true Center, and we are reduced, as it were, to nothing, for He is all.

Is religion subjective? Nay, its soul is in objectivity, in an Other whose Life is our true Life, whose Love is our love, whose Joy is our joy, whose Peace is our peace, whose burdens are our burdens, whose Will is our will. Self is emptied into God, and God in-fills it. In glad, amazed humility we cast on Him our little lives in trusting obedience, in erect, serene, and smiling joy. And we say, with a writer of Psalms, "Lo, I come: in the book of the law it is written of me, I delight to do Thy will, O my God" (Ps. xl. 7–8). For nothing else in all of heaven or earth counts so much as His will, His slightest wish, His faintest breathing. And holy obedience sets in, sensitive as a shadow, obedient as a shadow, selfless as a shadow. Not reluctantly but with ardour one longs to follow Him the second half. Gladly, urgently, promptly one leaps to do His bidding, ready to run and not be weary and to walk and not faint.

Do not mistake me. Our interest just now is in the life of complete obedience to God, not in amazing revelations of His glory graciously granted only to some. Yet the amazing experiences of the mystics leave a permanent residue, a God-subdued, a God-possessed will. States of consciousness are fluctuating. The vision fades. But holy and listening and alert obedience remains, as the core and kernel of a God-intoxicated life, as the abiding pattern of sober, workaday living. And some are led into the state of complete obedience by this well-nigh passive route, wherein God alone seems to be the actor and we seem to be wholly acted upon. And our wills are melted and dissolved and made pliant, being firmly fixed in Him, and He wills in us.

But in contrast to this passive route to complete obedience most people must follow what Jean-Nicholas Grou calls the active way, wherein we must struggle and, like Jacob of old, wrestle with the angel until the morning dawns, the active way wherein the will must be subjected bit by bit, piecemeal and progressively, to the divine Will.

But the first step to the obedience of the second half is the flaming vision of the wonder of such a life, a vision which comes occasionally to us all, through biographies of the saints, through the journals of Fox and early Friends, through a life lived before our eyes, through a haunting verse of the Psalms—"Whom have I in heaven but Thee? And there is none upon earth that I desire beside Thee" (Ps. lxxiii. 25)—through meditation upon the amazing life and death of Jesus, through a flash of illumination or, in Fox's language, a great opening. But whatever the earthly history of this moment of charm, this vision of an absolutely holy life is, I am convinced, the invading, urging, inviting, persuading work of the Eternal One. It is curious that modern psychology cannot account wholly for flashes of insight of any kind, sacred or secular. It is as if a fountain of creative Mind were welling up, bubbling to expression within prepared spirits. There is an infinite fountain of lifting power, pressing within us, luring us by dazzling visions, and we can only say, The creative God comes into our souls. An increment of infinity is about us. Holy is imagination, the gateway of Reality into our hearts. The Hound of Heaven is on our track, the God of Love is wooing us to His Holy life.

Once having the vision, the second step to holy obedience is this: Begin where you are. Obey now. Use what little obedience you are capable of, even if it be like a grain of mustard seed. Begin where you are. Live this present moment, this present hour as you now sit in your seats, in utter, utter submission and openness toward Him. Listen outwardly to these words, but within, behind the scenes, in the deeper levels of your lives where you are all alone with God the Loving Eternal One, keep up a silent prayer. "Open thou my life. Guide my thoughts where I dare not let them go. But Thou darest. Thy will be done." Walk on the streets and chat with your friends, offering yourselves in continuous obedience. I find this internal continuous prayer life absolutely essential. It can be carried on day and night, in the thick of business, in home and school. Such prayer of submission can be so simple. It is well to use a single sentence, repeated over and over and over again, such as this: "Be Thou my will. Be Thou my will," or "I open all before Thee. I open all before Thee," or "See earth through heaven. See earth through heaven." This hidden prayer life can pass, in time, beyond words and phrases into mere ejaculations, "My God, my God, my Holy One, my Love," or into the adoration of the Upanishad, "O Wonderful, O Wonderful, O Wonderful." Words may cease and one stands and walks and sits and lies in wordless attitudes of adoration and submission and rejoicing and exultation and glory.

And the third step in holy obedience, or a counsel, is this: If you slip and stumble and forget God for an hour, and assert your old proud self, and rely upon your own clever wisdom, don't spend too much time in anguished regrets and self-accusations but begin again, just where you are.

Yet a fourth consideration in holy obedience is this: Don't grit your teeth and clench your fists and say, "I will! I will!" Relax. Take hands off. Submit yourself to God. Learn to live in the passive voice—a hard saying for Americans—and let life be willed through you. For "I will" spells not obedience.

III. Humility and Holiness

The fruits of holy obedience are many. But two are so closely linked together that they can scarcely be treated separately. They are the passion for personal holiness and the sense of utter humility. God inflames the soul with a craving for absolute purity. But He, in His glorious otherness, empties us of ourselves in order that He may become all.

Humility does not rest, in final count, upon bafflement and discouragement and self-disgust at our shabby lives, a brow-beaten, dog-slinking attitude. It rests upon the disclosure of the consummate wonder of God, upon finding that only God counts, that all our own self-originated intentions are works of straw. And so in lowly humility we must stick close to the Root and count our own powers as nothing except as they are enslaved in His power.

But O how slick and weasel-like is self-pride! Our learnedness creeps into our sermons with a clever quotation which adds nothing to God's glory, but a bit to our own. Our cleverness in business competition earns as much self-flattery as does the possession of the money itself. Our desire to be known and approved by others, to have heads nod approvingly about us behind our backs, and flattering murmurs which we can occasionally overhear, confirms the discernment in Alfred Adler's elevation of the superiority motive. Our status as "weighty Friends" gives us secret pleasures which we scarcely own to ourselves, yet thrive upon. Yes, even pride in our own humility is one of the devil's own tricks.

But humility rests upon a holy blindedness, like the blindedness of him who looks steadily into the sun. For wherever he turns his eyes on earth, there he sees only the sun. The God-blinded soul sees naught of self, naught of personal degradation or of personal eminence, but only the Holy Will working impersonally through him, through others, as one objective Life and Power. But what trinkets we have sought after in life, the pursuit of what petty trifles has wasted our years as we have ministered to the enhancement of our own little selves! And what needless anguishes we have suffered because our little selves were defeated, were not flattered, were not cozened and petted! But the blinding God blots out this self and gives humility and true selfhood as wholly full of Him. For as He gives obedience so He graciously gives to us what measure of humility we will accept. Even that is not our own, but His who also gives us obedience. But the humility of the God-blinded soul endures only so long as we look steadily at the Sun. Growth in humility is a measure of our growth in the habit of the Godward-directed mind. And he only is near to God who is exceedingly humble. The last depths of holy and voluntary poverty are not in financial poverty, important as that is; they are in poverty of spirit, in meekness and lowliness of soul.

Explore the depths of humility, not with your intellects but with your lives, lived in prayer of humble obedience. And there you will find that humility is not merely a human virtue. For there is a humility that is in God Himself. Be ye humble as God is humble. For love and humility walk hand in hand, in God as well as in man.

But there is something about deepest humility which makes men bold. For utter obedience is self-forgetful obedience. No longer do we hesitate and shuffle and apologize because, say we, we are weak, lowly creatures and the world is a pack of snarling wolves among whom we are sent as sheep by the Shepherd (Matt. x. 16). I must confess that, on human judgment, the world tasks we face are appalling—well-nigh hopeless. Only the inner vision of God, only the God-blindedness of unreservedly dedicated souls, only the utterly humble ones can bow and break the raging pride of a power-mad world. But self-renunciation means God-possession, the being possessed by God. Out of utter humility and self-forgetfulness comes the thunder of the prophets, "Thus saith the Lord." High station and low are levelled before Him. Be not fooled by the world's power. Imposing institutions of war and imperialism and greed are wholly vulnerable for they, and we, are forever in the hands of a conquering God. These are not cheap and hasty words. The high and noble adventures of faith can in our truest moments be seen as no adventures at all, but certainties. And if we live in complete humility in God we can smile in patient assurance as we work. Will you be wise enough and humble enough to be little fools of God? For who can finally stay His power? Who can resist His persuading love? Truly says Saint Augustine, "There is something in humility which raiseth the heart upward." And John Woolman says, "Now I find that in the pure obedience the mind learns contentment, in appearing weak and foolish to the wisdom which is of the World; and in these lowly labours, they who stand in a low place, rightly exercised under the Cross, will find nourishment."

But God inflames the soul with a burning craving for absolute purity. One burns for complete innocency and holiness of personal life. No man can look on God and live, live in his own faults, live in the shadow of the least self-deceit, live in harm toward His least creatures, whether man or bird or beast or creeping thing. The blinding purity of God in Christ, how captivating, how alluring, how compelling it is! The pure in heart shall see God? More, they who see God shall cry out to become pure in heart, even as He is pure, with all the energy of their souls.

This has been an astonishing and unexpected element for me. In this day of concern for social righteousness it sounds like a throwback to medieval ideals of saintliness and soul-combing. Our religious heroes of these social gospel days sit before a battery of telephones, with full office equipment, with telegraph lines to Washington and London and Tokyo and Berlin. And this is needed. Yet there is in the experience of God this insistent, imperative, glorious yearning—the craving for complete spotlessness of the inner self before Him.

No average goodness will do, no measuring of our lives by our fellows, but only a relentless, inexorable divine standard. No relatives suffice; only absolutes satisfy the soul committed to holy obedience. Absolute honesty, absolute gentleness, absolute self-control, unwearied patience and thoughtfulness in the midst of the ravelling friction of home and office and school and shop. It is said that the ermine can be trapped by surrounding it with a circle of filth. It will die before it will sully its snowy coat. Have we been led astray by our fears, by the fear of saccharine sweetness and light? By the dangers of fanatical scrupulousness and self-inspection and halo-hunting? By the ideal of a back-slapping recommendation of religion by showing we were good fellows after all? By the fear of quietism and of that monastic retreat from the world of men's needs which we associate with medieval passion for holiness of life? Nay, tread not so far from the chasm that you fall into the ditch on the other side. Boldly must we risk the dangers which lie along the margins of excess, if we would live the life of the second half. For the life of obedience is a holy life, a separated life, a renounced life, cut off from worldly compromises, distinct, heaven-dedicated in the midst of men, stainless as the snows upon the mountain tops.

He who walks in obedience, following God the second half, living the life of inner prayer of submission and exultation, on him God's holiness takes hold as a mastering passion of life. Yet ever he cries out in abysmal sincerity, "I am the blackest of all the sinners of the earth. I am a man of unclean lips, for mine eyes have seen the King, Jehovah of Hosts." For humility and holiness are twins in the astonishing birth of obedience in the heart of men. So God draws unworthy us, in loving tenderness, up into fellowship with His glorious self.

IV. Entrance into Suffering

Another fruit of holy obedience is entrance into suffering. I would not magnify joy and rapture, although they are unspeakably great in the committed life. For joy and rapture need no advocates. But we shrink from suffering and can easily call all suffering an evil thing. Yet we live in an epoch of tragic sorrows, when man is adding to the crueller forces of nature such blasphemous horrors as drag soul as well as body into hell. And holy obedience must walk in this world, not aloof and preoccupied, but stained with sorrow's travail.

Nor is the God-blinded soul given blissful oblivion but, rather, excruciatingly sensitive eyesight toward the world of men. The sources of suffering for the tendered soul are infinitely multiplied, well-nigh beyond all endurance. Ponder this paradox in religious experience: "Nothing matters; everything matters." I recently had an unforgettable hour with a Hindu monk. He knew the secret of this paradox which we discussed together: "Nothing matters; everything matters." It is a key of entrance into suffering. He who knows only one-half of the paradox can never enter that door of mystery and survive.

There is a lusty, adolescent way of thought among us which over-simplifies the question of suffering. It merely says, "Let us remove it." And some suffering can, through more suffering, be removed. But there is an inexorable residue which confronts you and me and the blighted souls of Europe and China and the Near East and India, awful, unremovable in a lifetime, withering all souls not genuinely rooted in Eternity itself. The Germans call it Schicksal or Destiny. Under this word they gather all the vast forces of nature and disease and the convulsive upheavals of social life which sweep them along, as individuals, like debris in a raging flood, into an unknown end. Those who are not prepared by the inner certitude of Job, "I know that my Avenger liveth" (Job xix. 25), must perish in the flood.

One returns from Europe with the sound of weeping in one's ears, in order to say, "Don't be deceived. You must face Destiny. Preparation is only possible now. Don't be fooled by your sunny skies. When the rains descend and the floods come and the winds blow and beat upon your house, your private dwelling, your own family, your own fair hopes, your own strong muscles, your own body, your own soul itself, then it is well-nigh too late to build a house. You can only go inside what house you have and pray that it is founded upon the Rock. Be not deceived by distance in time or space, or the false security of a bank account and an automobile and good health and willing hands to work. Thousands, perhaps millions as good as you have had all these things and are perishing in body, worse still, in soul today."

An awful solemnity is upon the earth, for the last vestige of earthly security is gone. It has always been gone, and religion has always said so, but we haven't believed it. And some of us Quakers are not yet undeceived, and childishly expect our little cushions for our little bodies, in a world inflamed with untold ulcers. Be not fooled by the pleasantness of the Main Line life, and the niceness of Germantown existence, and the quiet coolness of your well-furnished homes. For the plagues of Egypt are upon the world, entering hovel and palace, and there is no escape for you or for me. There is an inexorable amount of suffering in all life, blind, aching, unremovable, not new but only terribly intensified in these days.

One comes back from Europe aghast at having seen how lives as graciously cultured as ours, but rooted only in time and property and reputations, and self-deluded by a mild veneer of religious respectability but unprepared by the amazing life of commitment to the Eternal in holy obedience, are now doomed to hopeless, hopeless despair. For if you will accept as normal life only what you can understand, then you will try only to expel the dull, dead weight of Destiny, of inevitable suffering which is a part of normal life, and never come to terms with it or fit your soul to the collar and bear the burden of your suffering which must be borne by you, or enter into the divine education and drastic discipline of sorrow, or rise radiant in the sacrament of pain.

One comes back from Europe to plead with you, you here in these seats, you my pleasant but often easy-living friends, to open your lives to such a baptism of Eternity now as turns this world of tumbling change into a wilderness in your eyes and fortifies you with an unshakable peace that passes all understanding and endures all earthly shocks without soul-destroying rebelliousness. Then and then only can we, weaned from earth, and committed wholly to God alone, hope to become voices crying in this wilderness of Philadelphia and London, "Prepare ye the way of the Lord. Make straight in this desert a highway for our God" (Isa. xl. 3). These are old truths. But now is no time for enticing novelties but for a return to the everlasting truths of life and suffering and Eternity and unreserved commitment to Him who is over all.

The heart is stretched through suffering, and enlarged. But O the agony of this enlarging of the heart, that one may be prepared to enter into the anguish of others! Yet the way of holy obedience leads out from the heart of God and extends through the Valley of the Shadow.

But there is also removable suffering, yet such as yields only to years of toil and fatigue and unconquerable faith and perchance only to death itself. The Cross as dogma is painless speculation; the

Cross as lived suffering is anguish and glory. Yet God, out of the pattern of His own heart, has planted the Cross along the road of holy obedience. And He enacts in the hearts of those He loves the miracle of willingness to welcome suffering and to know it for what it is—the final seal of His gracious love. I dare not urge you to your Cross. But He, more powerfully, speaks within you and me, to our truest moments, and disquiets us with the world's needs. By inner persuasions He draws us to a few very definite tasks, our tasks, God's burdened heart particularizing His burdens in us. And He gives us the royal blindness of faith, and the seeing eye of the sensitized soul, and the grace of unflinching obedience. Then we see that nothing matters, and that everything matters, and that this my task matters for me and for my fellow men and for Eternity. And if we be utterly humble we may be given strength to be obedient even unto death, yea the death of the Cross.

In my deepest heart I know that some of us have to face our comfortable, self-oriented lives all over again. The times are too tragic, God's sorrow is too great, man's night is too dark, the Cross is too glorious for us to live as we have lived, in anything short of holy obedience. It may or it may not mean change in geography, in profession, in wealth, in earthly security. It does mean this: Some of us will have to enter upon a vow of renunciation and of dedication to the "Eternal Internal" which is as complete and as irrevocable as was the vow of the monk of the Middle Ages. Little groups of such utterly dedicated souls, knowing one another in Divine Fellowship, must take an irrevocable vow to live in this world yet not of this world, Franciscans of the Third Order, and if it be His will, kindle again the embers of faith in the midst of a secular world. Our meetings were meant to be such groups, but now too many of them are dulled and cooled and flooded by the secular. But within our meetings such inner bands of men and women, internally set apart, living by a vow of perpetual obedience to the Inner Voice, in the world yet not of the world, ready to go the second half, obedient as a shadow, sensitive as a shadow, selfless as a shadow—such bands of humble prophets can recreate the Society of Friends and the Christian church and shake the countryside for ten miles around.

V. *Simplicity*

The last fruit of holy obedience is the simplicity of the trusting child, the simplicity of the children of God. It is the simplicity which lies beyond complexity. It is the naïveté which is the yonder side of sophistication. It is the beginning of spiritual maturity, which comes after the awkward age of religious busyness for the Kingdom of God—yet how many are caught, and arrested in development, within this adolescent development of the soul's growth! The mark of this simplified life is radiant joy. It lives in the Fellowship of the Transfigured Face. Knowing sorrow to the depths it does not agonize and fret and strain, but in serene, unhurried calm it walks in time with the joy and assurance of Eternity. Knowing fully the complexity of men's problems it cuts through to the Love of God and ever cleaves to Him. Like the mercy of Shakespeare, "'tis mightiest in the mightiest." But it binds all obedient souls together in the fellowship of humility and simple adoration of Him who is all in all.

I have in mind something deeper than the simplification of our external programmes, our absurdly crowded calendars of appointments through which so many pantingly and frantically gasp. These do become simplified in holy obedience, and the poise and peace we have been missing can really be found. But there is a deeper, an internal simplification of the whole of one's personality, stilled, tranquil, in childlike trust listening ever to Eternity's whisper, walking with a smile into the dark.

This amazing simplification comes when we "center down," when life is lived with singleness of eye, from a holy Center where the breath and stillness of Eternity are heavy upon us and we are wholly yielded to Him. Some of you know this holy, re-creating Center of eternal peace and joy and live in it day and night. Some of you may see it over the margin and wistfully long to slip into that amazing Center where the soul is at home with God. Be very faithful to that wistful longing. It is the Eternal Goodness calling you to return Home, to feed upon green pastures and walk beside still waters and live in the peace of the Shepherd's presence. It is the life beyond fevered strain. We are called beyond strain, to peace and power and joy and love and thorough abandonment of self. We are called to put our hands trustingly in His hand and walk the holy way, in no anxiety assuredly resting in Him.

Douglas Steere wisely says that true religion often appears to be the enemy of the moralist. For religion cuts across the fine distinctions between the several virtues and gathers all virtues into the one supreme quality of love. The wholly obedient life is mastered and unified and simplified and gathered up into the love of God and it lives and walks among men in the perpetual flame of that radiant love. For the simplified man loves God with all his heart and mind and soul and strength and abides trustingly in that love. Then indeed do we love our neighbours. And the Fellowship of the Horny Hands is identical with the Fellowship of the Transfigured Face, in this Mary-Martha life.

In this day when the burdens of humanity press so heavily upon us I would begin not first with techniques of service but with the most "Serious Call to a Devout Life," a life of such humble obedience to the Inner Voice as we have scarcely dared to dream. Hasten unto Him who calls you in the silences of your heart. The Hound of Heaven is ever near us, the voice of the Shepherd is calling us home. Too long have we lingered in double-minded obedience and dared not the certainties of His love. For Him do ye seek, all ye pearl merchants. He is "the food of grown men." Hasten unto Him who is the chief actor of the drama of time and Eternity. It is not too late to love Him utterly and obey Him implicitly and be baptized with the power of the apostolic life. Hear the words of Saint Augustine, as he rued his delay of commitment to Him. "Too late loved I Thee, O Thou beauty of ancient days, yet ever new! Too late I loved Thee! And behold, Thou wert within and I abroad, and there I searched for Thee; deformed I, plunging amid those fair forms which Thou hadst made. Thou wert with me but I was not with Thee. Things held me far from Thee which, unless they were in Thee, were not at all. Thou calledst and shoutedst, and burstedst my deafness. Thou flashedst, shonest, and scattered my blindness. Thou breathedst odours, and I drew in breath and pant for Thee. I tasted, and hunger and thirst. Thou touchedst me and I burned for Thy peace. When I shall with my whole soul cleave to Thee, I shall nowhere have sorrow or labour, and my life shall live as wholly full of Thee."

THE BLESSED COMMUNITY

When we are drowned in the overwhelming seas of the love of God, we find ourselves in a new and particular relation to a few of our fellows. The relation is so surprising and so rich that we despair of finding a word glorious enough and weighty enough to name it. The word *Fellowship* is discovered, but the word is pale and thin in comparison with the rich volume and luminous bulk and warmth of the experience which it would designate. For a new kind of life-sharing and of love has arisen of which we had had only dim hints before. Are these the bonds of love which knit together the early Christians, the very warp and woof of the Kingdom of God? In glad amazement and wonder we enter upon a relationship which we had not known the world contained for the sons of men. Why should such bounty be given to unworthy men like ourselves?

By no means is every one of our friends seen in this new and special light. A wholly new alignment of our personal relations appears. Some men and women whom we have never known before, or whom we have noticed only as a dim background for our more special friendships, suddenly loom large, step forward in our attention as men and women whom we now know to the depths. Our earlier conversations with these persons may have been few and brief, but now we know them, as it were, from within. For we discern that their lives are already down within that Center which has found us. And we hunger for their fellowship, with a profound, insistent craving which will not be denied.

Other acquaintances recede in significance; we know now that our relationships with them have always been nearer the surface of life. Many years of happy comradeship and common adventures we may have had together, but now we know that, at bottom, we have never been together in the deep silences of the Center, and that we never can be together, there where the light of Eternity shines still and bright. For until they, too, have become wholly God-enthralled, Light-centered, they can be only good acquaintances with whom we pass the time of day. A yearning over them may set in, because of their dimness of vision, but the eye-to-eye relationship of love which binds together those who live in the Center is reserved for a smaller number. Drastically and re-creatively, Fellowship searches friendships, burning, dissolving, ennobling, transfiguring them in Heaven's glowing fire.

Not only do our daily friendships become realigned; our religious friends are also seen anew. Many impressions of worth are confirmed, others are reversed. Some of the most active church leaders, well-known for their executive efficiency, people we have always admired, are shown, in the X-ray light of Eternity, to be agitated, half-committed, wistful, self-placating seekers, to whom the poise and serenity of the Everlasting have never come. The inexhaustible self-giving of others of our religious acquaintances we now understand, for the Eternal Love kindles an ardent and persistent readiness to do all things for, as well as through, Christ who strengthens us. In some we regret a well-intentioned, but feverish over-busyness, not completely grounded in the depths of peace, and we wish they would not blur the beauty of their souls by fast motion. Others, who may not have been effective speakers or weighty financiers or charming conversationalists or members of prominent families are found to be men and women on whom the dews of heaven have fallen indeed, who live continuously in the Center and who, in mature appreciation, understand our leaping heart and unbounded enthusiasm for God. And although they are not commissioned to any earthly office, yet they welcome us authoritatively into the Fellowship of Love.

"See how these Christians love one another" might well have been a spontaneous exclamation in the days of the apostles. The Holy Fellowship, the Blessed Community has always astonished those who stood without it. The sharing of physical goods in the primitive church is only an outcropping of a profoundly deeper sharing of a Life, the base and center of which is obscured to those who are still oriented about self rather than about God. To others, tragic to say, the very existence of such a Fellowship within a common Life and Love is unknown and unguessed. In its place, psychological and humanistic views of the essential sociality and gregariousness of man seek to provide a social theory of church membership. From these views spring church programs of mere sociability and social contacts. The precious word *Fellowship* becomes identified with a purely horizontal relation of man to man, not with that horizontal-vertical relationship of man to man *in God*.

But every period of profound re-discovery of God's joyous immediacy is a period of emergence of this amazing group inter-knittedness of God-enthralled men and women who know one another *in Him*. It appeared in vivid form among the early Friends. The early days of the Evangelical movement showed the same bondedness in love. The disclosure of God normally brings the disclosure of the Fellowship. We don't create it deliberately; we find it and we find ourselves increasingly within it as we find ourselves increasingly within Him. It is the holy matrix of "the communion of the saints," the body of Christ which is His church. William C. Braithwaite says, in the Rowntree Series, that it was a tragic day when the Quakers ceased to be a Fellowship and became a Society of Friends. Yet ever within that Society, and ever within the Christian church, has existed the Holy Fellowship, the Blessed Community, an *ekklesiola in ekklesia*, a little church within the church.

Yet still more astonishing is the Holy Fellowship, the Blessed Community, to those who are within it. Yet can one be surprised at being *at home?* In wonder and awe we find ourselves already interknit within unofficial groups of kindred souls. A "chance" conversation comes, and in a few moments we know that we have found and have been found by another member of the Blessed Community. Sometimes we are thus suddenly knit together in the bonds of a love far faster than those of many years' acquaintance. In unbounded eagerness we seek for more such fellowship, and wonder at the apparent lethargy of mere "members."

In the Fellowship cultural and educational and national and racial differences are leveled. Unlettered men are at ease with the truly humble scholar who lives in the Life, and the scholar listens with joy and openness to the precious experiences of God's dealing with the workingman. We find men with chilly theologies but with glowing hearts. We overleap the boundaries of church membership and find Lutherans and Roman Catholics, Jews and Christians, within the Fellowship. We re-read the poets and the saints, and the Fellowship is enlarged. With urgent hunger we read the Scriptures, with no thought of pious exercise, but in order to find more friends for the soul. We brush past our historical learning in the Scriptures, to seize upon those writers who lived in the Center, in the Life and in the Power. Particularly does devotional literature become illuminated, for the *Imitation of Christ,* and Augustine's *Confessions,* and Brother Lawrence's *Practice of the Presence of God* speak the language of the souls who live at the Center. Time telescopes and vanishes, centuries and creeds are overleaped. The incident of death puts no boundaries to the Blessed Community, wherein men live and love and work and pray in that Life and Power which gave forth the Scriptures. And we wonder and grieve at the overwhelmingly heady preoccupation of religious people with problems, problems, unless they have first come into the Fellowship of the Light.

The final grounds of holy Fellowship are in God. Lives immersed and drowned in God are drowned in love, and know one another in Him, and know one another in love. God is the medium, the matrix, the focus, the solvent. As Meister Eckhart suggests, he who is wholly surrounded by God, enveloped by God, clothed with God, glowing in selfless love toward Him—such a man no one can touch except he touch God also. Such lives have a common meeting-point; they live in a common joyous enslavement. They go back into a single Center where they are at home with Him and with one another. It is as if every soul had a final base, and that final base of every soul is one single Holy Ground, shared in by all. Persons in the Fellowship are related to one another through Him, as all mountains go down into the same earth. They get at one another through Him. He is actively moving in all, co-ordinating those who are pliant to His will and suffusing them all with His glory and His joy.

The relation of each to all, through God, is real, objective, existential. It is an eternal relationship which is shared in by every stick and stone and bird and beast and saint and sinner of the universe. On all the wooing love of God falls urgently, persuadingly. But he who, having will, yields to the loving urgency of that Life which knocks at his heart, is entered and possessed and transformed and transfigured. The scales fall from his eyes when he is given to eat of the tree of knowledge, the fruit of which is indeed for the healing of the nations, and he knows himself and his fellows as comrades in Eden, where God walks with them in the cool of the day. As there is a mysterious many-ing of God, as He pours Himself forth into the universe, so there is a one-ing of those souls who find their way back to Him who is their home. And these are in the Holy Fellowship, the Blessed Community, of whom God is the head.

This community of life and love is far deeper than current views based upon modern logic would suppose. Logic finds, beneath every system of thought, some basic assumptions or postulates from which all other items of belief are derived. It is said that those who share in a system of thought are those who hold basic assumptions in common. But these assumptions are of the intellect, subsequent products, efforts to capture and clarify and make intelligible to ourselves and to others some fragment of that immediacy of experience which is the soul of life itself. Such assumptions we must make, but they are experimental, variant, conditioned by our culture period. But Holy Fellowship reaches behind these intellectual frames to the immediacy of experience in God, and seeks contact in this fountainhead of real, dynamic connectedness. Theological quarrels arise out of differences in assumptions. But Holy Fellowship, freely tolerant of these important yet more superficial clarifications, lives in the Center and rejoices in the unity of His love.

And this Fellowship is deeper than democracy, conceived as an ideal of group living. It is a theocracy wherein God rules and guides and directs His listening children. The center of authority is not in man, not in the group, but in the creative God Himself. Nor do all members share equally in spiritual discernment, but upon some falls more clearly the revealing light of His guiding will. "Weighty Friends," with delicate attunement both to heaven and to earth, bulk large in practical decisions. It would be a mistake indeed to suppose that Holy Fellowship is chained fast to one political system, or bound up inextricably with the fortunes of any one temporal structure of society. For the swaying fortunes of democracy and of fascism and of communism are of time, but the Fellowship in God is of all times and is eternal. It is certainly true that some temporal systems are more favorable than are others to the flowering of the Fellowship. But within all groups and nations and creeds it springs up, smiling at differences, for, existing in time, it is rooted in the Eternal One.

No single person can hold *all* dedicated souls within his compass in steadfast Fellowship with equal vividness. There are degrees of Fellowship, from wider, more diffused relations of love to nearer, more intense inter-knittedness. As each of us is at a point in space which compels us to a perspective relationship to all things, some near, some far, so each of us is dear to some and remote from others in the bonds of love.

Within the wider Fellowship emerges the special circle of a few on whom, for each of us, a particular emphasis of nearness has fallen. These are our special gift and task. These we "carry" by inward, wordless prayer. By an interior act and attitude we lift them repeatedly before the throne and hold them there in power. This is work, real labor of the soul. It takes energy but it is done in joy. But the membership of such special groups is different and overlapping. From each individual the bonds of special fellowship radiate near and far. The total effect, in a living Church, would be sufficient intersection of these bonds to form a supporting, carrying network of love for the whole of mankind. Where the Fellowship is lacking, the Church invisible is lacking and the Kingdom of God has not yet come. For these bonds of divine love and "carrying" are the stuff of the Kingdom of God. He who is in the Fellowship is in the Kingdom.

Two people, three people, ten people may be in living touch with one another through Him who underlies their separate lives. This is an astounding experience, which I can only describe but cannot explain in the language of science. But in vivid experience of divine Fellowship it is there. We know that these souls are with us, lifting their lives and ours continuously to God and opening themselves, with us, in steady and humble obedience to Him. It is as if the boundaries of our self were enlarged, as if we were within them and as if they were within us. Their strength, given to them by God, becomes our strength, and our joy, given to us by God, becomes their joy. In confidence and love we live together in Him. On the borders of the experience lie amazing events, at which reputable psychologists scoff, and for which I would not try any accounting. But the solid kernel of community of life in God is in the center of the experience, renewing our life and courage and commitment and love. For daily and hourly the cosmic Sacrament is enacted, the Bread and the Wine are divided amongst us by a heavenly Ministrant, and the substance of His body becomes our life and the substance of His blood flows in our veins. Holy is the Fellowship, wondrous is the Ministrant, marvelous is the Grail.

Frequency of personal contact in this Fellowship is not imperative, although desirable. Weeks and months and even years may elapse, yet the reality remains undimmed. Conversations within the Fellowship gravitate toward Him who is dearer than life itself. Yet the degree of self-disclosure which we are given to make to others is variable with time and place and person. And never is it complete. For as it nears completeness, words no longer help, but hinder, and the final pooling of joy and love in Him is accomplished in the silences of the Eternal.

All friendships short of this are incomplete. All personal relations which lie only in time are open-ended and unfinished, to the soul who walks in holy obedience. Can we make *all* our relations to our fellows relations which pass *through Him?* Our relations to the conductor on a trolley? Our relations to the clerk who serves us in a store? How far is the world from such an ideal! How far is Christian practice from such an expectation! Yet we, from our end of the relationship, can send out the Eternal Love in silent, searching hope, and meet each person with a background of eternal expectation and a silent, wordless prayer of love. For until the life of men in time is, in every relation, shot through with Eternity, the Blessed Community is not complete.

ON LISTENING
TO ANOTHER

by Douglas V. Steere

EDITOR'S PREFACE

I have not composed an introduction for Douglas Steere's *On Listening to Another* as I did for each of the other eight classics in this series. In this instance such an introduction seems unnecessary and perhaps inappropriate. Being a contemporary writing, first published in 1956, *On Listening to Another* speaks clearly and forcefully to our own setting without interpretation. In it Douglas V. Steere, for many years Thomas Wistar Brown Professor of Philosophy and, since 1964, Professor Emeritus at Haverford College, unapologetically shares with us the deep and abiding insights of Quaker meditation.

I think it not inappropriate to say here, however, that the Church owes a great debt to Douglas Steere for his contribution to spirituality. A man of obvious brilliance—Rhodes Scholar at Oxford (1925–27), Phi Beta Kappa—and honored in many ways in the academic world, he has channeled his best thought and experience into a search for the Eternal in the midst of our lives. It is fitting that one of his own writings should be included in a collection of devotional classics, because he has done so much to direct others to these great works. In *Doors Unto Life* he introduced five classics. Before Westerners had become acquainted with Kierkegaard, Steere translated what many would consider his most significant religious writing. He assembled the speeches or essays for Thomas Kelly's *Testament of Devotion*. In addition, he has studded his own writings with gems mined from wide reading in great religious literature.

But I would be remiss if I did not mention what has impressed me more than anything else in my personal contacts with Douglas Steere. He has a sense of that presence which comes through his own meeting with the divine. I never go away from a meeting with him but that I feel uplifted. It does not matter what he or I say—or whether we say anything. He may admonish or reproach me, as John Woolman sometimes did his contemporaries. Still, I feel uplifted. I've often mulled these experiences over in my mind. What is Douglas Steere's secret? I think he comes very close to telling us in *On Listening to Another*.

—E. GLENN HINSON

INTRODUCTION

In the Journal of John Woolman, there is a well-known scene which took place in an Indian village along the upper Susquehanna River in Pennsylvania. John Woolman rose to pray in a religious meeting held among the Indians and an interpreter who stood up to render Woolman's words into the Indian language was asked to sit down and let the prayer go untranslated. After the meeting, the Indian chief, Papunehang, approached Woolman and through an interpreter said of the prayer whose English words he had not understood, "I love to feel where words come from."

If we could learn the art of listening which Chief Papunehang witnessed to, we should be led to the ground of all true conversation, of prayer, of worship, of vocal ministry and of the divine accent on things to be done which Friends have called "concerns." This lecture is published in England under the title of "Where Words Come From," and I am most grateful to the Swarthmore Lecture Committee for their kind consent to the change in title in the American edition. A portion of it was delivered in England as the 48th annual Swarthmore Lecture on May 20, 1955, at the opening of the London Yearly Meeting. The lecture is devoted to an examination of what is involved in listening and in being listened to. It seeks a fresh approach to an interpretation of the genius of Quaker worship and to its articulation in vocal ministry and in practical concerns in terms of the process of listening.

Haverford, Pa.
July 17, 1955   *Douglas V. Steere*

Have you ever sat with a friend when in the course of an easy and pleasant conversation the talk took a new turn and you both listened avidly to the other and to something that was emerging in your visit? You found yourselves saying things that astonished you and finally you stopped talking and there was an immense naturalness about the long silent pause that followed. In that silent interval you were possessed by what you had discovered together. If this has happened to you, you know that when you come up out of such an experience, there is a memory of rapture and a feeling in the heart of having touched holy ground.

Have you ever been writing a letter when your capacity to listen to the other and to his situation suddenly comes into focus and all you have been saying or meant to say is swept up into something infinitely more important? You have listened and you have been listened to and you have heard, even though a complete recasting of what you had set down before is now exacted of you.

Have you ever talked with someone who listened with such utter abandon to what you were trying to tell him that you were yourself made clearer in what you were trying to express by the very quality of his listening? Have you ever found this listening changing what you started out to tell and moving it over into quite a different channel? Perhaps you had begun to speak of the loveless character of your own religious group, of how little they cared for each other, and at bottom, how little concerned they were for what happened to each. In the course of telling this, although your listening companion had scarcely spoken a word, it may be that little by little it began to dawn upon you that you were describing not so much the situation of your religious group as the condition of your own heart. Now you began to see what was required of you, and you found yourself reduced to silence. You may have begun by describing your own inner agonies which had been mounting up until they finally blotted out all hope. You had meant to complain bitterly against a fate that had pressed you to such a state of desperation. You had meant to collect a litre or two of sympathy. But as you talked, and as your friend listened with that perfect understanding love which gave you his complete attention, the true state of things dawned upon you and you no longer needed sympathy or a towel for your tears. Painful as the insight was, you now saw things from another perspective and you stopped talking. You no longer needed to talk, or if you did continue, it was now on another theme and level.

Perhaps you had sought out a friend to confess something you could no longer keep in the solitary confinement of your own heart. You were not sure you would have the courage to admit how low you had fallen and you began in evasively safe regions, not sure either of yourself or of your friend. But the utter and easy attentiveness, the free and open listening of your friend lifted the latch on the gate and it swung open noiselessly and effortlessly, and all that you had held back tumbled out. Now it was out and now it was over and you had died a little death, but in the patient eyes of the friend which you scarcely dared to lift your own to look into, you discovered that you were still in the land of the living.

Have you had the contrary experience? Have you ever talked to a person on a subject that was of burning importance to you, something that you felt that you must enable him to feel, and in the course of it had the choking, stifling realization that he was not listening to you at all, and that his responses to what you said were purely automatic and mechanical? In February, 1941, I went to see one of the highest placed officials in the American Government to ask him to use his good offices to soften the American embargo to the extent of letting some American food get through to Southern France where the general population, and particularly the depressed groups like the Jewish refugees and the refugees from Franco Spain, were slowly starving to death. I had just returned from this region and had seen these people with my own eyes and I tried to help him to see what our embargo was doing.

I had only begun speaking when he apologized and reaching for his telephone asked his secretary to make appointments for him with certain senators. He jotted down things on his pad that had nothing to do with our interview. I faced his body. He said "yes" and "no," now and then. But his mind was elsewhere. He had no interest in this concern. I was unable to draw his attention to its relevance. I went away sad and chastened that I had not been given the grace to draw him to listen.

More often the situation is not so crass as this. The listener is involved in the conversation but he is involved only to the degree that he is eager to give his own opinion. He listens to what is said only sufficiently to inject his own already-fashioned view at the earliest possible moment. He listens only with the outer ear. With the rest of him, he is preparing his own speech. In this situation there is no real listening. We have only two tangential monologues in process and neither person is in the least affected by the exchange.

Levels of Listening and the Price They Exact

In order to listen discerningly to another, a certain maturity is required, a certain self-transcendence, a certain expectation, a patience, and openness to the new. In order really to listen, there must be a capacity to hear through many wrappings, and only a mature listener, listening beyond the outer layer of the words that are spoken, is capable of this. How falsely a listener may construe what we say if he takes only our words. Our words are often halting and many times plainly not what we mean. Back of what we mean on the conscious level, there is almost always a deeper unconscious meaning that is at work.

A young minister in his first year of service tells his friend that he cannot bear the work and wishes he would find a place for him with some good farmer. Does he mean that he is not strong enough to stand the nervous toil that the work of a busy minister of the gospel involves? Does he think that he really is meant for agricultural work instead of the ministry? This is what his words have indicated. But in all probability he means neither the one nor the other. What does he mean? Only the listener who cares and who has the patience of his caring and the faith of his patience will ever know. In the presence of this understanding patience, he is soon telling that what he really means is that there is no let-up to grief in this work, no limitation to the hours he is on duty, and that he feels utterly inadequate to the troubles people open to him, the faith they have in him, the opportunities that are about him night and day, and he wonders if he can ever measure up to them. If the truth were known you could not drive him from the work. Underneath in his hidden life, he senses that the noose of his own commitment is tightening and is closing around more and more of his life as he is being drawn into a situation where there is less and less chance to extricate himself, hence the above-surface ripples of what in words are complaint, but what in truth are signs that the calling he has chosen is taking him over. The harness is beginning to tighten as the pull of the wagon behind makes itself felt.

What old veteran in religious service has not confided to a companion that he will not bear the grief of it any more! He is going to quit and look out for himself for a while. The Curé d'Ars ran away periodically from his parish and his twenty-hour-a-day vigil in the confessional only to return promptly when the parish sent some peasant parishioner after him, as they always did. What parties to a marriage have not at moments had their long thoughts, "All for you, and nothing for me," as the music-hall ballad puts it. What occupation has not at moments looked less attractive to one in the midst of it than other careers around it? But the patient listener soon finds that these "moments" so vociferously described, are not really what the person is meaning to say at all. He knows that at heart he is trying to tell him what he himself does not yet consciously know, namely, that the marriage needs another child, or another level of understanding or tenderness. The occupation may need a fresh dedication or another set of undertakings to change its aspect. The shoemaker may need a fresh vision of what his service means to those who go through life shod by his ministrations. But these unconscious meanings are only dimly felt by the speaker and they do not formulate well in words. Complaints and threats are so much easier to express. Only before an open listener do they disclose what they really mean, do the complaints and sighs give way to further understanding.

A Finn once suggested to me that in every conversation between two people there are always at least six persons present. What each person said are two; what each person meant to say are two more; and what each person understood the other to say are two more. There is certainly no reason to stop at six, but the fathomless depth of the listener who can go beyond words, who can even go beyond the conscious meanings behind words and who can listen with the third ear for what is unconsciously being meant by the speaker, this fashion of attentive listening furnishes a climate where the most unexpected disclosures occur that are in the way of being miracles in one sense, and the most natural and obvious things in the world, on the other.

The Spectator Listener Within the One Who Speaks

This favourable climate for self-disclosure is a rare situation. For in all that has been mentioned, it is in the mind and heart of the speaker that the disclosures must finally come, and these disclosures come strangely enough because there is not only a listening friend sitting near, but because there is also a spectator listener within every speaker that listens while he speaks. That inward listener seems able to grasp what is going on at all levels at once so that it hears the words, it hears the conscious meaning of the words, and it even hears in a throbbing but inarticulate way, the unconscious meaning of what is being spoken of, and all three of these simultaneously. Without this inner unity, there would be no possibility of self-disclosure, no breaking through of the hidden unconscious meaning into the speaker's conscious life.

There is a great shyness, a profound reticence about this inward spectator listener. It is acutely tuned to the situation in which the speaker is engaged as he speaks and another listens. It is tuned, however, not only to these levels within the speaker himself and to the speaker's sincerity in what he says. Curiously enough, it is also focussed with almost equal intensity upon these different levels within the outward listener. What is going on in the outward listener's conscious mind, as well as what is occurring in the outward listener's unconscious is never fully veiled to the speaker's inward spectator listener. Is it any wonder then that disturbances in the outward listener that escape completely the most delicate outward seismographic recorder may yet profoundly affect the situation of self-disclosure to the speaker? And is it any wonder that this favourable climate is so rare?

For in what listener is there the constant abundance of charity that springs from the depths of his own unconscious, that floods and illumines his conscious intelligence and understanding, making him a tuned and concentrated instrument that is able to reach through the words and even the conscious meanings to the unconscious meaning of the friend who is speaking, and to answer to it?

In what listener are there not vast stretches of bored inattention when the listener rests, or tries to rest, or wonders when, if ever, the speaker will subside? In what listener are there not temptations early in the conversation to classify what is being said, to label and file it, and once in this frame, to give it only such attention as this frame calls for? There is then no longer a person before him, but a type. There is no longer a creative unconscious solution that neither speaker nor listener sees but that could be disclosed if they reached the depths out of which it might come. There is now only a predictable automaton before him whose symptoms and course of development he is all too familiar with.

In how many listeners is there not some adverse judgment on what is being revealed, some comparison between the listener's own standard of assessment and that of the one who is speaking, a judgment which places the speaker at a point on a scale and neatly seals him off from the listener? In what listener is there not aroused by some remote congruity with what the speaker has mentioned, a compulsion to impose upon the speaker a detailed account of his own personal experiences?

In what listener is there not upon listening to another, some involvement of his own unconscious meanings and intentions, some stirring up of his own unfaced fears, or evaded decisions, or repressed longings, or hidden aspirations, that flare up and involve him so completely that the speaker is scarcely present for him any longer? This may not be a negative reaction. On the contrary it may indicate that the listener is alive, is involved, cares, and has himself begun to speak whether he utters a word or not. But this inward speaking of the outward listener, genuine and moving as it may be, unless it is in the same direction as the speaker's concern may become an intrusive force in the situation.

There is no need to detail the role of the professional listener who, having studied a recent technique by which he has learned not to involve himself but to seek to act exclusively as a resonant Swiss valley, sends back an accurate echo to the speaker of what he has said and leaves the rest to him. Happily, few professional listeners are capable of any such total impassivity, and those that are, manage quite readily to uncover the mechanical character of their services to those who visit them. Yet in all of these situations that have been described, the rarity of the favourable climate for listening bears down even more formidably as the grounds for it become more apparent.

If all of these deficiencies on the part of the listener were heavily cloaked from the speaker and only rarely detected by him, it would be one thing. But as has already been noted, the vigilant inward spectator listener in most speakers never relaxes its surveillance. There is little in the outward listener that it misses. And when the outward listener is not really open, there is usually a closure effected in the speaker himself, a watering down to the conventional level, a safety factor is invoked, a self-preservative function that prevents more than surface exposure. Now we begin to realize what "holy listening" involves, how it differs from what passes for listening, and some of the diseases that afflict it.

The True Listener Is Vulnerable

But we have not yet plumbed it. We have still to look at this condition of openness in a genuine listener which the inward spectator listener in the speaker so swiftly recognizes and responds to, this condition that opens doors in the speaker, this condition that brings the climate for self-disclosure, this situation where the deepest longings in the heart of the speaker feel safe to reveal themselves, this atmosphere where nothing needs any longer to be concealed. The truth of the matter is that there are not perfectly open listeners. Yet in those who approach this degree of openness, it is clear at the outset that they are involved. In some way I, the speaker, matter for them. Neither of us is a ventriloquist's dummy for the other. Both of us affect each other and cannot come out of this encounter unscathed. Even the professional physician admits that he can only work at his best when the patient is convinced that he matters for him. The practice of old Dr. Wooster in Waltham, Massachusetts, who would turn his calls over to an adequate assistant and serve with his own hands an old patient who was dying, relieving the nurse of the most menial and loathsome tasks, is a symbol of this involvement. The speaker matters to the listener. The listener is vulnerable. Behind any words of his, there is a quality of life which shows that this is the case.

The genuine listener must not only care. It greatly assists the openness if the speaker knows that the listener himself has been through some testing that is comparable to his own. When Father Damien on Molokai, after years of energetic service to the lepers there, began his sermon in the chapel one Sunday with "We lepers," a new note of reality entered his relationship with the community. When at her missionary hostel in England, Florence All-shorn listened to countless furloughed missionaries telling of their inner numbness after years of taxing duty on the field, they knew that she had once been one of them and that they could be sure they were not simply being ridiculous or betraying the name of the exacting vocation they had chosen. The help that is given by members of the Alcoholics Anonymous to each other; by newly-founded bands of alumni of mental institutions to those who have just come out; by parents who have lost children of their own through cancer and who make themselves available to parents whose children have newly entered the hospital and who are facing the same ordeal; by nurses in tubercular institutions who have been cured of the disease themselves, is a clue to how openness is assisted by the assurance of a similar testing on the part of the listener.

In the depression days of 1931 when the merchants and business community of Morgantown, West Virginia, were in a state of utter confusion and despair, a Quaker woman named Alice Davice came into the community to help in a child-feeding programme. Soon after her arrival, she was asked to speak at a widely-attended luncheon club meeting. In the course of her talk she described to them what conditions were like and yet how much was able to be done in a comparable Russian city where she had worked, between 1921 and 1927, under conditions so infinitely worse than any they were experiencing that it seemed comparatively easy for them to trust this relative stranger with their confidences. Openness is assisted by the confidence that the listener, too, has been through the fire.

Acceptance, Expectancy and Constancy in Human Listening

A listener extends openness when he accepts the person who is speaking, when he relinquishes all buffing and finishing operations and takes the man as he comes. Such acceptance is no toleration born of indifference but is rather a positive interest in this person, an interest that is so alive that judgment is withheld.

In South Africa a white person who was deeply concerned for the improvement of the relations between the races confessed to me that in the situation there, the disease of racial prejudice was so deep that even people like himself who went about crossing lines had become so self-conscious about it as to cancel out all virtue and meaning from the gesture. He begged me to try to persuade some people whose acceptance of the other race was so natural and genuine as to be beyond this stage of self-consciousness to come out to South Africa and by their example to help to make such an attitude contagious. It is that kind of unconscious acceptance to which my friend referred, that a sensitive speaker requires of the open listener.

This acceptance, however, does not wither or dwarf the deep expectancy on the part of the listener for the partially concealed capacities which are within the speaker. At the best, the listener by something that is almost akin to divination reaches through to these capacities in the speaker and evokes them. This very expectancy immeasurably assists the speaker in his response to the listener's openness. When Thomas Kelly came to Haverford College for graduate study in 1914, he sought out Rufus Jones, and under the glow of the unfailing sense of expectancy which Rufus Jones seemed able to direct toward those who visited him, Thomas Kelly, all restraints aside, bared his secret dream that in some way he wanted to make of his life a miracle.

This sense of expectancy in a listener must, however, have a durable quality, a constancy about it in order to have an authentic ring. If it is to vindicate itself, it must reappear again and again, no matter what the evidence against it. It must have an infinite patience grounded in faith in what the person may become. A seasoned well-digger is not put off by the soiled muddy water which first appears in the pipe when he strikes a flowing well. He knows that given time, it will run clean.

Even Mathilde Wrede, the Finnish prisoner's friend, who went on forgiving and believing when the same ex-prisoner failed her, deceived her and cheated her, not once, but time after time, could testify that only as she held firmly and patiently to the expectation of what that man might become, could her listening matter. Her own confessions of her frailty in this regard are shattering to the rest of us in our humiliation before her patent purity.

But as the circle of these qualities that are all of a piece is rounded, we return to the first which undergirds and nourishes all the rest. It is the listener's capacity to care, to care enough to be involved. For the listener who knows what he is about, there is a realization that there is no withdrawal half way. There is every prospect that he will not return unscathed. There is no lead apron that can protect his own life from being irradiated by the unconscious level of the one he engages with. A friend of mine who has spent many years in listening admits that in the course of it, he has learned something of what the Bible and the Apostles' Creed refer to as the "descent into hell" and is quite frank in confessing that for him each act of listening that is not purely mechanical is a personal ordeal. Listening is never cheap. Only the listener who can say "for what else was I born" can fulfill this vocation.

Beyond Human Listening

It should be more than apparent after the things that have been said about what open listening exacts from the listener, why such listeners are scarce and why they are so deeply prized. To "listen" another's soul into a condition of disclosure and discovery may be almost the greatest service that any human being ever performs for another. But in this scrutiny of the business of listening, is that all that has emerged? Is it possible to set forth the perfect listener without a flash of realization that we have been engaged in something more? Is it blasphemous to suggest that over the shoulder of the human listener we have been looking at, there is never absent the silent presence of the Eternal Listener, the living God? For in penetrating to what is involved in listening do we not disclose the thinness of the filament that separates men listening openly to one another, and that of God intently listening to each soul?

In his *Purity of Heart,* Søren Kierkegaard gives an image that compellingly reveals this emergence of the Eternal background in listening from the human foreground. There he is speaking of how a devotional address should be listened to, but his image will illumine the way of listening to all vocal ministry. The natural way to listen to such a message, Kierkegaard suggests, is to consider oneself as seated in the audience and the one giving the message as an actor on the stage. The listener is therefore quite free as a member of the audience to criticize both the content of the message and the art, or the lack of it, in the one who delivers the message. But Kierkegaard insists that this is not the right way to listen. And until it is reversed, the exercise of listening is likely to have little result, no matter how habitually it is practiced. To listen correctly, we must radically shift the roles. Now it is not the deliverer of the message who is performing before me, but I myself am on the stage speaking the part. Now there is only a single listener in the audience. That listener is God. But where in this altered scene has the deliverer of the message been placed? In the wings, where he belongs. He has no more than the role of the prompter on the old Danish stage who stood in the wings and spoke over the actor's lines in a low voice so that if the actor missed them at any point, he could recover them with this assistance.

Kierkegaard could have gone on with his figure if he had chosen to do so and could have indicated that this reversal of roles in listening to a religious message was not alone something that a man by an act of his own will could do for himself. He might quite as readily have pointed out that when a religious message reaches not only the ears but the soul of a man, that apparently without any effort of will whatever on his part, this very reversal of roles is precisely what happens within him. The message-bearer has been in the focus of his attention as he has been listening, perhaps even critically listening. Then suddenly the message-bearer drops out of sight and the man who a moment ago thought he was the listener is now face to face with the compassionate presence of the listener from whom nothing is hid but who, in spite of all, loves and accepts him.

There is no deeper spiritual insight in Kierkegaard's writings than this vision of a man placed squarely before God, the Listener, and he continually returns to it in his works. Finally we shall be alone with God and there will be no hurry. Finally there will be no crowd to hide in, no favourable comparisons with others to draw about us like a protective coat, no more self-deception. Finally we shall realize that we cannot evade him. In walking on the Jutland heath, Kierkegaard had seen great stretches of land without a tree or a bush that could conceal a man. Finally it will be like that. Kierkegaard might well have evoked the witness of the 139th Psalm:

O Lord, thou hast searched me and known me.
Thou knowest when I sit down and when I rise up.
Thou discernest my thoughts from afar.
Thou searchest out my path and my lying down,
And art acquainted with all my ways.
Even before a word is on my tongue
Lo, O Lord, thou knowest it altogether.
Thou dost beset me behind and before
And layest thy hand upon me.
Such knowledge is too wonderful for me;
It is high, I cannot attain to it.
Whither shall I go from thy Spirit?
Or whither shall I flee from thy presence?
If I ascend up into heaven, thou art there!
If I make my bed in Sheol thou art there!
If I take the wings of the morning
And dwell in the uttermost parts of the sea
Even there thy hand shall lead me,
And thy right hand shall hold me.
If I say, "Let the darkness cover me,
And the light about me be night,"
Even the darkness is not dark to thee
The night is bright as the day,
For darkness is as light to thee.
Search me, O God, and know my heart!
Try me and know my thoughts!
And see if there be any wicked way in me,
And lead me in the way everlasting. (Psalm cxxxix. 1–12, 23–24)

Here in the 139th Psalm, a clarified man is speaking. Like the prophet Amos, he has had a vision of the Lord standing beside a wall with a plumb line in his hand. He has recognized the Listener for who he is and gratefully abandoned all concealment. Now he is listened to with a listening that hears as no stethoscope has ever been devised to hear. Now he is known not as he thinks himself to be, not as his friends think him to be, nor as his enemies depict him, but as he is. And with this has come a wave of liberation.

Search me, know me, try me, lead me: these are the stages of disclosure and discovery which the Psalmist has revealed. To speak to a Listener from whom it becomes progressively clearer that nothing can be concealed; to talk on and on before such a Listener until our silence answers his, until disclosure and discovery come, is a longing that is so universal that it could be called one of the "givens" of all human experience.

Clarification and the Eternal Listener

How many attempts there have been to portray the stripping, the cleansing and the final valley of decision which marks this experience of confronting the One who listens. I came across a striking example of this portrayal some years ago in the form of a painting by a German Quaker artist, Eberhard Tacke, who with his little family lives in East Berlin. He has painted a scene where a vision of the crucified Christ appears to three men who stand holding their masks in their hands. The vision has stripped them of this covering. In their freshly exposed eyes there seems to be a mingled look of yearning and of fear: yearning to give what this figure asks of them, fear of what such giving would cost. "Search me, know me, try me, lead me."

The German writer Bergengruen has given a thinly veiled portrait of the listening God in his *A Matter of Conscience* where the various figures accused of a capital crime painfully unwind their tangled skein of deception and truth before the Prince who knows the truth from the beginning. The clarification of those involved comes about because there is present an incorruptible Listener to whom all is known.

Perhaps nowhere is this condition more powerfully described than in the Grand Inquisitor scene in Dostoevsky's *Brothers Karamazov*. There Jesus Christ appears again in the streets of the sixteenth-century Seville, and by his acts of healing is joyously recognized by the common people. He is promptly arrested by the Inquisitor's guard and brought to the Inquisitor's prison to face the Inquisitor Cardinal alone. There the Cardinal begins his "I accuse." And there in response to wave after wave of rationalization and self-justification of the course that has been taken by the Church in order to correct his original work, Jesus is completely silent. He does not in turn accuse, he does not defend any more than he did before Pilate. He only is what he is, and listens. Slowly his listening penetrates to the core of the Cardinal and reduces him to silence. There is a final violent thrust: the threat of invoking the death penalty if Jesus does not go at once.

In Dostoevsky's scene, Jesus then crosses the room, kisses the aged Cardinal on his bloodless lips, and disappears. Seldom in any literature has the course of the human spirit when it confronts the Eternal Listener been more magnificently depicted than here. Yet even here, the Cardinal has spent himself, has had his own arguments and defenses revealed for what they are in the presence of the silent, patient, all-knowing, all-loving one but we are not told that he has come to the end of himself. The Cardinal has entered the valley of decision but has turned back or he would have fled in search of his visitor that he might follow him.

In a lighter vein, the gay, saucy, sparkling Italian post-war fantasy *The Little World of Don Camillo* brings Don Camillo regularly before the crucifix to expound, to argue out and to defend his preposterous and ethically dubious proposals. In spite of the delicate line between humour and blasphemy which this novel often bends, if it does not transgress, the course of this unorthodox priest's pleas before the crucified one is intensely revealing. Slowly and surely as he argues, the assurance wanes, the insistence weakens, and the real course is reluctantly but finally seen and accepted. The Listener has silenced and clarified the petitioner until the petitioner yields and is transformed.

With the exception of Bergengruen's symbolic portrait of the Prince, and possibly even this is no exception, each of these examples has given us a further confirmation that all that we discovered earlier about ordinary listening is even more characteristic of the greatest listening of all. For it is not merely in being perfectly known that the Listener finally brings the speaker to silence and to the discovery of what is his deepest yearning. It is in being what he is and confirming what he is by what he does that the Listener becomes something more than a Roentgen machine. And what he is in the Christian experience is one that cares infinitely for the speaker. He speaks to the speaker's condition because he has loved him from the beginning of the world.

Vulnerability, Acceptance, Expectancy and Constancy in the Eternal Listener

It was this unremitting love of the Listener for the speaker that Pascal was inwardly swept by three hundred years ago on the memorable night of November 23rd, 1654, and it was this experience which authenticated his declaration that Jesus would suffer in agony for men until the end of the world. For one who has listened to another person with a bowed mind and tendered heart, how much is vindicated, is inwardly confirmed and made alive by the gospel story of the Listener entering flesh and blood and caring so deeply as to consent to have it stripped from him again in order to arouse men to his infinite caring. Phillips Brooks once said, "If you want to know the worth of a human soul, try to save one." He might as well have said, "try to listen one into life." For to listen, there can be no bottom to the caring for the other. Yet we know that this caring cannot be a verbal affair. It must be sealed by some unmistakable material evidence of vulnerability on the part of the Listener.

Bishop Stephen Neill told once of hearing an Indian village evangelist telling the story of the prodigal son and allowing himself some of the liberties of interpretation which his vivid imagination begged for. The evangelist explained how the prodigal's real change had not come about when he made his own decision in the far country to return to his Father. And it had not come about when, to his astonishment, his Father had come out to meet him and welcomed him home with loving tears and a feast. The real change of heart had not come about until some days later when in looking at his Father, the prodigal realized in a flash that the Father's hair had turned grey since he had gone away.

The Abbé Huvelin once told Friedrich von Hügel that no Sermon on the Mount, even when guided as it was by the most sublime instruction on earth, could ever have redeemed men. When God himself wanted to redeem man he could not do it by any other means than by dying. For God himself there could be no arranging a cheaper form of convincing man that he cared supremely.

Throughout the experience of listening, this evangelical witness is confirmed again. The speaker's silent demand that the adequate listener be tested by sharing some comparable experience to his own is not left without a witness: "tempted in all things as we," "conceived," "born," "suffered," "dead and buried." How materialistically literal are the words of the incarnation. Yet, without this testing, could the Listener have opened the hearts of all conditions of men throughout all the ages and released them to pour out their inmost depths to him in order that under his compassionate listening they might come to themselves as the sons of God?

The speaker's need to be accepted as an original, as having a worth of his own, as one who is above classification and who requires that routine judgment be suspended, withheld, is met beyond measure in the Listener. "Our good Lord showed me," Mother Julian of Norwich relates, "that it is his full pleasure that a silly soul come to him naked, plain and homely."

Where is the evidence for unqualified acceptance more complete and convincing than in the figure who moved easily and without self-consciousness among publicans, tax-gatherers, prostitutes, people who were national and racial outcasts of his own fiercely zealous national community and who in his death between two thieves accepted and welcomed the one who came "naked, plain, and homely" bidding him to be with him in paradise?

This sense of expectancy that we found furnishing such an important part of the favourable climate which the listener supplies to the speaker has never been more conspicuously evident than in the figure of Jesus. His easy unselfconscious acceptance of men and women seemed always to be linked to this power of divination into what they might become.

Is it possible to exaggerate what this expectancy of the Listener did to the impetuous vacillating Peter, to Mary Magdalene, to the despised Quisling-like tax contractor Zaccheus, to those who had despaired of ever again having either their sight or sanity or bodily wholeness? He stubbornly rejected their surface appearances. He ignored the nicely calculated probabilities of society's judgment of what one might expect of them. He penetrated even the heavy wrappings of what they had themselves settled for in their lives and pierced through to what in their deepest yearnings they still longed to become. He drew this out, confirmed it, and those we have named acknowledged it and accepted it. He answered expectantly to that of God in each of them and they felt and responded to the quickening.

The constancy of this figure needs little more than mention in passing, it is so transparently evident. The human listener at his superb best aspires to this costly patience, this durable steadiness in his faith and expectancy toward the speaker, but he lapses so lamentably and so often. Even in the greatest of saints, our mirrors of the active love of God in each generation, how often are they clouded. Even in Francis of Assisi or Theresa of Avila, how given to bursts of despair or exasperation at the conduct of those who go on in their wayward speaking while they must continue listening.

In contrast even to these chosen ones, what constancy is found in the One who revealed the nature of the Listener himself. The disciples go out to preach and heal and return to confess their impotency. The populace, like water, rises and falls in its favour toward him. The last night with his own disciples, they are quarrelling over issues of precedence in the kingdom. One of them betrays him. He leaves this little band fearful, scattered, fleeing and in utter dismay, yet these are all that there are to carry on the work he has begun. His constancy, like a regnant acid, dissolves away film after film of their disbelief until it breaks in upon them that they are the children of God and are called to live joyously together in his kingdom and to share it with all the world.

Beneath all that has been said of the living Listener, as of human listening, there is no concealing the fact that what in the listener acts most deeply upon the speaker either to release or to bind him is not only the costly things that the listener does, nor is it exclusively what in his depths the listener is. What really matters is rather what the listener is in what he does. This cleanses the situation from the outset by distinguishing it from any pseudo-listening which is reducible to some readily transmissible technique that makes no appreciable demand on what the listener is. It also throws light on a strange occurrence in the ordinary listening that men do for each other as well as in the spiritual situation in which each man is open before the living Listener. For while the least semblance of an act of self-conscious judgment on the part of the listener destroys and renders sterile the relation to the speaker, yet there is no denying that there is a kind of judgment going on continually between listener and speaker.

The Inner Encounter with the Eternal Listener

The speaker in the presence of a human listener is never unaware of the judgment of what the listener is upon his own life, and in turn, the listener's own life cannot resist the judging effect of what the speaker is upon his own life. Here are fields of radiation that interpenetrate each other and that leave neither party unprobed. Nietzsche in his *Thus Spake Zarathustra*[1] declares incisively that "In one's friend, one shall have one's best enemy," an enemy that rebukes and judges that which is unauthentic or merely imitative in the friend.

In the listener, then, if he be a true friend, a true listener, there is inevitably an enemy to much that is in the speaker. But this "enemy" in the listener is not the re-introduction of any level of conscious judgment, any weakening of the listener's complete acceptance of the speaker. This enemy is an effortless, unconscious influence which rises up out of what the listener is in what he does. It may be all very well to say as Nietzsche does that "many a one cannot loosen his own fetters, but is nevertheless his friend's emancipator."[2] But the odds are heavily against any such miracle. For it is only the listener whose own fetters, if not shattered, have at least been loosened, who seems able effortlessly to irradiate the level of existence of the speaker in such a way as to move him toward release. Any minimizing of the maturity required of the listener may lead to the most tragic consequences. Furthermore it is only the mature listener who without disturbing the listening situation can submit both humbly and fearlessly to the counter radiations of the speaker to which he is continuously subjected.

Yet even this does not seem to get to the bottom of the matter. It penetrates to a genuine inner encounter between two friends who speak and who listen to each other, and it rightly draws attention to the searching unconscious interplay which takes place between the deep life of each as they listen to each other. But where it fumbles and becomes confused and unsure of itself is that it leaves out of all account the living Listener who "stands behind our lattices and waits." It ignores the hidden presence, the patient, all-penetrating Listener, the third member of every conversation whose very existence, if it is not ignored, rebukes and damps down the evil and calls out and underlines the good, drawing from the visible participants things they did not know they possessed. It does this not in a conspicuous fashion, as an orchestra leader tones down the brass with a menacing downstroke of his baton or calls forth the strings with a beckoning, pleading upward gesture, but does it more like the quietly permeating influence of a person of patent purity sitting silently in a conversation, saying almost nothing, but whose presence there changes all. The New Testament gives a vivid picture of this in describing the scene on the Emmaus road and at the inn where the presence of the mysterious stranger on the road and at the table changed all and left the travellers' hearts glowing as it withdrew.

Rarely does this business get itself adequately articulated. Common as the experience is, it seems to take a Bernard of Clairvaux to lift it up above the threshold of consciousness and to write of it, "He is living and full of energy. . . . He has quickened my sleeping soul, has aroused and softened and goaded my heart which was in a state of torpor and hard as a stone. He has begun to pluck up and destroy, to plant and to build, to water the dry places, to illuminate the gloomy spots, to throw open those that were cold as also to straighten its crooked paths and make its rough places smooth."

The living Listener who is "living and full of energy" seems able to take fearlessly the speakers' own diseased irradiations, lethal though they may be, to absorb them, and to transform them. Here is a kind of alchemy by which base metals are transformed into gold by a reagent whose power is as lavishly and recklessly poured out upon men as it is fathomless. Jesus' acts of healing, as in the case of the woman with the issue of blood or the many cases of demented spirits, seemed to involve just such a fearless interchange of radiations and the healing power he revealed moves in our world today to those who are wakened to it.

The more we come to realize the extent of the penetrating influence which our own hidden life and the hidden life of our friend exert upon each other, the more acutely do we come to appreciate how inadequately prepared we are to listen, no matter how mature we may be. The deeper this sense of humbling inadequacy soaks into our minds, the more open we are to realize the wisdom of seasoned spiritual guides like François de Sales or

George Fox who both insisted that the task of all spiritual guidance is to take men to Christ, to bring them to the living Listener, and to leave them there. With this realization, too, the well-known remark of Max Chaplin's comes freshly to life when he reflected that all the deepest friendships ultimately bear within themselves the seeds of tragedy unless both persons have their lives open to a power that is infinitely greater and purer than themselves.

The more conscious a listener becomes of the influence of the living Listener in searching both speaker and listener and in drawing out both to confirm in the other what is high and to reject in the other what is low, the more certain he is that only the cleansing radiations of an utterly loving and charitable one will do. Human listening then becomes what it is: a preciously thin point in the membrane where the human and divine action can be felt to mingle with the least opaque cloud of concealment. The human action can begin at any point, the conversation can start where it will, but if it goes on, the living Listener's presence may almost imperceptibly rise into awareness and with that awareness the total situation is altered.

The Living Listener in Prayer and Worship

How true this experience is of prayer. Prayer may begin as a soliloquy in which a stream of petitions is poured out. "I cannot bear the loneliness of my station. I live alone. I have been cut off by distance or death or estrangement from all persons who care for me. I cannot bear the company of my odious self day after day. Why has such a sad lot come to me of all people? It is wrong and the wrong should be corrected." Until now, this has been the outpouring of a person who feels choked with unhappiness tinged with a downright sense of injustice. There are those who insist that such a petition is blasphemy and should be sternly discouraged and certainly denied a place in the legitimate life of prayer. But such purists happily have little encouragement from either the Bible or the masters of prayer.

When they pray, men have to begin where they are. If they are obsessed and clogged up with loneliness and self-pity and a feeling of injustice, how can they be sincere if they do not pour out these sentiments? Veterans of prayer are not shocked at these things. They only insist that the person persevere, continue in the prayer, pray it through until the foreground becomes aware of the background. For in prayer, real prayer, what a man brings is irradiated by a power that loosens the arms that are carrying all these bundles of defective goods, bent on returning them to the merchant with bitter abuse, and the arms relax, and the bundles fall away, and the errand seems unimportant, in fact ridiculously unimportant and the question arises "What is God willing to have me learn from this time of aloneness? What new step of yielding is he asking of me now? What can I do for him in my situation?" And the person stops talking and begins to listen. What does it matter how self-involved a prayer or a conversation begins if it beats its way through to such an awareness? For in this tendered openness, the membrane between the soul of man and the living Listener is almost as if it did not exist at all.

The situation in corporate worship is closely akin to that described in private prayer. The company assemble in order to be made freshly aware of God, of their dependence upon him, of what they owe to him for his constancy, and of what focus of life and plans, if they can discover it, he would draw them into. They are nominally gathered to experience these things afresh. In fact, they come heavy with freight and often far from any worshipping frame of mind. They may be cumbered with cares, bruised and shamed at the state of their lives, physically and nervously tired, all in all hard-driven by life. Or they may feel dull, torpid and stale, sated with the routine of life and of their carefully secured and reserved station in it. Is this any condition in which to come to worship? Would it not be better if they stayed at home until they could get themselves sorted out and come only when their hearts were full and brimming, when they longed to praise and thank and adore God? As with private prayer, only the religious Pharisee dares even to put such a question. For a service of religious worship that is not able to take men where they are and draw them into an awareness of what they secretly seek has a place only on the drafting boards of religious romanticists. "Come unto me all ye who are weary and heavy laden and I will give you rest," Jesus declared, and if the place of religious worship is not a place to bring the rucksacks of care that are strapped to our backs, we are not likely to appear there often.

A service of corporate worship is for those who are weary and heavy laden, it is for sinners, for apprentices and journeymen, as well as master workmen, and what we begin with does not matter. What matters is, are we brought to such a focus of attention that our claimful cares are made aware of being petty chatterers in the presence of the patient Listener? What matters is, does this awareness of the Listener change their course, re-order them, drop them into the background, and finally reduce them to silence as the worshipper becomes still enough to hear God speak? Newman in his *Dream of Gerontius* speaks of the twin disclosure, the "two pains so counter and so keen" which all Christian experience of worship, at its deepest, testifies to:

> There is a pleading in His pensive eyes
> Will pierce thee to the quick and trouble thee.
> And thou wilt hate and loathe thyself; for though
> Now sinless, thou wilt feel that thou hast sinn'd
> As never thou didst feel; and wilt desire
> To slump away and hide thee from His sight.
> And yet wilt have a longing ay to dwell
> Within the beauty of His countenance.

All exercises of worship, all vocal ministry, all growth of concern find their focus here. Do they serve to bring the worshippers into a corporate attentive awareness of the living Listener? Do they keep the worshipper there until he has both spoken out his cares and been brought himself to listen? Do they encourage the "knowing Joy" of dwelling within the beauty of his countenance together with the inward "quickness" that comes when a man dares "to see myself His friend" as Vaughan and Traherne speak of the silent worshipper in the presence of the living Listener? Like the Franciscan Brother Giles embracing the Franciscan tertiary King Louis, their looking long and lovingly into each other's faces, and then parting silently, no words having been spoken or required, but both touched to the quick by the other's presence, a true service of worship should open the worshipper to such a moment. And finally does the service of worship having silenced the worshipper's cares, searched out and purified his frailties, encouraged the enjoyment and adoration of God, does it bring the worshipper to listen with his whole being for the word that may speak out the meaning of his present experience, for the divine accent or the holding back on his inward leading, for the sense of quickened responsibility for his fellows and for "thy kingdom come on earth"? If a service of worship, if vocal ministry can draw ordinary men and women regularly into this kind of renewal, they have performed their function.

The Order of Formal Worship in the Presence of the Living Listener

When it comes to the apparatus of worship that can renew men and women in attentive awareness to the living Listener, the classical Quaker practice of corporate silent waiting on God seems stark indeed to those who are used to the elaborate forms of a liturgical or even a free church service. I can still remember the heartiness of an Italian Franciscan monk's laughter that resounded from the walls of the tiny refectory at the Carceri near Assisi as he told me over our Easter dinner of the time he had been called to Rome in 1914 to be inscribed and granted exemption from the military, and being there "not really on church business" had broken over and visited the American Protestant Church in Rome. They had sung hymns, prayed, read the Bible, heard a sermon and sung again, and then to his utter amazement, it was all over, and the people went home. There had been no mass at all—and they thought that they had had a religious service! He could not see how anything could be more ridiculously funny. I wondered what he would have thought of a Quaker meeting.

But it is not what is missing, but what is present that makes this plain Quaker form of corporate renewal so natural and so adequate. For the worshippers are present, and the living Listener is present, and the worshipper's needs are there in abundance, together with the needs of the community and of the world, and the living Listener's magnetic transforming caring is present and able to meet those needs and to draw the worshippers into his service. Present also is not only this little company, this fellowship of those who know each other in that which is Eternal, but the spirits of all of the vast company of the faithful, living and dead whose inward ministrations are not wanting.

The most ardent free churchman or devoted adherent of a liturgical church would be the first to admit that the Quaker type of lay religious fellowship with its worship of silent waiting and its waiting ministry is spared certain problems which afflict their forms of worship. When the late Dean Willard Sperry of the Harvard Divinity School in what is generally acknowledged to be his finest book, *Reality in Worship,* begins to detail some of the defects and troubles of free church worship with its elements that are "assembled and not grown"; with its "pilfered prayers secured through predatory raids on the liturgy"; its responsive reading of blood-curdling Psalms that cannot but outrage the discerning, or if expurgated of these elements, excite the criticism of the "whole-Bibleists"; its prefabricated sermons; its prayers over the collection; the garbled architecture and the treacly hymns, a Quaker may have some ground to give a grateful sigh. The liturgist, too, with his problems of rote and purely mechanical habits that groove both clergy and congregation, often enough inoculating them with a kind of assured immunity to the meaning and to the costly surrender which the words demand, presents another set of obstacles that are not found to disturb a Quaker service of corporate waiting worship.

But in the conduct of both of these types of public worship, whose frailties their most honest adherents do not try to conceal, it is of first importance to note that there is an objective rhythm, a sequence of outwardly guided exposure of the worshipper to stages in the worship of God that are of deep significance. There is, of course, some minor variation between the practices of denominations, but more striking than the variation are the elements of praise, penitence, assurance of forgiveness, thanksgiving, petition, intercession, vocal message of edification, consecration, and benediction that are common to them all. Assisted by music and some vocal participation on the part of the congregation, the clergyman guides them through these movements. They are the outward invitations to inward states of soul, to inward stages of experience, which if they laid hold of the worshipper as they are intended to do would bring him into the presence of the Listener and renew and refresh his life.

Freedom and the Discipline of Interior Order in Quaker Corporate Worship

In laying them aside as Quakers do in their silent waiting worship, there is a responsibility whose magnitude it is scarcely possible to exaggerate that is placed squarely upon the Quaker worshipper himself. Here indeed is a service of worship that demands that every believer be his own priest. For in the Quaker meeting for worship, the member must still his body, still his mind, must attend to the presence of God, must thank and adore him for being what he is, must feel the incongruities in his own life that are out of keeping with such a presence, must long for their removal and for forgiveness, must be inwardly absolved, must become conscious of persons and situations in special need and draw them into this presence, must wait in utter stillness before God, and if some even deeper insight into his own condition should be discovered to him by any vocal ministry that may occur in the meeting or by the unhurried stay in the presence of the Divine Listener, he must be ready to yield to what is required of him.

It is sobering to reflect that unless the Quaker worshipper who has laid aside these outward aids used by his fellow Christians has learned their interior equivalent and has grasped the gentle art of guiding his own spirit through such an hour of worship, guiding it in such a way that it can resist outer and inner distractions or can recover from their ravages if he has succumbed; can draw himself out of the drowsy, day-dreaming, wool-gathering states; can resist what Augustine refers to so tellingly as the state of "dispersion, in which I turned from Thee, the One, and was vainly divided"; can dare to enjoy God and bear what is asked of his life as the cost of company in such a presence, this silent waiting worship can disintegrate for him into a boring state of deadness, into a situation of vegetative stagnation, or what is more likely, can be replaced by a period of strictly mental effort on a variety of themes that is not to be distinguished from intellectual application in any secular setting. For alas, the silent waiting worship of Quakerism is not above its own catalogue of frailties, different as they may be from those of other Christian groups.

I know of nothing more inspiring than an utterly free school where a truly great educator dares to trust the teachers and pupils to the point where the disciplines become inner ones instead of the usual authoritarian "whistle and bell" type that are imposed. I have visited such free schools under remarkable Quaker educators like the late Per Sundberg. But I know of nothing more tragic than such a progressive school when death or illness or transfer has removed the inspirer of these inner disciplines, when they have been allowed to atrophy away, or when a new generation of students has come in demanding the old freedom but ignoring the inward order that the great pedagogue inspired. The resulting absence of any effective order either inward or outward is not easy to endure.

In the Quaker waiting silence, there is a freedom and an absence of externally guided order which is both baffling and deceptive to one on first acquaintance with it. Only slowly do the inner forms of discipline of this form of worship make themselves known, for too little has been written about them. Friends feel almost as if they were becoming morbid even to examine them, and they seem instinctively afraid to look at this inner order too carefully lest they become self-conscious and in some sinister way their spontaneity in worship be interfered with.

One thing, however, is clear. This type of free worship can only be creative in a company of people who are intimately aware of and intimately gathered round the living Listener who knows all yet cares, who shares, and whose expectation never wavers in its constancy. It was to this that they rallied from the beginning. All of the inner order and discipline is a reflection of that. Without it this free silent waiting worship is unthinkable. And without that at the centre these forms of inner order become the cold artificial psychological devices that Friends in their most fearful moments have suspected them of being. The dilemma which anyone seeking to explain Quaker worship faces is that only when this inner ordering has dropped into the background as we are swept up into the presence of the Listener himself, only when what was wilfully and consciously begun, has been crowded out of consciousness by something to which it led, can the real significance of the preparation become apparent, and yet by that time this inner ordering seems like trivial scaffolding compared with what has now been discovered.

On deeper reflection and greater maturity, we can, nevertheless, be brought to see that what is consciously and voluntarily done by us in moving ourselves into the silent waiting worship is not to be scorned or ignored. The fact that we gather for corporate worship at all is a violation of complete spontaneity. God is quite capable of laying hold of us anywhere. Why should we gather at an appointed time to seek to become aware of his presence unless some wilful order on our part is called for?

Voluntary and Involuntary Attention in Quaker Corporate Worship

If we go back to the simplest act of attention on our part, we find it contains both a voluntary, self-induced phase, and if the attention is favoured, an involuntary phase where the object of attention itself takes over and our own effort falls away. The more I know of a subject, the more experience of concentration I have had, the more support I get for this preliminary stage of voluntary attention and the less difficult it is for me to place myself before the subject. If I want to write a letter, I usually get the materials and sit down at my table and call to my mind the person I am writing to. I may read over thoughtfully his last letter. I may think very especially of some things I want to reply to or some experiences of my own I want to share. In the early lines of the letter I may find it hard to get under way. I am easily distracted. I may even give up. But if I stay put, these distractions usually pass and before long I am totally engrossed in this relationship with my absent friend. I have forgotten where I am, what else I have to do, how hard it was to have gotten under way. Then I may emerge and find the letter only partly finished, and again be distracted. In the engrossed phase my attention was given involuntarily. Now I must rely on voluntary attention once again, and I give it. Then another burst of communication comes and I am again absorbed and my attention is wholly involuntary. This may happen several times before I seal up the finished letter.

Does this mean that the fact that I had to use voluntary attention to get placed and under way and again to continue in the breathing patches of my letter is any sign that I do not care for my friend? On the contrary, these voluntary stretches are signs that I am a free person and that I have chosen to spend my freedom on this person for whom I care. Unless I did care enough tó use this voluntary guidance, the involuntary stretches would be most unlikely to come.

In the Quaker discovery of an inward order, an inward discipline that would bear a worshipper into the heart of the silent corporate waiting, much can be learned from such a study of the nature of attention. For it is the focussing and refocussing of attention upon the Divine Listener that is the small part which the frail worshipper can perform and which he must perform if this form of service is to be fruitful for him. The presence of a group of earnest worshippers is of itself a great encouragement to him. But it is not enough. He must do more than bring his body to the place where others have also gathered. He must learn the art of voluntary attention either as a child brought up in it until it becomes a natural thing to enter into the silence, or if this training has not been adequate or is totally wanting, then he must learn it in adult life.

Those Friends to whom this gift of voluntary acts of attention is second nature would do well not to take it too much for granted in newcomers to the meeting. It was not alone a barrenness in worship and ministry among birthright rural American Friends in the mid-nineteenth century which led to the return of a considerable portion of American Quakerism to the conventional free Protestant type of service led by a pastor. It was quite as much the entry into those groups of persons from other denominations to whom the silent waiting worship was foreign and who were never helped to learn the way to participate in it, that led to their adding their voices toward its rejection.

The characteristic reticence of Quakers to speak of these voluntary acts of attention on the part of Quaker worshippers has a further root in their sound realization of the drastic variations in temperament and in personal needs in so intimate a matter as coming into the presence of God. In any suggestions that could be made, it is assumed that the order may need to be changed, there may be some areas that need dropping out entirely, and other forms of help that are not mentioned at all may be especially needed. Yet after all this has been said, and rightly said, there are certain common elements in this matter of taking the spirit by the hand and leading it gently into the presence of the Great Listener and from time to time softly drawing it back there again, elements that should be able to be stated with a minimum of complexity and adornment.

Steps in the Practice of Quaker Corporate Worship

It can be assumed that having been seated on a meeting house bench, the worshipper's first act is to get Brother Ass, the body, properly tethered and out of the way. Many have found it a help if the legs are crossed at the ankles instead of the knees, and the body placed in a posture that neither strains nor droops into an inert slouch. Kagawa is said to advocate keeping the eyes open in prayer, but most worshippers find that closing them aids concentration.

When this is done, how can a beginning of worship be better made than to remember into whose presence we come; "Draw nigh unto God, and he will draw nigh unto you." Several years ago, I was asked to go to Lambarene to visit Albert Schweitzer. I had heard him speak and play the organ when I was a student, twenty-five years before, but I had never met him personally. In the meantime, he had come to embody for me much that was most admirable in our time. I suppose that I would rather have met him than any man living today. Yet as I approached the Lambarene hospital, coming up the Ogowe River in a small boat, my heart was so full I was almost fearful of the meeting. I was thankful for the climb up the steep path before we got to the building in which he had his room. It seemed especially good that we did not have to hurry. For to prepare to go into the presence of such a man, one wants to be inwardly tidied up and ready. I wanted to be inwardly quiet and open when I met him, and not with loose, random talk on the lips. If such a feeling is authentic about meeting a great contemporary, how much truer is it of coming into the presence of the living God?

Distractions and Their Control

To keep recalling the greatness of God whose cosmic ordering of the infinite spaces is as fathomless as his love, and to prepare to sit quietly in his presence here and now in this company of worshippers, is not only a helpful exercise in entering the silent worship but one that again and again, as outer or inner distractions draw at our minds, is a positive restorative of telling strength.

Most Friends know how worse than futile it is to fight against distractions or to feel despondent at their presence as a sign that they are not fitted for this form of worship. There is no noise-free meeting-place. There are no persons, no matter how saintly, who are not subject to persistent mental distractions. These noises and these inner mental intrusions are a part of our outer and our inner lives that are simply there. If accepted, acknowledged and quietly ignored as we move on into worship, they fade into the background. Some prefer to enfold outer distractions into a prayer, "Oh God, may my heart wing its way as swiftly to Thee as the flight of the jet plane whose moan has punctured our silence." "Oh God, kindle in our hearts here and now a childish joy that will match that of those gay playing children whose shouts we have heard," and with this they get on with their worship.

Some find it helpful to ask God what this mental distraction, if it is persistent, is really able to communicate to them, what unfaced fear, what unfulfilled obligation, what leading into greater faithfulness is concealed in it, and find themselves back in his presence having been opened even more deeply to his will by this intrusion. Most Friends, however, acknowledge and ignore these distractions, leaving them to furnish a cloud frame over their worship but one to which their attention is not centrally directed. As they quietly return to the centre, these distractions may even have served to renew their naked intent to yield themselves to the presence of God.

It is a rare Friend whose own personal needs do not operate to draw him inwards when he has made a beginning in worship. The Listener hears the language of the heart that often has much to tell: the infidelities of the week, the decision still pending, the heart of stone, the withheld consent. In his hearing, how differently these things appear! How far from the mark! How deep the abyss! Mercy, forgiveness, a fresh approach are required. Such silent worship is not for the good, if there are any. It is for sinners. Before the Listener, how clear beyond a shadow all sin becomes, yet the forgiveness is already given before it is asked. The healing is there, even the strength for the renewal, for the ignition of this supposedly noninflammable man. "The light that shows us our sins is the Light that heals us." But this light is no sun lamp. It is an X-ray beam. It is deep therapy.

The Role of Adoration in Worship

Thankfulness for such a Listener's ministrations is something many Friends find a natural response to the occasion. This is not a mere counting of one's blessings, although that is an exercise not to be sneered at. It goes deeper, however, and there is thankfulness for the Listener himself, for his love, his constancy, his caring, for being what he is. It is at this point that regular touch in private with the Bible and a fresh sense of the meaning of Jesus' life and ministry and death and resurrection and inward accessibility can furnish a reminder of countless grounds for gratitude. This can also pierce the torpid envelope around the worshipper's soul with a sense of how much God cares. Thankfulness at this level passes readily into adoration, into the quietness of which Fox speaks when we are instructed to be "still and cool from our own thoughts," simply open-hearted at being in the company of the living Listener. We are known, we are accepted, we are thankful to be silent before him. The Psalmist's "Search me, know me, try me, lead me" are all laid aside. We do not want his gifts. We want only himself. We want only to enjoy him.

Yet in this presence, in this very enjoyment, there is no snug coziness. In the adoration of him, we find ourselves always quivering before a mysterious depth that we cannot get to the bottom of. The Negro spiritual declares: "God is so high, you can't get above him. God is so low, you can't get beneath him. God is so wide, you can't get around him" and the experience of adoration confirms this. If in a friend or in one we love there is always a final solitude, a final depth that we forever approach but never penetrate, is it surprising that in the living God, we find an abyss of being that in adoration brings us into a mingled sense of awe and of glad creatureliness? How good to be the creatures of such a creator, the branches of such a vine, the friends of such a Friend!

Corporate Worship and the Redemptive Community

But Quakers enter the service of silent waiting not alone or in a series of separate reveries but in a company of worshippers. They know something of the needs of their fellow worshippers; they know something of the sufferings and needs of the world. Often they are conscious of a whole redemptive company of faithful departed ones who are engaged in this all-embracing struggle as well. This realization and these needs are gently brought into the worship in the form of intercession, of brothering the souls of men. "We must be saved together. Together we must be presented before Him. Together we must return to the Father's house," Charles Péguy has his *Joan of Arc* declare. Often Friends have been able to cross the threshold into true worship in bringing into the Listener's presence the needs of others rather than their own. But if I do not know my fellow members, if I do not call on them, if I am not concerned for them, if my mind and all of my personal resources are not at the disposal of both near and distant situations of need at other times, this leading of the spirit to bring before the presence of God these needs has neither sincerity nor deep intent behind it.

Russell Maltby, speaking of his own prayers of intercession, says he heard through them a voice that queried "How long hast thou cared for him?" Often in intercessory prayer we are brought to realize how little we care, and how much God cares, and how lightly we had asked for "the ordination of the pierced hands." But in this very insight we are suddenly before the Listener again and we have been stabbed by the painful realization of how long he has cared.

There is finally an offering of what we are and what we have to the Listener, a holy pliability, an inward agreement to the one thing needful, a waiting on him for some accent, some quickening that will draw us more usefully into the intricate skein of human relationship in which each of us stands. To leave a meeting without this offering is to leave too soon.

Now in speaking of these voluntary acts of attention that Friends may well learn how to apply inwardly to their own spirits as they sit in a corporate waiting silence; the acts of aspiration in remembering into whose presence they come; of penitence; of thankfulness for absolution; the acts of adoration; of intercession and consecration, and of openness to concern, we have been speaking of those little-mentioned inner disciplines which this free form of religious worship asks of its participants. But these inner disciplines have all presupposed the active moving presence of the living Listener. And the Society of Friends needs nothing as much today as a fresh baptism of inward realization of who it is that truly sits at the head of the Meeting.

The Gathering That Is Beyond Voluntary Attention

For the gentle inward leading of the mind by the Quaker worshipper over the ground which in outward symbols and words is faithfully patrolled by our fellow Christians in their services of worship is immeasurably assisted when again and again what is begun as a voluntary, subjective act of guided attention on our parts is lifted from our hands, and our souls wheel through this course drawn irresistibly by the living power of the all tender One whom we confront in worship. Then we know inwardly what Angelus Silesius meant by his Christian imperative, "Bloom, frozen Christian, bloom. May stands before thy door." Now what we have done, and rightly done inwardly in the way of gentle leading, of praying, is both superseded and confirmed. The Russian Orthodox Saint Seraphim of Sarov could not have put more simply what the experience of Quaker corporate worship has learned: "We must pray only until God the Holy Spirit descends . . . when he comes to visit us, we must cease to pray."

It is good to come to the Friend's house of worship. It is good to have remembered him very especially at this time and to have brought my body and my mind and all I possess to this celebration in his honour. It is good to have placed myself quietly in his presence and to have remembered all he has done for me, all he has done for others, all he does for the cosmic universe, and to have opened my needs and the needs of the world to him. But how infinitely better it is when in the course of this, I and my fellows feel ourselves gathered up and our true conditions discovered to us, feel ourselves brought low, tendered, renewed and strengthened and perhaps even commissioned to take a step that we might have ignored or hesitated over, had this occasion been wanting.

Now there is no contempt for having learned the inner guiding that brought us to his presence. Now there is no confusion of these rehearsals with the performance itself. Now there is no scorn for the outward practices of other groups. There is only the query: "Did you finally find the Listener taking over? Did he clarify your speech? Did he bring you to insight? Were you at last silent before him, broken and silent, and yet joyous and infinitely grateful?"

Where Words Come From in Free Vocal Ministry

No mention has been made in the description of the corporate waiting silence gathered to himself by the living Listener, of the part which vocal ministry plays in the Quaker service of worship. Luther once declared, "Where God's word is not preached, it would be better that no one should sing or read or come together." If this were to be taken literally as referring to vocal ministry, Quakers would repudiate it vigorously. For the meeting for worship can and occasionally does conclude without any offering of vocal ministry at all, yet with the word of God so mightily preached in the hearts of the assembled company that few present are not touched by it.

Quaker experience repeatedly verifies the fact that without any outward preaching, the corporate silent waiting on God can of itself become a crucible where the slag is separated from the pure ore and where precious metal is refined and cleansed. Again and again such a worshipping company has been baptized into a feeling sense of "where words come from" and has been spoken to directly by the Word and not by words.

One of the tragedies of formal Protestant services is their wordiness, their forensic character. It is so easy for Protestants to confuse the Logos, the Word which God speaks to the heart of the world, with the words of the preacher. When Jesus gave his command, "Go ye into all the world and preach the gospel" it is highly doubtful if he had a global speaking tour in mind. In his own ministry, healing and prayer, friendship, common meals, common festivals and even his final decision to die, all give the appearance of having been in his estimation on a level quite comparable to his speaking. Stanley once declared of Livingstone, "He made me a Christian and he never knew he was doing it."

There is an old story of a boy who joined the Franciscan Order longing to become a friar preacher. He was put to work in the kitchen for the first months and got more and more restive and impatient to get on with learning to preach. Finally Francis himself drew him by the arm one day and asked him if he would like to go into the village with him to preach. The boy's heart was full as they set out. They stopped on the way to see a man whose son needed work in the town, then to call on an old woman who was sick and lonely, and to visit with a peasant at work in his fields. In the town, they saw a merchant about a post for the son, they begged some food for the brothers at home, they talked with some people in the market place, and then Francis turned to the boy and gaily proposed that they return to the friary. "But when are we going to preach?" asked the boy in an anguish of concern. Francis slipped his arm about him and said, "Why my brother, we've been preaching all the time."

When all of this has been said, however, and Friends have always had a very special tenderness for the forms of ministry that are executed in deeds rather than in words, it cannot be denied that both Jesus and Francis did try to convey, in the precious vehicle of human communication supplied by words, what God's love and caring was like. But both were men who knew silence. Jesus by night, Jesus in the desert, Jesus on the mountain returned to silence. Francis on the middle slopes of Mt. Subasio or on the jagged Bibbiena hills at La Verna did the same. Theirs was a speech that came up out of the silence, the silence before the living Listener where their lives were being continually renewed and restored. Their words were rimmed with this silence, with this presence, and therefore they carried an authority and a power that contrived, detached words never possess.

A contemporary German philosopher, Martin Heidegger, in a happy phrase refers to language as "the dwelling place of being." Language is indeed the foreground of reality, its articulate shore. But back of language and clinging to it, when it is real, is the receptive sea of silence. Language is always tempted to make reality more articulate than it is. And the words of language are always being rebuked and overrun and swallowed up again by the silent ocean of existence from which they once emerged. It is obvious that without some form of language, existence would be hidden and mute, but only when words come up fresh and breathless, come up still moist and glistening from the sea of existence, do they carry power and authority.

If this is true, it cannot surprise us that words made from other words, books written from other books, sermons preached from other sermons lack this authentic ring and power. Language torn away from the background of silence, of existence, becomes stale, emaciated, and powerless. When words speak to the centre of existence in a listener and call for a recasting of his life, they must have come freshly out of the same centre of existence which the speaker has touched.

At no point is this more patently self-evident than in vocal ministry. Bede Frost in his *St. John of the Cross* goes as far as to say, "The exercise of preaching is spiritual rather than vocal. For although it be practised by means of outward words, its power and efficacy reside not in these but in the inward spirit," and he goes on to add, "It is a common matter that so far as we can judge here below the better is the life of the preacher, the greater the fruit is produced." There is an old adage that declares, "a holy priest makes a perfect people; a fervent priest, a pious people; a decent priest, a Godless people. Always a degree less of life in those who are begotten." In these remarks about the preacher's life, the reference seems to be to the issue of whether his "inward spirit" comes from the source of power itself. It is as if the preacher, like a disc of cobalt, could only beam through diseased tissue and radiate healing when he had been long in the atomic pile and had become a transmuter of what was received there. The Quaker insistence that vocal ministry which occurs in its corporate silent waiting worship shall first grow up out of the hidden life that is moving in the meeting and that before it is released it shall be held in this life, shaped in this life, and confirmed by this life, is an expression of the same temper.

This relation of words to the Word has been a central problem for Quakerism from the beginning. For it soon enough became clear that a meeting for worship that was habitually "starved for words," habitually silent, tended to wither and dwindle. A Swiss writer, Max Picard, suggests that "the perfect silence is heard to echo in the perfect word." In a meeting for worship, in spite of exceptions, the silence is likely to be most vital when it is not habitually mute but when it comes to fruition in vocal ministry and in turn enfolds this ministry in the labouring silence which follows.

This normal expectation of vocal ministry on the part of a lay body like the Quakers has profoundly tempted it at periods in its life, and in the last half of the nineteenth century went so far as to lead one large group in the Society to secure such ministry by engaging professional ministers to supply it, as is done in other denominations. This same expectation in the silent waiting type of worship has also had the effect of tempting some of its members to speak words that have lacked the inward baptism that was spoken of above, resulting in a chatty, conversational type of contrived homily or the word of ethical counsel directed at the worshipper's conscience. There has never been a time, however, when some flash of the strain of prophetic ministry has not been present to reverse Gresham's law that bad money drives out the good. This prophetic ministry has had an authentic mark about it and while its leafy structure has altered from generation to generation it has been marked by a common stem.

A Corporate Listening Silence and a Prophetic Ministry

What is that common stem? What is the common trait that characterizes a prophetic ministry and makes the varied accents of the generations fall away before its invariableness? A prophetic ministry is a listening ministry. It has learned what is meant by "Listen before you speak, see before you say." Because it is a listening ministry, it is a ministry that has come freshly from a first-hand experience of the good news it proclaims. It has been preceded not, as in most services, by a period of worship on the part of the congregation with the minister carrying through his professional routine in the prescribed way. Here there is no longer a division of minister and worshipper.

In this Quaker mutation, ministry has been preceded by the whole company, including those who may minister, being gathered in worship and the very ministry rising up out of this listening silence. Here the living God has listened this organ of the gathered meeting into a condition of openness. The meeting has been listened into a readiness to receive. It has been listened into a corporate drawing toward the loving One whose presence can reconcile all enmity, melt all hatred, and kindle into active love every power that seems to resist it.

Here is the common stem that George Fox and Isaac Penington in the seventeenth century; John Fothergill, John Woolman and Job Scott in the eighteenth; Thomas Shillitoe and Stephen Grellet in the nineteenth; and John Wilhelm Rowntree, Rufus Jones and John William Graham in our own time, in spite of the vastly different accounts of the human mind which they might have given, could all have agreed upon.

A Balance Sheet on Quietism's Answer to Where Words Come From

The most extravagant eighteenth-century Quaker Quietist who sought to treat the mind in worship and in preparation for ministry as a tabula rasa, as a blank sheet of paper, or as a hollow tube, a horn through which God could blow, becomes less unintelligible to us today if we recognize what he was protesting against. It was a ministry of words, a ministry that had not been freshly tempered, hammered out, and reshaped in the powerful forge of the silent listening meeting. They were pleading instead for longer and more attentive listening to keep the forward, wordy part of themselves back and to be penetrated by the all-searching, all-transforming presence of the eternal Christ who could be met only in that way. They were asking those who lead others to stay seated in that presence until their own frosted hearts were melted down and they were fused with the needs of those immediately present and of those everywhere who suffer. These men rightly sensed that it was not words alone, or the minister alone, but rather a hidden man in the worshipping minister that is called out and quickened in the course of the group-listening to speak to the hidden man in his fellows.

Job Scott who, like John Woolman before him, died in middle life of smallpox while on a foreign journey in the ministry, was one of that Quietist company. Of his own witness, a memorial minute from the Meeting in Dublin, Ireland, that is attached to his Journal says: "He was a diligent waiter to experience renewed qualification to service, before he attempted to move either in ministry or in the transactions of the discipline; as well knowing that without a fresh anointing, any endeavours to act must prove ineffectual and tend to a lifeless formality: against which he was zealously concerned to bear testimony."

To read the journals of such men as Job Scott, John Fothergill or John Churchman, to name only three, is to come into a fresh realization of how much they have to teach us about unhurried waiting until the surface mind has been stilled and the deeper levels of our being are drawn out. Such a reading, however, will not close our eyes to the need for prizing more highly than they do, the gifts which the Quaker worshipper brings to the ministry, nor will it tempt us to belittle, as they did, what these gifts in God's keeping can contribute to ministry.

It would seem that the principal ground for this Quietist error lay in their curious psychology that failed to distinguish between an inward clarification in which the ministering worshipper was indeed given an insight to be shared, and the different levels on which this insight might be searched and communicated. Failure to distinguish between these, resulted in the first place in a radical depreciation of all natural and cultivated gifts which the ministering worshipper might lay in God's hands for use in searching and communicating this disclosure. It also ignored the results of all previous dedication. Such a ministering worshipper may have been brought to live by the hour and the day and the year as one who was more and more attentive to "the pulses of the divine whisper," and therefore may have arrived at the meeting for worship so prepared that when he had felt the inward exercise of the meeting, and when the Divine Listener had brought his inward conversation to clarity, his mind and life presented a supple instrument that was fitted to search and to share this insight in such a way that the hidden power of God could charge the words used.

Laying the Fire in Vocal Ministry

To admit freely that the precise words, the illustrations, the capacity to quote scripture, or the telling lines of some poem have been drawn from the worshipping minister's lifetime of preparation is in no sense to minimize the source of the insight which they are used to search and to communicate. George Fox was an assiduous student of the Bible and knew it almost by heart. The mighty works of God recorded in Scripture were always before him and this knowledge was always at the disposal of the inward insights that were given to him. Fox was also a man of prayer, a man who was "energized in secret for life in the open world." By being continually open to inward guidance, the exercise in the meeting for worship was a natural one for him and he came to it attentive and inwardly gathered. The practice of regular prayer and a continual intent to listen for the deeper meaning in everything that happens in life is an indispensable preparation for this type of ministry.

It is said of John Woolman that he was a hard reader all his life and his ministry and writings reveal an appreciation for and a discernment of the views of others that reflects this form of outward preparation. Bonaventura, when asked by Thomas Aquinas to show him his library, took him to his prayer cell where a crucifix hung. The incident is significant in putting first things first. But a look at a sermon that Bonaventura preached would show that he brought to that prayer cell a disciplined mind and spirit that knew the best that the ages could give, and that he brought this with him in order to lay it at the foot of the cross as he knelt to remember the sacrificial love of Jesus.

This in no sense suggests that formal education necessarily cultivates or prepares the spirit for ministry or that the humble spirit-tipped word of an utterly unlearned man or woman or child in a meeting may not minister to its deepest need, but it does propose that nothing is too good for God and that over the years there is no preparation of the mind and heart and will that God cannot use and use with power to further his ministry.

As I think of the vocal ministry of two great Quaker spirits of our time, Rufus M. Jones and Henry T. Hodgkin, and of their outward preparation for ministry, I know how they stored their minds and hearts not only first and foremost with the Bible, but also with the best books of their generation. Books of poetry, literature, religious history, and especially biography were always on their tables, and Rufus Jones's personal collection of books which are now in the Haverford library are full of heavy pencil-markings and marginal notes, showing the intimacy of his encounter with these books. Henry Hodgkin took the first hour each morning for a time of silent prayer, for reading the Bible or some devotional book, and then for writing his heart out in a commonplace book that no one ever saw but that enabled him to set down some of the insights that had come to him.

Gratry in an old book called *The Well Springs* speaks of this discipline of listening and writing which Henry Hodgkin practiced. "What, you will ask of me, is the meaning of listening to God? . . . What am I to do in reality? Here is my answer. You are to write. . . . St. Augustine begins his *Soliloquies* thus, 'I was a prey to a thousand various thoughts and for many days had been making strenuous efforts to find myself, my own good, and the evil to avoid, when on a sudden . . . it was said to me, "If you find what you are seeking, what will you do with it? To whom will you confide it?" "I shall keep it in my memory," answered I. "But is your memory capable of treasuring all that your mind has conceived?" "No, certainly it cannot." "Then you must write, that this offspring of your mind may animate and strengthen you!"'"

Not only may the storing of the memory, the wide reading, the life of prayer, and the discipline of writing like a well-laid fire in the life of the worshipping minister be consumed in worship, but his own faculties are of importance as well. The power of reason to interpret a spiritual insight and put it convincingly is a precious gift. When John Churchman declares, "I let in reasoning, and so departed for a time from my inward guide and safe counsellor," it is well to recall Isaac Penington's classic remark that, "Reason is not sin; but a deviating from that from which reason came is sin." Churchman is referring to precisely this deviating of reason from that from which it came, but the Quaker Quietists generally neglected the more precise distinctions of Penington and denounced the faculty itself.

To learn how to use the full preparation and the full faculties both before and after the inward tendering and the inward accent is, and always must be, the condition of a sound Quaker ministry. Theresa of Avila once wrote, "God gave us our faculties for use; each of them will receive its proper reward. Then do not let us try to charm them to sleep, but permit them to do their work, until divinely called to something higher."[3] When Friedrich von Hügel wrote in the opening lines of the preface to his monumental work *The Mystical Element of Religion* that it "embodies well nigh all the writer has been able to learn and to test, for the matter of religion during now some thirty years of adult life," he was speaking of what mature Friends who covet a powerful vocal ministry might long to have go with them to meeting and be laid before the flame of waiting silence. For to those who have been seasoned and prepared in this way and who bring with them to meeting all that they have been able to learn and to test in the years of their adult life, there is a mighty instrument and witness which the Listener may freshly anoint and use.

Vocal Ministry and the Ministering Worshipper's Own Commitment

Closely related to the prayer and study and the full use of a man's faculties and past experience in the waiting ministry is the depth of the ministering worshipper's own personal religious commitment. For the task of preparing for the Quaker ministry is one of preparing the person and not the message. It is not hard to believe that one of the most effective preparations for ministry is past faithfulness in response to divine leading. If this faithfulness has been tested by times when the man went against his own earthly advantage, it cannot but have left him more open, and to have made the fellow worshippers to whom he ministered more open because they knew the quality of his commitment.

The amazing itinerant lay ministry of the eighteenth century was carried on only at the heaviest cost to the Friends involved, and to their families. It affected the style of life and the choice of business which would free them from cumber that they might follow where they were inwardly led. The sheer fatigue of months and even years on horseback, the perils to health and the dangers attending travel by land and sea in that period, the long separation from their families, the willingness when widowed even to entrust their own children to others in order to set out dauntlessly on these journeys, was a powerful witness to those with whom they entered the silent worship that these men and women were committed to the Inward Guide and that they cared deeply for the welfare of their souls.

The words of the young wife of Job Scott, the lay minister, tell of one form of this cost in a way that few could miss. As she lay dying she said to him, "I have several times thought I should have been willing to have taken the care of these dear children a little longer, if it had been the Divine Will; and I have thought, if it might have been so ordered, I could have given up everything that might have been called for; even if it had been to give thee up to travel in truth's service, let the time be longer or shorter. I have always given thee up with a good degree of cheerfulness, and have been supported in thy absence beyond my expectation; and yet I have often thought since thy return from thy last journey, that I did not know that I could ever give thee up again, or bear up in thy absence. But in this sickness I have felt as though I could give up all, if I might be spared a little longer to help along in the care of children. It has seemed to me that I should give thee up, my dear husband, to go wherever the Lord may lead thee; it has seemed so, but maybe it would not be so with me, if I should be tried with it; and perhaps I shall be taken away, that thou mayest be set more at liberty to attend to the Lord's requirings, in whatever part of the world he may see meet to employ thee."[4]

John Churchman having been on a journey in the ministry in Britain, Ireland and Holland records, "In this visit I was from home four years and twelve days, having travelled [on horseback] by land nine thousand one hundred miles and attended about a thousand meetings." On finally landing in Wilmington, Delaware, after this long absence he says, with his characteristic restraint, "I went home that evening, where I found a kind reception."[5]

The equivalent in miniature of this kind of service today by which a concern for the fellow-worshippers of our meetings may lead us to find the necessary time to know them, to visit them, to have them in our homes, and to make their needs our concern is a tested preparation for ministry of the highest importance. A person who throughout the week thinks of the approaching meeting for worship and holds up inwardly some of the needs of those who attend, is being prepared for that kind of participation in the meeting for worship that may open the way for helpful ministry. Ministry is often deepened by our natural exposure to those in greatest need, whether it be physical need, as in a constant visiting of the poor, of those in prison, of those whom group prejudice segregates, or to the poor in spirit, those who face mental turmoil and inner problems. Few who feel this kind of responsible love for the meeting do not in the course of the week find some experience, some insight, something they have read that has helped them, some crushing burden they know some member or some group is bearing which they have held up to the Light, without these things appearing as seeds out of which ministry could grow.

What Turns the Waiting Worshipper into a Minister?

But all of this girding up of the worshippers who gather is preparation, and no more. When they enter the meeting, they proceed as any worshipper to open themselves before the Listener. Once William Penn is said to have begun to preach on the way up the aisle, as he was taking his seat in meeting. But for a message truly to come up out of a meeting for worship, it must have been held in its inner tempering power. While it is not a matter of time, few meetings can gather in less than a quarter of an hour and some find it takes at least twice that long before a deep level is reached. Tempered ministry, then, must rise out of a gathered meeting, and it is not surprising that it seldom comes until after this gathering has taken place.

What happens to the worshipper that turns him into a minister? He may have brought with him certain seeds out of which ministry could flower or he may have come without any expectation that he would that day be called into the ministry. What he is and what moves in him is slowly disclosed before the living Listener, who gathers the meeting to himself, and there in that tendering presence an ordering takes place.

He may and often does feel that all that he brought with him is not in the tide that is running or he may feel that something that had seemed important has now become enormously more important but in quite a fresh way. His mind may be drawn to this in such a way that he sees its implications for his own life with an icy clarity, and the consequences for him may be all too apparent. Should such a personal message then, be shared with the meeting? It may be, but this is not necessarily the case. Much is given us for our own use and testing before it is given us to publish as truth.

Job Scott says so simply, "I was shut up as to words but had clear openings. It is sometimes wisely ordered, that precious and divine openings are treasured up in the Lord's treasury: but how dangerous would it be . . . to lavish them out among people only because we are favoured with openings without the word of command, to deliver them to people."[6] John Churchman, too, relates that, "I began to see there was a difference between seeing what was to be done, and being bidden to do the thing shown . . . being made sensible that every opening or vision which the Lord is pleased to manifest to his servants is not for immediate utterance."[7]

I have yet to see the time when some moving insight that came into a worshipper's mind in meeting but that was not suitable for immediate sharing, was ever lost. For if it goes into the life of the worshipper it will bear ultimate fruit in his own faithful preparation for later ministry, and if it is meant for the meeting but seems at this time to lack the compulsion to be publicly shared, it is sure to gather strength and power and one day be drawn forward when it is in the life and to be charged with added strength for having been held back at the Listener's disposal.

In another worshipper, however, there may be an accent placed on something that has grown up in his mind in worship and a great tenderness rise up in him toward those that are gathered in worship. This may grow until he feels a deep sense of the inward need to which this message that is springing up within him might speak. As in John Woolman's call to visit the Indians on the Susquehanna, so in genuine ministry, "Love was the first motion." John Churchman writes how in his experience the call to vocal ministry came: "As I sat in one of our meetings, I felt a flow of affection to the people . . . in which extraordinary flow of affection I had a bright opening."[8]

This inward caring for those to whom one is to minister and this inward disclosure of conditions and of need is a most important part of the preparation to speak. For in that moment of being drawn into speech by the Listener, the opaque veil that separates us from each other in so much of life seems swiftly to be lifted as this life and power courses through us.

Where Words Come From

The insight that has come must be clothed. The early Christians were counselled to "take no thought for what you are to say" and there are often times when in a flash all is ready. Illustrations are there and the words with which to begin and to close this exercise in the ministry have all unbidden tumbled into place. Far more often however the message grows, and in the growing, the worshipper experiences the most creative moments of his life.

Count Keyserling declares somewhere that all of the luminous insights a man ever gets in his life can be cupped into a few fractions of a second. But in a gathered meeting this miracle may happen countless times in a single life. In the company of the Divine Listener and of the silent worshipping community, the worshipping minister sees a focussing take place and sees non-essentials trimmed away. Arnold Toynbee once criticized a sketch which his mother had drawn, complaining that she had omitted some foreground detail that his eye could see in the scene that she had drawn. She replied that in sketching the first principle one had to learn was what to leave out. Here this operation of what to leave out takes place without effort. A hidden meaning that at first disclosed only a part of itself, and the least important part, now may be drawn forward; an example falls into place; a verse he had not recalled for years; a confirmation of Scripture that is unmistakable, are all there.

In this very moment a worshipper is more passive and more alive; more in the spell of Another, yet more intensely himself; more a living cell of the worshipping group, and yet more of a separated organ cut off in order that he may speak to its condition, than he can believe could be true of himself. When this centering process has done its work there is a gathering of compulsion that the message should be given. In some, this compulsion heightens the breathing and is as inwardly perceptible as any physical arousal of adrenalin in its preparation of the body for action. In others it is a quieter compulsion that goes on at the mental level. If this is steadily resisted, the compulsion may fade, but the worshipper is not likely to escape the sense of his infidelity to the call that came to him, and restless days may follow.

In his *Faith of a Quaker,* John William Graham has dared to set down with admirable frankness the experience of a mature Quaker in being drawn into ministry in a meeting. The long paragraph is so revealing that no sound account of this exercise could well omit it: "It comes by waiting. When I sit down in meeting I recall whatever may have struck me freshly during the past week. This is, initially at least, a voluntary and outward act. It means simply that the outward man is ready to run if he is sent. It means that the will is given up to service; and it is quite possible to stop everything and take an opposite attitude. So thoughts suggest themselves—a text that has smitten one during the week—a new light on a phrase, a verse of poetry—some incident private or public. These pass before the door whence shines the heavenly light. Are they transfigured? Sometimes, yes; sometimes, no. If nothing flames, silence is my portion. I turn from ideas of the ministry to my own private needs. From these sometimes a live coal from off the altar is brought, suddenly and unexpectedly and speech follows. Sometimes it does not. Again there are times when the initial thought strikes in of itself from the Inner Man beyond the will. These are times to be thankful for. Often two or three thoughts that have struck home during the week are woven together in unexpected ways. When the fire is kindled, the blaze is not long. In five minutes from its inception the sermon is there, the heart beats strongly and up the man must get. How trying is any interruption during those few rapt and fruitful minutes, when the whole scheme is unfolding itself, and flashing itself up the brain. There are the five or six main points, the leading sentences of thought are there, the introductory expository teaching, the generalization, the illustration, the final lesson and appeal, they fall into place. The sermon is made, but I, the slow compiler, did not make it."9

The content of this ministry can never be prescribed from without. There is no Quaker liturgical cycle of the Christian year. Yet it can be said that a meeting whose members read and inwardly digest the Bible, who pray, and who are exposed to the needs of one another and of those who suffer in the world around them, will not fail to be drawn down into the great Christian themes of the love, the joy and the greatness of God; of suffering, sin, redemption, atonement and resurrection. The passionate new interest among younger Friends today in Christian theology has come in part because these great themes have been too much neglected in the Quaker recent past. But this fresh accent on theology will not be enough. I recall how Agnes Tierney once told of passing a bookshop in Philadelphia and noting a sign in the window which read "Second-hand theology for sale". It will only be when these great themes come up out of a baptism of inner experience, that they will speak to the needs of meetings for worship in our time. Only then can they help to lift and frame all that we do.

The content of these messages when it is authentic fulfills the requirements of existential preaching. It exposes to light, demolishes, and makes uninhabitable for the future, comfortable hollow logs where we had long been snugly hibernating. I remember hearing of how the schoolmaster in Le Chambon, at a farewell dinner for André Trocmé who was leaving his long pastorate there, described their previous two fine pastors who had been able to give them weekly sermons to which, he insisted, one could really look forward. After them you could go home and enjoy a big Sunday dinner. But in 1934, Pastor Trocmé came and changed all that. Since then he had never, not for a single Sunday, been permitted to leave the church in complacent content with himself. "I see the wrong that round me lies, I feel the guilt within," wrote Whittier, and existential preaching touches this spring in us. To interpret the tireless and utterly adequate reconciling love of the one who stands at the door and knocks, to move the springs of human compassion, to take away fear and restore vulnerable love, is content enough to sustain any worshipping group.

In the preparation of a worshipper to minister, the influence of the corporate waiting, of the worshipping group, is not a small one. Those psychically sensitive Quietist members were often silent in meeting after meeting because they felt a darkness in the group that stifled them. Job Scott wrote of such an experience, "I was enabled to sound an alarm among them." A worshipping group that contains a number of persons who are in a state of lassitude and torpor, or in a condition of numbness induced by the dispersed character of their ordinary living, or in a condition of exclusive absorption in their own internal problems, or in a state of critical testiness toward each other and toward any one who may speak, does not fulfill the requirements of positive collective expectancy out of which real worship and real ministry may come.

A medical doctor once refused to give a bed-ridden college professor patient of his a most helpful book, saying that it would serve no purpose, because he would only tear it to pieces with his critically poised mind. For every plant there is a degree of frost beyond which it will winter-kill, and the tender plant of vocal ministry is no exception. It is when the worshipping group is open and loving, it is when it is abandoned to the inner exercise that may take place in it, when there is a movement at its heart expressed in Guy Butler's lines, "We wait, we wait the catalyst, we wait, we wait, we wait," that it becomes possible for one member to arise and express the very moving which half a dozen others may have felt, albeit not in their own words. In such an atmosphere when ministry is brief and does not try to exhaust the insight, others may rise and add to it until something grows that no single speaker could have presented, and the meeting closes with a feeling of blessing and unity.

How blessed any Protestant minister might feel if he could have the privilege of sitting for an hour in silent waiting with a little inner company of his congregation that week. How that message might be clipped, how it might be refocussed, and upon occasion how it might be completely recast as he was swept by a deeper sense of both the need of his group and of the abundance of God's power to meet the need. In such an experience, how it might be charged with power!

How helpful, too, it might be if this occasion might become a regular spring and source of his ministry, if ministry were required of him that week, or a place where one of the lay group sitting with him might from time to time be inwardly drawn to discharge the vocal ministry of the meeting and on that occasion relieve him of that exercise. If to this little group could in time be added the whole congregation who would all gather with him to wait in this way, with the freedom to minister shared still more widely, and the message come straight from a freshly touched mind and heart, is it impossible to see some, at least, of the steps by which this Quaker treasure of a silent waiting ministry could be shared with the whole free church family?

Quaker Worship and the Unfolding of Concerns

But the experience of worship and of ministry has not done its full work until there is a kind of inner "regrouping of one's resources," as Gabriel Marcel so effectively expresses it, until in the life of the worshipper there is produced a state of "disponibilité," a condition of being expendable, of being at the disposal of the Listener and of one's fellows who are infinitely precious to him. This tendering of the heart and being drawn into a fresh sensitiveness to the needs of others, this malleable willingness to be used in meeting that need, is the condition in which what Friends have called a "concern" may arise.

The word "concern" is often used too lightly today. Friends may refer to any whim or fancy of an individual to do some act or to champion some cause as that person's "concern." In its truest form, a concern refers to a costly inner leading to some act that in the course of its fulfillment may take over the very life of the one it engages. At this level, it can be said that in a genuine concern, a person has been drawn into the living inward linkage of man and God, of man and man, and of man and creation. For to be brought into a condition of awareness of the compassion of the living Listener is to have disclosed to the worshipper a realization of the redemptive order of love that girdles our world for its healing. Is it surprising then that men and women who have been listened into life should be called upon not only to serve as a delicate litmus solution to record and point to outer and inner needs, but should be drawn as well to set about the process of meeting the needs that they or others have detected?

This does not mean to depreciate those exercises of worship and ministry which culminate in stirring the level of being of the worshipper himself. This result is more than ample justification for them. But it does imply that when the Listener who has been revealed by Jesus Christ changes the level of our being, Friends over the centuries have found an accompanying passion of love and concern for their fellow creatures that has not remained vague and abstract but has frequently drawn them into specific and concrete expressions of it.

The order of the unfolding of a concern has not been identical. Occasionally the concern has put its finger on a specific thing to be done and on the initial steps of carrying it out. When Joseph Sturge in his inner agony over the steadily worsening relations of England and Russia and the impending Crimean War felt personally drawn to visit the Czar and to labour with him, the concern and the means seemed clear and specific. More often the concern has laid hold of the person in terms of a deep inner distress over the wrongness of some situation or a yearning to minister to some condition of need without more than the first minute step being clear to him as to how to deal with it. A person may have a leading to go or to offer to go to some situation of need. He may go and remain there for some time, and perhaps when he has returned may go again before the specific steps to be taken become clear to him. If the first step that is laid upon him is not undertaken, the later ones are not disclosed. As Adrienne Speyer says in her commentary on the Gospel of John, "It is hardly ever possible to see from the start all that God is to mean to one. . . . Once open to the light, he may ask God to claim him more essentially and more profoundly. But on one condition, that he does not refuse the first small act God demands of him."

"The first small act" is sooner or later known to every worshipper. The first act may be a visit, or a letter, or a gift, or it may be a first alert to clear the decks of one's engagements for orders that are still sealed. The mysterious thing of it all is that in God's eyes there are no "little" things. Everything matters and everything leads to something further. Even when a concern is as specific as Joseph Sturge's, the disclosure is still progressive. How little he knew at that time, the humiliation and misunderstanding that his journey to Russia was to cost him in the months and years of patriotic fervour that came with the Crimean War. How little he could forsee that out of that humiliation and inward chastening was to come his call to Finland to release a chain of reconciliation that has not yet fully spent its force.

The revisions to major concerns which subsequent reflection or the wise provision of the Quaker requirement that these concerns be laid before a gathered meeting for their counsel and acceptance, or which the measured judgment of wise Friends who may be personally consulted may make to help shape the course of a concern, have in practice been found only to result in refining it. If the delay entailed by this process of scrutiny should whittle the concern away to nothing and it should wither in the mind of the one on whom it was laid, then its authenticity can be viewed with considerable suspicion. For a genuine concern is marked both by its persistence and, strangely enough, by its flexibility and openness about the means by which it is to be carried out.

Meister Eckhart's remark that "a man can only spend in good works what he earns in contemplation" is not unconnected with the Society of Friends' experience in the matter of concerns out of which its acts of service have risen. For only as these services have sprung from, and been shaped and consummated in the life of such inward concerns have they left any lasting residue that has quickened men to the love of God and their fellows, and to an implementing of vital peace. For that reason our times call Friends to a fresh season of inward waiting on the Divine Listener who can alone draw out and redispose of our tightly clutched lives and our personal and institutional plans and programs.

The Society's experience, however, has been that those who from the first entry into a concern have learned to listen, have learned to keep open, have asked the question about each turn of events, "What may I learn from this? What has this to teach me about the way I am now to go?" have been the ones whom nothing could deter, and have had operating in them a process of correction which did not fail them in any situation that arose. The faith in the accessibility of the Divine Listener that has marked the carrying out of Quaker concerns and the subsequent listening temper with its flexibility and openness to admit error and to correct it, have had a cleansing effect upon the diseases of private fanaticism that may readily infect such action. This openness to continual correction has had the practical effect of revealing to many who followed a concern how brittle and fragile was the thread of their commitment when they undertook it and how far the Divine Listener had used this concern to draw them on into his redemptive action and to cleanse and clarify them, a process that worship alone had only begun. For our action like our words is being listened to not only by our fellows but by the Eternal One, and it is only as we feel his scrutiny and respond to his illumination in what we do that we become a part of the redemptive circle that longs to draw not only all men but all creation into its healing power.

NOTES

1. I. 14.
2. Ibid.
3. Theresa of Avila, *The Interior Castle*, 4:3.
4. *Journal* of Job Scott (London, 1815), pp. 284–85.
5. John Churchman, *An Account of Gospel Labors* (Philadelphia, 1882), p. 189.
6. Scott, op. cit., p. 137.
7. Ibid., p. 52, 196.
8. Ibid., p. 137.
9. John William Graham, *The Faith of a Quaker* (Cambridge, London, 1920), pp. 245–46.